CREATIVE TEACHING

CREATIVE TEACHING

Ideas to Boost Student Interest

James P. Downing

1997
Teacher Ideas Press
A Division of
Libraries Unlimited, Inc.
Englewood, Colorado

TEACHER IDEAS PRESS
A Division of
Libraries Unlimited, Inc.
P.O. Box 6633
Englewood, CO 80155-6633
1-800-237-6124
www.lu.com/tip

Production Editor: Kay Mariea
Copy Editor: Jan Krygier
Proofreader: Suzanne Hawkins Burke
Indexer: Christine J. Smith
Design and Layout: Pamela J. Getchell

Library of Congress Cataloging-in-Publication Data

Downing, James P., 1947-
Creative teaching : ideas to boost student interest / James P. Downing.
xiii, 224 p. 22x28 cm.
Includes bibliographical references and index.
ISBN 1-56308-476-7
1. Creative thinking--Study and teaching. 2. Creative ability in children. 3. Creative activities. 4. Teaching--Aids and devices. I. Title.
LB1590.5.D68 1997
370.15'7--dc21 97-11676
CIP

CONTENTS

Part 2: Skills and Tools for Creative Teaching

Part 3: Applications of Tools for Creative Teaching

PREFACE

The idea of creative teaching may call to mind the image of a stand-up comedian in front of the class keeping students amused or a yarnspinner telling wildly entertaining stories or an "artsy" teacher who advocates "doing your own thing." But these are not very good examples of creative teaching. Although highly gifted people often make good teachers, being naturally theatrical or artistic is not always synonymous with good teaching. Taking on the role of entertainer will surely make a teacher popular, but this approach automatically puts the student into the passive role of observer, not participant. Creative teaching is hard to define because creativity is elusive and generally misunderstood and because many people—perhaps even most—hold serious misconceptions about what constitutes effective teaching. In a nutshell, creative teaching is a set of practices that result in everyone in a group of students being fully engaged in productive learning for an entire lesson or project. At times, the creative teacher may tell dramatic, entertaining stories or even sing. More often, students will direct their own investigations; solve open-ended problems; construct schematics; draw blueprints; hold debates and seminars; write interviews, stories, and imaginary excursions; and, in general, participate in constructing a mental and emotional network of concepts, processes, facts, ideas, and skills that have personal significance and individual meaning to them.

Creative teaching is a natural extension of effective teaching. Extraordinary creativity is not required; ordinary creativity is sufficient. The techniques of creative teaching presented in this book can be learned by anyone who has the prerequisite disposition, sensibilities, and knowledge to teach. I say this not with casual optimism but from experience. In the opening session of the teacher education class I teach at the University of Colorado, "The Art of Creative Teaching," I frequently hear comments such as "I don't know why I'm taking this course; I don't feel particularly creative, and I'm not sure I like standing up in front of groups." By the end of the course, however, after overcoming their own creative blocks and learning the mechanics of a dozen or so practical tools for teaching creatively, students are giving final presentations in costume, enacting scripts they have written about a historical person, scientist, or author. These are the same people who said a few months before that they didn't feel particularly creative!

In teaching current and prospective teachers, I have tried several textbooks but found them unsatisfactory for my purpose, which is to train and inspire teachers to teach in a way that fosters creative thinking and expression in students by engaging them fully in their own learning. *Artistry in Teaching* by Louis Rubin (1985), a well-known lecturer on teacher education, is an interesting book, chock-full of keen observations and anecdotes about the art of teaching. An astute commentator, Professor

Rubin is more the lecturer about education in the abstract than a frontline practitioner of the art. Consequently, *Artistry in Teaching* is short on examples for everyday classroom use. Another book about creative teaching, *Creativity in the Classroom: Schools of Curious Delight* by Alane Starko (1995), provides essential background knowledge to teach creatively. It is a well-researched textbook that contains many ideas for creative teaching and some sidebars entitled "Thinking about the classroom." Unfortunately, Professor Starko's hefty, jargon-burdened text often drags like a dissertation and stops short of providing skill-building activities for the reader and firsthand tips for the practice of creative teaching.

Over the last several years students have graciously given my teacher education course an A+ and encouraged me to put the course material in book form. This is my main reason for writing this book: to present a complete model of creative teaching that can be learned with patience and practice and applied to teaching any age group. *Creative Teaching* is uniquely practical because it is written by a full-time schoolteacher for fellow teachers and prospective teachers. The material grows out of both theory and practice. Many of the tools for creative teaching presented here are my own inventions, developed during my 26 years as a classroom teacher and my after-hours work as amateur actor, playwright, novelist, photographer, and coach. For the last seven years, I have taught concurrently in a public school and a university, trying out and fine-tuning every teaching tool in this book. (Some other tools and techniques didn't work, so I abandoned them.)

In writing this book, I have always kept the "real world" teacher in mind. I have written the material in an easy-to-read, conversational style, free of technical vocabulary as much as possible. Knowing the importance of constructing knowledge rather than passively receiving it, I have provided more than 40 activities that the reader can use to practice the skills explained, tips for using these skills, and information on potential problems that could arise. I would have loved to include more examples of these teaching tools for each grade level and subject, but space constraints prevented it.

This book is laid out in three parts: Part 1: The Nature of Creativity; Part 2: Skills and Tools for Creative Teaching; and Part 3: Applications of Tools for Creative Teaching. The value of this book will be enhanced if the reader will do the activities, choose a target audience (a given age group and subject area such as eighth-grade social studies), and work out applications and adaptations of this material for the chosen group of students.

I offer thanks to many people for their roles in developing this book. Special thanks to my friend and colleague Joyce Gellhorn, with whom I co-taught "The Art of Creative Teaching" for three years; my brother David and my friend Rick Thomas for their help and encouragement on this and other projects; Donna Haglin for her valuable suggestions on an earlier draft; my sister Marobeth Ruegg for her spunky cartoons and overflowing creativity; my illustrator Gary Raham; Stan Converse for his scripted enactment of John Muir; Silvia Kjolseth for her photography; Bill Kalinowski for enacting Galileo; John Zola for his many valuable suggestions; Carol Sheehey, Director of Credit and Special Programs, Division of Continuing Education, for establishing "The Art of Creative Teaching" at the University of Colorado; and my students at Boulder High School and the University of Colorado for their enthusiasm, positive feedback, and helpful suggestions.

ACKNOWLEDGMENTS

Grateful acknowledgment is made to the following for permission to reprint from their publications:

The line from "anyone lived in a pretty how town," copyright 1940, (c) 1969, 1991 by the trustees for the e e cummings Trust, from *Complete Poems: 1904-1962* by e e cummings, edited by George J. Firmage. Reprinted by permission of Liveright Publishing Corporation.

Cartoon from *Close to Home*, John McPherson/Dist. of Universal Press Syndicate. Reprinted with permission. All rights reserved.

Excerpts from "Tentative (First Model) Definitions of Poetry" from Good Morning, America, copyright 1928 and renewed 1956 by Carl Sandburg, reprinted by permission of Harcourt Brace & Company.

and quotations from

A Man for All Seasons by Robert Bolt, (c) by Robert Bolt, 1960, Random House, Inc.

Of Mice and Men by John Steinbeck. Copyright 1937, renewed (c) 1965 by John Steinbeck. Used by permission of Viking Penguin, a Division of Penguin Books USA Inc.

Colorado Model Content Standards for Geography, (c) 1995 by Colorado State Board of Education.

Module 1

Creativity's Many Faces

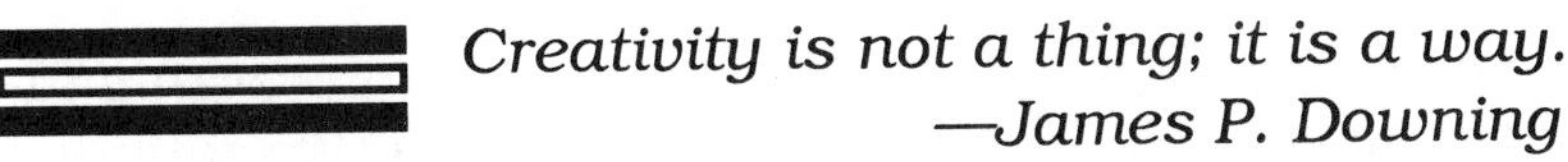

Creativity is not a thing; it is a way.
—James P. Downing

THE NECESSITY OF RENEWING WONDER

What happens to the sense of wonder that fills the lives of children when they grow up? To children, the world is an enchanted place, an unknown continent to explore, a magical realm to experience and enjoy. Why does growing up take away the wonder of the world? Do the social forces that shape us into citizens hammer the sense of wonder out of us? Or, does school life sober us and stamp out our sense of imagination? Does maturation demand that we adopt the standard picture of "real life" and give up playing with other versions of reality?

What would it take for an adult to be re-christened in wonder, to wake up one day to find the world transformed and life filled with all sorts of wondrous and amazing things? How could a person who has lived long and learned about the world—the whole lovely, rude story—ever experience wonder again with the freshness of a tender-aged child, innocent of rough truth and free of personal memories of being bullied by misfortune?

If wonder is a destination, you can't get there from here—not unless you go back to what you were, not unless you find a way to start again. To renew our sense of wonder requires a transformation of how we see ourselves in relation to the world. To replenish the sense of newness that makes every breath of air feel fresh demands energy and sacrifice of some cherished notions. The journey to the source of creativity requires the freedom to play and, as Rollo May, the eminent psychoanalyst put it, the courage to create.

But wait! This book is about creative teaching, isn't it? What about a list of creative projects? What about *tips* and *potential problems* and "*how to*" examples? Wouldn't that be enough?

Not really. Better to aim high and fall short than to shoot at an easy target and score all bull's-eyes without stretching. I remind you of the scope and sanctity of our mission, which is not less than to change the future of the world. We must teach the right things in the right way at the right time. Yes, we can choke on paperwork and get smothered in far-flung duties, but never forget that we strive for timeless aims. Our task is to guide young people toward visions of a better world and to give them the skills to build it. To accomplish such a task, we must locate in ourselves a new vitality; we must rekindle our own creative spirit and convey it to others.

Because I remember my own schools days not entirely fondly, it's a bit surprising that I turned out to be a teacher. The process of schooling left me feeling restless and alienated. I was restless because I had to fight tendencies to move around, to play with the material, to change activities, to work with others as a team, and in general to have more fun. The alienation arose from the feeling that the work I did at school was irrelevant to my life and interests. I had to take on a secret identity at school, pretending to be someone I wasn't, and that led to a deep sense of self-betrayal. School shouldn't be like taking foul-tasting cod liver oil to benefit from the vitamins it contains.

Gradually, over several decades of teaching, I gave up suppressing the playful, creative part of myself and began incorporating creative activities into my classroom. Not only has it boosted student motivation but it has also raised achievement levels, and my students and I feel more satisfied with our work.

This book offers some ideas and skills as a foundation to initiate creativity in the classroom. In these pages you'll find a bit of theory on creativity, the principles of creative teaching, and more than 40 activities to use for practice in applying the tools for creative teaching. These ideas and techniques are powerful, and I worry about the misuse of them. There are no formulas for correct teaching, let alone creative teaching. All projects done under the umbrella of creativity are not necessarily wonderful. Creativity is not a gimmick, nor is it a means to some other end—for example, building self-esteem—though that is an important goal. Research has shown that when creativity is used as a reward or as a diversion from a lesson, achievement goes down (Davis and Thomas 1989). A halfhearted application of these ideas and techniques or a skimpy, pick-and-choose manner of using them is not good enough. The purpose of this material is to strengthen teaching and to make learning more enjoyable without sacrificing one iota of quality or compromising achievement standards in any way.

The route to the fountainhead of creativity is a challenging, yet familiar path going backward in time. Before children enter school, they are very creative; they sing and dance, draw pictures, invent stories and imagine themselves in other places. But children grow up, "and down they forgot as up they grew," as the poet e e cummings put it. Creative teaching rests on the discovery of play. Play is joyful, unself-conscious interaction with a person or thing. That's the first priority in renewing wonder: to make a habit of playing without feeling awkward or unproductive.

But the journey to the source of hidden creativity is not only learning to play. It is a craft as well, acquired with practice and patience, like learning to play a musical instrument or even taking up a religious quest. If you want to recover your creativity and rediscover wonder, you must make a decision to do so and hold fast to your commitment even when the mood is not right, the energy is not there, and the whole project seems hopeless. If you succeed in recovering your sense of wonder and play, that will be reward enough. But consider the effect you will also have on others.

Your sense of wonder and play will make you a much better teacher. If you are already teaching—no matter what age group, pre-school to doctoral students—I invite you to rediscover the inner source of the creative spirit, trust it, and let it work for you.

TEACHING CREATIVELY

A journey of a thousand miles begins with the first step, says a Chinese proverb. To teach creatively, begin by recognizing that you have hidden creativity, that you want to explore it, and that you want to help young people do likewise. Creative teaching is a complex skill and cannot be learned in a short time. There are three steps to teaching creatively.

Step 1: Understand the nature of creativity.

Step 2: Practice your own creativity.

Step 3: Use teaching strategies that nurture creativity in your students.

Of course, it goes without saying that creative teaching (or any other teaching methodology) is no substitute for knowledge in a subject area. Being an expert in a subject area does not automatically make you a good teacher; on the other hand, you can't be an effective teacher unless you are knowledgeable in your subject area. Creative teaching allows you realize your full potential as a teacher, but only if you have mastered that subject area yourself.

A Note on Using This Book

Although this book contains sample lessons and teaching activities, it is not an activity book. This book discusses the process of teaching at any level or about any subject. A sage once said, "Catch someone a fish, and you provide a meal; teach someone to fish and you provide food for a lifetime." This book is meant to be a skill-building book—"food for a lifetime"—that provides teachers with the ability to generate endless creative lessons, rather than an activity book specific to a grade level and subject area. I am making a distinction between teaching *with* creativity and teaching *for* creativity. In the first case, the teacher's creativity is central. Artistic or performing creativity is especially appropriate for certain activities such as dramatic readings and enactments. But the more important kind of classroom creativity by far is teaching *for* creativity—that is, stimulating students to rediscover their hidden creativity and showing them how to use that creativity fully. Of course, these two approaches are not separate. Teaching students to be more creative works best if the teacher has "been there" and knows firsthand the joys and pitfalls of creativity.

This book adopts the premise that a teacher must rediscover his or her own creativity and then apply it to help students find and enjoy their own creativity. To this end, more than 40 sample lessons and activities are provided. These activities fall into four categories: (1) *Growth activities*, that assist the teacher in developing his or her own creative abilities; (2) *Concept development activities* that help the teacher understand a foundational idea; (3) *Skill development activities* that provide practice in a specific technique of creative teaching; and (4) *Classroom activities* that can be used with students. Many of these activities put the teacher in the student's role. Having done an activity, a teacher can then reflect on how he or she felt about the task and what was easy or hard, relevant or irrelevant, about it. For any teacher, this information could be valuable in adapting material to one's own use and setting.

What Is Creativity?

To first-century Christians, *charisma* was the mark of a divine gift of healing or prophecy. The word *charisma* means "a gift." Persons blessed with the gift could be easily identified by their extraordinary deeds. The question arises: *Is creativity a specific quality, a gift that sets apart the fortunate few from ordinary folk as distinctly as charisma set apart the chosen seers and healers of the distant past?*

Perhaps we could turn to science to discover the essence of creativity using the method of organic chemists who grind up rose petals, extract the scent-bearing oils, and refine them down to a single chemical essence. If creativity were a single potent ability that gave its owner special powers, this reductionist approach might well work. But creativity is less like the rose petal extract than the iridescent tropical butterfly in flight, elusive and hard to study in action. As we will soon see, creativity is complex; that is, it results from a mixture of specialized abilities, motivations, habits, and circumstances that are present in everyone to some to degree but are most noticeable in "gifted" people.

The word *creativity* often evokes the image of theatrical creativity, which is associated with the personal panache and charisma of Hollywood or Broadway stars, a magnetic power that attracts unmerited devotion. In reality, creativity is much broader and much less rare. To a degree, creativity is a natural part of everyone's mental process, though creativity differs, of course, in type and amount from person to person (Crutchfield 1973). There is no such thing, however, as a totally uncreative person. Any act of producing something new, even something as simple as a sentence that has never been spoken before, is an act of creation.

The answer to the question *What is creativity?* should be broad enough to include both spontaneous expressiveness and original thinking as manifestations of creativity. Here is a working definition:

> Creativity is the process of producing a *new whole* out of existing elements by arranging them into a new configuration.

This definition is broad enough to include discovery, imagination, invention of all kinds, and theories—political, religious, scientific, and psychological—as well as literary works, sculpture, painting, and great performances so often associated with creativity. Creativity can be subdivided into several categories:

- Artistic creativity
- Inventive creativity
- Theatrical creativity
- Constructive creativity
- Interpersonal creativity

Thus, Alexander Graham Bell, Marie Curie, Duke Ellington, Joan of Arc, Isaac Newton, and Martin Luther King Jr., were all creators as well as John Lennon, Leonardo da Vinci, and Audrey Hepburn.

Creativity's Many Faces

Learning to use all aspects of one's creativity is part of becoming a fully functioning person. Because creativity is a normal part of everyone's feeling, expression, and thinking, making creativity the centerpiece of an instructional model is totally appropriate. Creative teaching involves all five types of creativity.

Artistic Creativity

Teachers with a special talent in one of the arts, such as photography, music, writing, acting, drawing, or painting, can usually employ this talent in their teaching. At the very least, sharing these talents helps build

rapport. Yet, as far as teaching is concerned, artistic talent is the least useful form of creativity because it places the students automatically in the role of audience. No matter how great the artistic talent of the teacher, it should not be allowed to upstage students or reduce their opportunities to develop *their* talents and skills. Although observing a teacher's gift may inspire some students, it may also inhibit students and stir feelings of inadequacy. Special talents or creativity in the arts certainly have a place in the classroom, but this form of creativity is less useful than the other four types.

Inventive Creativity

Meeting the demands of an increasingly complex and rapidly changing society requires flexibility. People and societies that can adapt readily to changing conditions survive and prosper while those that cannot fall by the wayside. Inventive creativity results from divergent thinking, which can be enhanced, as research has shown, through practice. To teach adaptability is to teach inventive creativity and creative problem solving. Because

no one can predict the future even 10 years in advance, creative problem solving and designing can and should be taught in the classroom, in addition to factual content.

Theatrical Creativity

A teacher who skillfully employs theatrical devices will capture and hold the students' attention better than the same teacher using plain vanilla methods. Students' attitudes and task commitment improve when their assignments allow for some degree of self-expression. Otherwise, schooling is an unnatural, distasteful affair that turns students off to future learning and dissuades them from pursuing a subject on their own. Theatrical creativity introduces levity, a sense of fun, compassion, and a deeper contact with emotions. A high school literature teacher who puts on a colonial costume and reads a sermon of Jonathan Edwards in dramatic style turns potentially dry material into an event. A history teacher who can tell, indeed, *enact* history's important moments will help students make connections, especially emotional ones, where, before, there were none. A science teacher who illustrates the recipe for making a planet by having students wear large names tags identifying

them as quarks, protons, and atoms and bunching them together in different groups will leave a more lasting impression of the structure of matter in the students' minds than the transparency-flipping stooge who drones on and on. There is an inherent joy to the creative process that does not exist in rote learning. Classrooms should be humane and engaging centers of learning rather than the drudge shops we call classrooms in many schools.

Constructive Creativity

True learning, as opposed to mere training or mimicry, requires the construction of meaning and inherently involves an act of creation. Creativity is required for any type of synthesis because a unified whole must be constructed where none existed before. Students cannot make copies of the teacher's knowledge; they must build up their own understanding brick by brick, concept by concept. Students need activities that evoke a response and engage their whole capacity: heart, hands, and head. The result of true learning is a sturdy but flexible mental scheme, a large cognitive-affective framework that organizes and links knowledge, motives, and feelings into a meaningful whole. Creative activities such as reconstructive writing, flowcharts, invention grids, scripts, choice mapping, and interviews require a greater degree of constructive thinking than mere memorization.

Teachers today face a challenging task in motivating students to do their best work. This task is made easier when the lessons provided are interesting and meaningful. Creativity, if used effectively, enhances students' motivation to learn because they have the opportunity to achieve a synthesis where none existed before. The result? A deeply satisfying, personally meaningful learning experience. True learning satisfies the inner longing of the human being to discover meaning and make sense out of information and experience.

Interpersonal Creativity

Learning and teaching involve a high level of interpersonal interaction. Building a rapport, sensing the students' feelings about a lesson or assignment, and solving discipline problems without leaving a residue of bitter feeling are valuable skills some people naturally have in abundance. Any creative endeavor in the classroom requires both the inborn talent possessed by the teacher and techniques understood and practiced over time. Interpersonal creativity comes into play in engaging students one to one and in reading the mood of the day. Sensitivity to other's feelings not only prevents emotional blocks in students, but contributes to making learning an enjoyable process. John Dewey (1963) noted that the best classroom climate is one that inclines a student toward wanting to learn more about the subject rather than less. Emotional climate is a big part of achieving this goal.

Growth Activity 1-1: Practicing with Types of Creativity

Part A: Complete this chart.

Type of creativity	Person with this type	Icon or symbol for this type

Part B: Draw a cartoon or schematic diagram showing the icons of all five categories of creativity in one picture.

WHAT MAKES A PERSON CREATIVE?

Creativity is not an isolated characteristic, found in some people and absent in others, but a constellation of traits that all come to bear at once. Though creativity cannot be reduced to a single equation, a variety of writers and researchers frequently identify the same handful of factors that contribute to creative acts as widely diverse as writing poetry and devising mechanical inventions (Abra 1988; Amabile and Hennessey 1988; Tardif and Sternberg 1988). Creativity involves

- a *gift* for associating thoughts and feelings in unusual combinations;
- an *attitude* of playfulness, openness, and flexibility;
- *knowledge* of how the creative process works;
- *skill* in using the tools of the trade;
- persistent *effort* to keep trying until the result is satisfactory; and
- a *favorable setting* in which creativity can find free expression.

Gift

Extraordinary creative ability seems to be specific to a given domain such as music, mathematics, or writing. Although certain people may be endowed with multiple gifts, creativity does not give the gifted person the Midas touch in any and all fields.

Effort

"Genius is one percent inspiration and 99 percent perspiration," said Thomas Edison. Task commitment is as important to creative productivity as gift and skill. Confidence and attitudes that affect effort and willingness to keep trying are two of the easiest things that can be changed to improve output.

Knowledge and Skill

Much of the time, raw, creative impulses do not look very good until craftsmanship shapes them into symbols and images that can communicate something of value. To come to fruition, many creative products require specialized skills. These skills, along with sets of defined symbols and images, make up an artistic craft. Highly creative impulses may not translate into meaningful products because of ineptitude in a specialized skill. In the worst-case scenario, a person develops counterproductive habits that result in frustration of, not fulfillment of, the desire to create.

Attitudes

Cultural biases and stereotypes about creative persons can make being creative unappealing, despite the acknowledged rewards. Ego defense mechanisms develop naturally in human beings as a response to threatening circumstances. These psychological mechanisms, however, often outlive their usefulness. Becoming more creative involves re-discovering creative abilities and removing blockages that prevent their expression. To become more creative requires replacing unproductive attitudes with habits of mind that support, rather than block, the flow of creative juices.

Favorable Setting

If creativity is role-modeled, valued, and encouraged, young people will become more creative; if fault-finding criticism is replaced by the suggestion of alternatives, creativity will blossom in the classroom. As the ancient philosopher Plato put it, "What is honored in a country will flourish there."

Growth Activity 1-2: Identifying Elements of Creativity

Draw a pie chart showing the relative proportions of gift, effort, knowledge, skill, attitudes, and favorable setting needed to complete each of the following acts of creativity.

1. Creating a new perfume
2. Writing a workable peace treaty
3. Turning an abandoned factory into a science museum
4. Writing a 500-page novel
5. Designing a new computer game
6. Performing an improvisational comedy act
7. ____________________ (Choose your own activity)

CREATIVITY: A MULTISTAGE PROCESS

Creative products often seem to spring forth fully formed. Suddenly, an idea is just there. But the unexplained appearance of the inspired idea does not mean it happened all at once. Long before the shining "Eureka!" moment, the mind, both consciously and unconsciously, has been involved in a *creative process* that leads to the crucial moment of insight. Thus, the most productive approach to improving creativity focuses on this creative process.

In the early nineteenth century the versatile genius Heinrich von Helmholtz—physician, scientist, physiologist, and philosopher—identified three stages in the creative process: *saturation*, *incubation*, and *inspiration*. In the 1920s, psychologist Joseph Wallas added a fourth stage, *verification*. The Helmholtz-Wallas theory of the creative process does much to describe the steps in the process, although it gives no indication of how creativity works and provides no explanation of the inspiration stage. What initiates this stage, and what's going on between the saturation stage and the moment of inspiration? Surely, mere waiting is not enough to bring about an insight or fresh idea. Thus, the traditional Helmholtz-Wallas model of the creative process needs to be modified, breaking the saturation step into two separate stages: *pooling elements* and *searching for a synthesis.* Learning to be more creative and to teach others to be more creative requires a thorough understanding of each stage of the creative process.

Stages in the Creative Process

Sensing Dissonance

The creative process apparently begins with an incongruity or discrepancy and a deeply human need to make things right. When a chance discovery or unplanned outcome intrudes upon the status quo, the individual's equilibrium state is disturbed. The new element is an irritant that must be absorbed or eliminated to restore equilibrium. *Creativity is the psyche's response to an irritant, a response that seeks to restore balanced harmony to a disharmonious condition.* Less creative persons often ignore or reject any new element or strange event they encounter to avoid being thrown out of balance in the first place, whereas more creative people are able to tolerate the irritant for as long as it takes to reconstruct a new mental supporting structure and re-balance the situation. The function of the creative process is to bring order to a set of items that no longer fit together into a coherent structure. For the teacher, to be creative involves finding, for example, a new way to present a concept or dreaming up a new learning activity.

Pooling Elements

Elements having to do with the creative desire are collected at first without much organization. If any organization does exist, it is based on a shallow form of similarity or visual appearance as opposed to a deeper category such as substance or function. The pool takes time to fill up as information is gathered. Eventually, the pool will contain routine elements, novel elements, and elements that have been altered in some way using allowed transformation rules.

Greater creativity occurs when there is a richer, more varied pool from which to draw. Routine elements, items that readily come to mind, will not contribute much to the pool. Yet people often exhaust their first few ideas, then get stuck and quit seeking new elements for the pool. A merely token effort early in the process of creating will produce routine, uninteresting products. The pool of elements must be constantly expanded to build up sheer volume. This requires persistence.

The pool, however, can become choked with an oversupply of routine elements. It also must have diversity; that is, it must have many different categories of items. Take a simple case. Suppose the guest room of your house doesn't look right to you (sensing dissonance). You decide to get together a short list of possible ways to refurbish it (pooling elements). The *routine procedures* for refurbishing include: changing the existing drapes and carpet, painting, hanging new pictures on the walls, replacing the wallpaper, adding wood paneling, or getting new furnishings. *Novel procedures* are knocking out a wall; adding a doorway to an adjoining room; enlarging the window; adding a bay window or fireplace; changing the lighting; replacing the molding; building in wall shelves or cabinets; installing a fold-away bed, a desk, or a pull-down stairway into the attic; adding a skylight, window box, or aquarium; rounding the contours of the walls; adding a hanging sculpture; installing a model railroad on a shelf around the room; or building platforms to make a two-level floor.

Once the pool of elements has been built up, a third process begins: *modifying the elements* in the pool to produce new elements. Perhaps the idea of hanging a large framed picture evolves into the idea of enlarging favorite snapshots and using them to wallpaper one side of the room.

Searching for a Synthesis

Various elements are tried out together, consciously or unconsciously, and as elements fit together, they are set aside as chunks or clusters. Gradually, the pool of elements accumulates an assortment of clusters. Clusters of elements are then tried together. This step requires work. The search for synthesis involves groping, struggling, or stretching, which may not be comfortable. Some of the clusters may have to be broken down again, because a promising possibility can go bust. In some cases where a single piece refuses to fit anywhere and the person is stuck in a loop, trying essentially the same thing over and over, a period of *incubation* may be advised. Upon returning to the sticky part of the process, the person may take one quick look at the problem and immediately see how the stubborn piece must be modified to fit into the cluster. As Sigmund Freud once put it, "So many times an error is just the truth stood on its head."

Discovery of the New Whole

Sudden insight after a period of incubation may be due to the processes of the unconscious mind, which can work on the problem without any conscious involvement. Apparently, at a certain stage, conscious effort actually blocks the creative process. Perhaps incubation is productive because it provides a fresh look at the elements from a different vantage point. Upon returning from a break, perceptual blocks are absent, allowing the unity of the final image to emerge. Rollo May (1975) observes that incubation often involves a change of setting and the release of conscious effort. Many inventors and scientists have reported giving up on a problem or setting it aside and taking a walk or a trip to the beach. Without having any awareness of the creative process happening, suddenly, with a flash of illumination, the solution or final form of the project just leaps out, as if in three dimensions, from the background. After many futile attempts at pulling the parts together to make a new whole, conscious or unconscious, a combination is placed together, and that combination strikes a chord of harmony. It hangs together well. This is the "aha!" moment, the moment of illumination, the instant when swarms of separate elements unite into a single whole, filling a person with joy and a sense of well-being. May (1975) emphasizes that sudden illumination often occurs just after giving up concentrated attention on the project. Intense effort followed by relaxation of tension and release of conscious control seem to be key ingredients in the incubation process.

Verification

Once a cluster of clusters that hang together well has been recognized as a single unit, it still requires testing. This last stage is needed to see if the "aha!" moment was merely a false alarm or a signal that the discovery indeed has merit. Testing is really not part of the creative process in the sense of generating something new, but it is a necessary follow-up step because it answers the question of whether to return to the search for synthesis or to move on.

> *Creative teaching boils down to the process of taking students to the brink of discovery and then letting them discover how to put the pieces together into a whole. This process is inherently engaging and, in the end, pleasurable. The craft of creative teaching is the art of knowing how to embed the creative process in the work the students do.*

Flowchart for the Creative Process

Figure 1.1 on p. 14 depicts the creative process. The two activities below and on p. 15 provide practice in this process.

Growth Activity 1-3: Developing Stages in the Creative Process

Part A: Design a board game such as "Monopoly" or "Chutes and Ladders" based on the creative process. The game should have a goal, intermediate payoffs, boosts and setbacks, and a random factor.

Part B: Construct the board game according to your plan.

Part C: Make the board game on large sheets of cloth so that the students can move around on the board as in hopscotch.

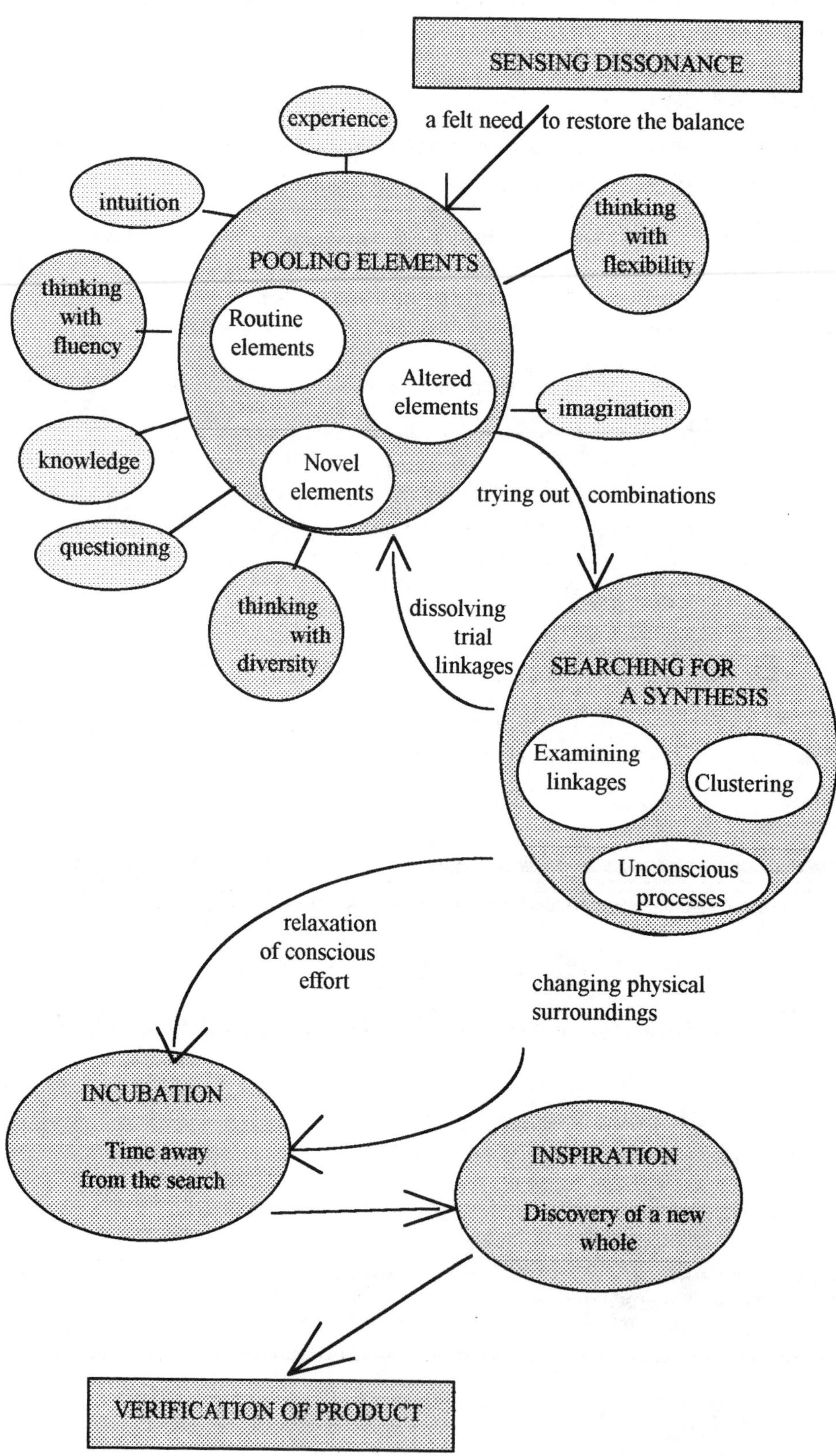

Fig. 1.1. Flowchart for the Creative Process

Growth Activity 1-4: Identifying Stages in the Creative Process

In the scenario below, an architect designs a building. Classify each action in the architect's creative process using the categories listed below, then place them in chronological order.

Pooling Searching for Synthesis Incubation Illumination Verification

Scenario: *An architect is retained to design an addition to an existing office building located on an odd-shaped piece of property in the heart of the city. Note: If two of the actions below fit one stage, place them in chronological order within the stage.*

- The architect suggests the plan first thing Monday to the client, and eventually her plan is adopted. That evening she takes her husband out to dinner to celebrate.
- Several days later, on Saturday, after having a cup of coffee, she tosses the newspaper aside. Something about the way it lands on the chair gives her an idea related to the new building and the odd-shaped parcel of land. What if the client could purchase the parcel of land across the street, which is for sale, and swap it with the city, which owns the land adjoining the office building? This change would allow the new addition to be built on a more regularly shaped lot. A building plan based on the combined lots would create sizable cost savings even including the land transfer fees and would allow for a more workable interior design and front elevation.
- She draws several different floor plans that meet the constraints of space and money. She studies the layout of the property, the city building codes, the location of utility lines, and the building's position in relation to the sun.
- She draws up entirely new floor plans and elevations. Still, nothing looks right. She is discouraged and wonders if there will ever be a suitable solution.
- She sets the project aside and takes up an entirely different project.

Types of Affect in the Creative Process

The creative process is deeply rooted in affect and connected to motives. Some of the important affective connections in the creative process are these:

Sensitivity to discrepancy, the feeling that things just aren't right. Environments that encourage the detection of inconsistencies are more likely to boost creativity.

Positive feelings toward taking up a challenge. Students may need to be reminded how good they feel when they are working on something that challenges them.

Openness to affect-laden memories and a willingness to suspend taboos, at least temporarily. This openness means being willing to recall any and all memories of the past. The person free of phobias and denial will be able to summon many connections and diverse responses, which may prove crucial later.

Tolerance of frustration and other negative affects. Creative work is never smooth or predictable. Creative people who quit in the face of opposition will not have much product to show for their effort.

Sensitivity to creative joy, the sense of victory that accompanies finding a solution or making a discovery. Creative joy, a wonderful sense of accomplishment, can be reviewed and savored. If the pleasure of finishing creative work is fully celebrated, then it is easier to take up the next project.

Processing emotions freely and integrating affect. Creative work involves using the imagination freely and getting in touch with the associated affect. This is the same process that operates when someone is enthralled by a movie or story and is free to feel and enjoy the emotional ups and downs that go with it. Positive affect in the classroom is as important to motivation as cognitive interest (Lozanov 1978). Although it is possible to set up a classroom environment of predominantly positive feelings, it is important not to deny negative affect. What is called for is authenticity—the recognition and acknowledgment of feelings, whatever they are—and a valuing of affect itself. Affect should neither be mocked or ignored but should be experienced in the right proportions; neither too little nor too much for the circumstance. This balancing process is a part of the process of becoming a complete human being. This is why Paul Torrance (1967) said that the exercise of creativity is part of becoming a fully functioning person.

Growth Activity 1-5: Identifying Affect in the Creative Process

Using the scenario in Growth Activity 1-4, identify when each of the above six types of affect enters the creative process.

REFERENCES

Abra, Jock. 1988. *Assaulting Parnassus: Theoretical Views of Creativity.* Lanham, MD: University Press of America.

Amabile, Teresa, and Beth Hennessey. 1988. The Conditions of Creativity. In *The Nature of Creativity: Contemporary Psychological Perspectives.* Edited by Robert J. Sternberg. New York: Press Syndicate of the University of Cambridge.

Crutchfield, Richard. 1973. The Creative Process. In *Creativity: Theory and Research.* Edited by Morton Bloomberg. New Haven, CT: College and University Press.

Davis, Gary A., and Margaret A. Thomas. 1989. *Effective Schools and Effective Teachers.* Boston: Allyn & Bacon.

Dewey, John. 1938, 1963. *Experience and Education.* New York: Collier.

Lozanov, Gregorii. 1978. *Suggestology and Outlines of Suggestopedeia.* New York: Gordon and Breach.

May, Rollo. 1975. *The Courage to Create.* New York: Bantam Books.

Tardif, Twila, and Robert Sternberg. 1988. What Do We Know About Creativity? In *The Nature of Creativity: Contemporary Psychological Perspectives.* Edited by Robert J. Sternberg. New York: Press Syndicate of the University of Cambridge.

Torrance, E. Paul. 1967. The Nurture of Creative Talents. In *Explorations in Creativity.* Edited by R. L. Mooney and T.A. Razil. New York: Harper & Row.

FURTHER READING

Amabile, Teresa. 1983. *The Social Psychology of Creativity.* New York: Springer-Verlag.

Barron, Frank. 1952. The Psychology of the Creative Writer. In *The Creative Process.* Edited by B. Ghiselin. New York: New American Library.

Bower, G. H. 1981. Mood and Memory. *American Psychologist* 36:129-48.

Csikszentmihalyi, M. 1990. *Flow: The Psychology of Optimum Experience.* Grand Rapids, MI: Harper & Row.

Gardner, Howard. 1982. *Art, Mind, and Brain: A Cognitive Approach to Creativity.* New York: Basic Books.

——. 1993. *Multiple Intelligences: The Theory in Practice.* New York: Basic Books.

Goleman, Daniel, P. Kaufman, and M. Ray. 1992. *The Creative Spirit.* New York: Dutton.

Kleinke, Chris. 1978. *Self-Perception: The Psychology of Personal Awareness.* San Francisco: W. H. Freeman.

Lazarus, R. 1991. *Emotion and Adaptation.* Oxford: Oxford University Press.

Masters, J., R. Barden, and M. Ford. 1979. Affective States, Expressive Behavior, and Learning in Children. *Journal of Personality and Social Psychology* 37:380-90.

Russ, Sandra. 1993. *Affect and Creativity: The Role of Affect and Play in the Creative Process.* Hillsdale, NJ: Lawrence Erlbaum.

Taylor, I. A. 1975. A Retrospective View of Creativity Investigation. In *Perspectives in Creativity.* Edited by I. A. Taylor and J. W. Getzels. Chicago: Aldine.

Torrance, E. Paul. 1976. Education and Creativity. In *The Creativity Question.* Edited by Albert Rothenburg and Carl R. Hausman. Durham, NC: Duke University Press.

Vygotsky, Lev. 1978. *Mind in Society: The Development of Higher Psychological Processes.* Translated from the 1930 original. Cambridge, MA: Harvard University Press.

Module 2

Rediscovering Your Hidden Creativity

The creative mind plays with the objects it loves.
—Carl G. Jung

IMPROVING YOUR CREATIVITY

Suppose you want to become more creative or, to put it in practical terms, to do more creative things. What is the best strategy for enhancing creativity? Should you try to *understand* creativity by isolating specific traits associated with creativity and work to acquire those traits? Should you view creativity as a *skill* like weaving which can be practiced—if not mastered—by practically anyone who is willing to expend the effort? Or should you regard creativity as an *aspect of personality* that either exists or doesn't exist?

The bad news is that it may be impossible to increase inborn creative talent. The good news is that you can definitely improve your creative productivity and get the most out of whatever gifts you have by revamping your approach to creativity, becoming more aware of how the hemispheres of the brain work, and building good creativity habits. For the vast majority of people, creativity is not lacking; it is merely blocked or hidden by socialization processes over the years. For instance, creativity runs high in preschool children, but the need for them to conform to group norms—a need they first experience in primary school—dampens creativity. The anxiety of puberty deepens the need for social acceptability, with competitive games replacing make-believe. Late adolescent abstract thinking, with its newly developed critical abilities, hounds any surviving creativity into hiding. So, by adulthood, the average adult's creative ability is covered by several levels of shielding and a mind-set that prevents creativity from showing itself.

Enhancing Your Creativity by Using Your Whole Brain

Anatomists have known for centuries that the right and left hemispheres of the human brain are different. Evidence from head injuries—war wounds, auto accidents, strokes—has helped scientists map out brain function to be mapped for various locations. Taking the process a step further, Michael Gazzaniga and Roger Sperry tested the brain functioning of patients whose right and left hemispheres had been surgically disconnected to treat severe epilepsy (Springer and Deutsch 1981, chap. 2). Studies of the split brain patients revealed that the two hemispheres do not duplicate each other's functions. Speech processes are located in the left hemisphere, whereas visual and nonverbal processes are located in the right hemisphere. Logic is processed by the left hemisphere, and analogic (the process of making and understanding analogies and humor) is processed by the right hemisphere. The tentative results of research on the location of brain functions are given in table 2.1.

Table 2.1. Functions of the Brain's Hemispheres.

Left Hemisphere	Right Hemisphere
Verbal	Nonverbal, visual-spatial
Sequential, temporal, digital	Simultaneous, spatial, analogical
Logic, analytic	Gestalt, synthetic
Rationale	Intuitive

From Springer, Sally, and Georg Deutsch. 1981. *Left Brain, Right Brain.* San Francisco: W. H. Freeman, p. 183.

"Why Can't Right-Brained People Like Me Do Math?"

The student who asked this question had made several assumptions: (1) that she couldn't do math, (2) that her dominant hemisphere is her right hemisphere, and (3) that brain dominance is total and permanent. These are common misconceptions. In the first place research has found that many of the brain's diverse and complex functions cannot be pinned down to one or the other of the hemispheres. Reading and speaking, for example, are dual hemispheric functions. Even the split-brain patients in whom the main connecting tract, the corpus collosum, was surgically severed to prevent seizures had considerable delocalization of brain functions. Both hemispheres in one patient known as P. S. could respond to questions. When tested by Gazzaniga and Le Doux, P. S. could answer verbally using either of his two hemispheres. The curious thing was that the answers to the question "What career would you like to pursue?" were different, depending on whether they asked the young man's right or left hemisphere. P. S.'s right hemisphere wanted to race cars, but the left hemisphere preferred to be a draftsman (Springer and Deutsch 1981, 185).

After several decades of research using varied techniques, scientists have come to realize that the two hemispheres of the brain do not usually operate independently. For virtually any complex function including creative activity, the brain hemispheres work together. Thus, there is no such thing as a totally right-brained or left-brained person. Unfortunately, misconceptions and misinterpretations of split-brain research are used in many cases to justify a lack of effort in learning a given subject. Although the concept of hemispheric dominance is a useful tool for understanding brain function, as popularly used it has become too much like astrology. Just as some view a birth sign as determining one's life, some people accept the over-simplified notion that brain dominance determines one's life.

Fluency in Using Both Modes of Brain Function

Striking the right balance is the central challenge for many activities of life: parenting, relating to friends and loved ones, making art. We are constantly asking ourselves where the balance lies. How much credibility should I give my critics? How should I divide my time between work and home, friends and self? Where is the balance between accepting how other people treat me and my being assertive enough to ask them for a change? Balancing requires not only using all the various capacities of the brain, but also being capable of moving freely back and forth from one hemisphere to the other. Indeed, it may turn out that creative people are those who can modulate smoothly back and forth between the right and left hemisphere.

The brain is tremendously adaptable; for example, people in their 80s can learn to "surf the Internet" if they want. But no one says that learning to use the whole brain is easy; in fact, it is quite difficult. But it is those very tasks that do not come easily that are the key to success. For someone to break out of a self-limiting loop or climb out of a rut requires new strategies in thinking.

> This is the central idea of this book, that anyone willing to change some strategies, sometimes cherished, but nevertheless self-limiting strategies, will enjoy a more satisfying and fulfilling experience in teaching and in life.

To become more creative means learning to use the whole brain to create new things and to examine old things in a new light. Using the whole brain means improving creative abilities and becoming skilled at using these abilities at the right time and place. This is the key to renewing wonder.

Removing Blockages to Creativity

Solid empirical research shows that certain blockages can be removed in a fairly short training program. Richard Crutchfield (1973) found that two blocks to creative problem solving in elementary children—*lack of confidence* and *getting stuck in ruts*—could be reversed within a span of months. The gains in problem-solving scores were nearly miraculous: The lowest scoring segment of the treatment group matched the highest scoring segment of the control group, which had not received the training.

Other more serious blocks than these—perceptual, affective, and social blocks—are more deeply rooted than lack of confidence and getting stuck in ruts and require considerably more time to overcome. The children in Crutchfield's study felt more confident about only the type of problem they were practicing, not more confident about solving problems in general. But whatever your level of inborn talent, you can enhance the creative process appreciably by re-discovering the creative play that you once engaged in as a preschooler. By doing so, you will probably feel the same as if you had increased your inborn creative talent because play reduces the exaggerated self-consciousness that interferes with the creative process. Courage to face up to inner patterns is required, but the payoff is great indeed: more inner freedom and an improved self-concept, not to mention the increased joy of creating.

BLOCKS TO CREATIVE THINKING

Creating is a highly complex process with many steps. If a bottleneck occurs anywhere along the way, the process doesn't work, and the flow of creative thoughts and feelings is halted. Blockages increase the sense of futility and reduce effort, which is the single most controllable part of the creative process. Blockages come in several different forms: cultural, social, perceptual, and affective.

Cultural Blocks

Cultural blocks are the result of lifelong conditioning concerning what constitutes being "normal." Quick answers may seem normal in a culture of impatience, but impatience works against individual creativity.

The False Belief That Creativity Is One Step from Insanity

In a widely circulated essay, "Genius and Insanity," written in 1864, Italian psychiatrist Cesare Lomboroso suggested a cause-effect relationship between genius and "insanity" (Lomboroso [1864]/1976). As evidence, he produced a long list of historical figures such as Caesar, Napoleon, Newton, and Mozart, geniuses who suffered bouts of what he called insanity. He did not account for the fact that all the figures chosen for study were famous. (Perhaps fame led to their "insanity," not their creativity.) Of course, Lomboroso had no primary data, merely the interpretive works of many different biographers. The vague umbrella term *insanity* has now been abandoned because it lumps eccentric behavior and other deviation from the norm with biologically caused mental illness. Since Lomboroso published his essay, various studies have shown the opposite correlation between genius and insanity. Havelock Ellis found that of 1,030 individuals listed in the *Dictionary of National Biography*, only 4.2 percent had any demonstrable mental illness (in Arieti 1976, 357). In a landmark longitudinal study by Lewis Terman of gifted children who were tested well into adulthood, gifted persons "showed a *lower* incidence of such psychological problems as 'nervous breakdown,' drug and alcohol abuse, and suicide than would a random sample" (Abra 1988, 53).

Unusual thinking processes or unconventional behavior may be found both in creativity and schizophrenia, but this fact does not link them by cause and effect; e.g., if all Germans are music lovers and all Americans are music lovers, it does not follow that all Germans are Americans.

Creativity does not cause harm. It does just the opposite; it helps a person adjust to life. Poet Virginia Woolf observed that mental problems develop when creativity is blocked, not when it is expressed. The unusual thought processes of gifted people produce high levels of anxiety (May

1975) that, if unrelieved, can worsen underlying mental health problems. The act of creation provides a catharsis for these unsettling thoughts and reduces stress. In this way, creativity protects the mental health of the highly creative individual (E. Fried, cited in Abra 1988).

Likewise, fantasy play in children is an important element in their normal development. "It is here that the child learns to act in a cognitive, rather than an externally visual realm by relying on internal tendencies and motives and not on incentives supplied by external things" (Vygotsky 1978, 97). In addition, "Play continually creates demands on the child to act against immediate impulse. A child's greatest self-control occurs in play" (Vygotsky 1978, 99). For example, if eating a piece of candy is forbidden because the rules of the game of make-believe state the candy is poison, the child must voluntarily renounce something he or she wants.

Play involves cognitive practice and the exercise of willpower, but it also has a strong affective component. Children's make-believe games, though apparently silly to adults, may be the child's way of dealing with the fear and confusion he or she experiences in daily life. "Children use play to gain mastery over traumatic events and everyday conflicts" (Russ 1993, 42). Through the cathartic activity of play, the unpleasant feelings associated with a traumatic event—once unmanageable—can become manageable. This process of turning around the affect, meliorating an unpleasant feeling until it no longer recurs, is called *integration of affect.*

Cultural bias against imagination, especially fantasy and daydreaming, is very strong. Daydreaming is considered slothful, and fantasy is often treated as though it were a drug that could destroy wholesomeness and incentive. As Rollo May (1975) points out, the act of creativity produces anxiety. Perhaps myths about creativity are generated out of fear of it. Prejudice against creativity, as with any form of prejudice, is generated out of fear of something poorly understood. This is one important reason why it is important to understand and teach about creativity. As for the value of imagination, consider what Albert Einstein (quoted in "Inside Einstein's Brain" by Don Colburn, in the March 6, 1985, edition of *Health/The Washington Post*) said in reference to how he came up with the far-out idea of relativity:

> The gift of fantasy has meant more to me than my talent for absorbing positive knowledge.

Overemphasis on Short-Term, Concrete Goals

Creativity cannot be focused. Having goals is generally positive, but creativity cannot flourish when projects are confined to regimens and narrow timetables. Yes, creative work must be accomplished within a framework of constraints, but those constraints must not be stated as immediate and concrete outcomes.

Being Conditioned to Expect Simple, Quick Solutions

Having experienced only concrete, algorithmic (step-by-step) problems, people don't realize that problems with multiple solutions exist. Many people end up compulsively reworking variations of same failed solution instead of seeking other solutions.

Social Blocks

Social blocks arise due to the need to get along in society. Asking too many questions isn't considered cool, even though asking questions is the beginning of the creative process.

Fear of Disgrace

People in our culture are rewarded for accomplishments, and a bonus of status is awarded to those who can make accomplishments look easy. When individuals fail to deliver immediately or succeed only through obvious effort, the response may be condescension or worse. This unspoken value makes people less inclined to take risks because creative groping is seen as indecisiveness or failure. A person may decide, perhaps unconsciously, not to take a chance on attempting something because control of the outcome is impossible. This choice shuts off creativity at the source by abandoning or suppressing incomplete or partially formed good ideas before they can see the light of day. Such an inability to take risks or accept and incorporate criticism is the result of the culture of image grooming, which blocks creativity in those who buy into the values of the culture.

The Social Stigma of Asking Too Many Questions

A student's anxiety over asking the wrong kind of questions or too many questions generates less, not more, creativity. The characteristic chosen by parents as most important for the school to teach their children was "consideration for others." Sadly, courage finished 13th and creativity didn't rank even an honorable mention (Torrance 1963).

Perceptual Blocks

Perceptual blocks involve an inability to shift perspective or to take a different point of view. Of course, creativity by its very nature requires perceptual fluidity, and rigidity of all kinds will block it. An inability to shift perspective results in going over and over variations of the same solution. To break out of the rut, a change of scenery is needed, or at least a change in point of view.

Seeing only what one expects to see—stereotyping—cuts down diversity at the knees. To this prejudicial tendency one can add such thought processes as "knowing what type someone is"; "I'll never be one of *those*"; "I'm not a science/computer/artsy/musically-minded/logical person; I'm a Leo."

Affective Blocks

Affective blocks result from desensitization to our own and to other people's feelings. The psyche, as a means of self-protection from pain or overwhelming emotion, simply blocks the mechanism of feeling; difficult feelings are "forgotten."

Unconscious Repression of Emotion

Affective blocks may occur for unconscious reasons that may be inaccessible. For example, speed skater and world record holder Dan Jansen had recorded the fastest time in the world in his event in 1988, yet failed to win a gold or even a bronze medal at the 1988 Winter Olympics; even more disturbing, he seemed to be taking uncharacteristic falls on the ice. It was as though he had lost his desire to win. Sadly, Dan's sister had been fighting leukemia for many months. She lost her fight on the same day as her brother's biggest race. After the Olympics, Dan became aware of his psychological blockage. With the help of a psychologist, Dan realized what had happened: He had felt subconsciously that had he won the gold medal and enjoyed the victory, he would have been making a statement to the world that he didn't care about his sister's death. Having identified and removed his psychological blockage, Dan came back to win a gold medal in the 1992 Winter Olympics.

Low Tolerance for Ambiguity, Chaos, or Struggle

Two of the strongest correlates of creative thinking are having a high tolerance for ambiguity and being at ease with a lack of closure. Creativity is learning to be comfortable with the uncomfortable.

The regression stage of the creative process requires suspension of ego control. You need an unconscious faith and optimism that makes letting go possible.

Lack of Confidence

Confidence comes with success. A lack of confidence in your ability to make a problem or project work out leads to a vicious circle of not trying. Failing for lack of practice and having a low level of confidence feed on each other. The best way to begin to break the cycle is to believe in yourself unconditionally: "I'll find a way to make this work."

ATTITUDES AND THE POWER OF SELF-PERCEPTION

For better or worse, people tend to live out their self-concepts. If people believe they are capable, they will make an effort to reach their goals. If not, they either won't try or will become easily discouraged and quit. Imagine the implications of a person saying, "I'm not any good at X," a judgment perhaps made years ago, under different circumstances, that has never been scrutinized, let alone updated or reversed. Johann Wolfgang von Goethe, the great German poet and playwright, didn't take up his craft until age 50. He didn't believe he could produce anything worthwhile until then. What a sad loss to the world if he had not revised his negative self-concept! Even though he got a late start, it was better than getting no start at all. It is ironic that you can't really judge your creative ability in the abstract; you know if you have the ability to do something only in retrospect.

Of course, actors have known for years how powerfully the imagination can work to shape mood and mind. The power that lies in imagining that you're someone else seems to rest in accepting what is already part of you.

This is a central premise of the Stanislavski acting method which transformed the way actors present their roles. With practice, it is possible to mentally create an inventive character role to enact before trying creative tasks. Role-playing opens the psychological doors to the inner self by temporarily suspending acquired inhibitions.

Growth Activity 2-1: Imagining Yourself as a Creative Character

Part A: Recall a character from a movie, TV show, or book who exhibited a lot of creativity; perhaps Mary Poppins, Kermit the Frog, or Robin Williams. List a half-dozen creative acts performed by that character.

Part B: Close your eyes and imagine you are the character. Fill in the details of what your outfit feels like, what the surroundings look like, and how you feel inside. Still imagining you are the creative character, walk around your house and react the way the creative character would to the sounds, smells, and sights of your environment.

Where Are You Now?

To find out where you are starting in terms of full utilization of your creative potential, take a few minutes to write out answers to the questions below.

Growth Activity 2-2: A Biographical Questionnaire on Creativity

1. When did you decide what your level of creative ability was? How did you make this decision?

2. Do you have any unfinished creative projects lying around? How many? Why did you start them? Why didn't you finish them?

3. When you have been satisfied with a project you finished, what was it about the project that was most satisfying?

4. Do you feel everything you do has to be perfect, or at least good quality? How did you acquire this value?

5. Do you ever sing or whistle as you walk down a sidewalk or in a public place? Do you stop doing it when someone approaches, then resume when he or she is gone? Why?

6. Have you ever been embarrassed by your creativity or a creative product? When? Why were you embarrassed?

7. Is playing make-believe childish?

8. When was the last time you spent at least several minutes daydreaming—for example, imagining that you lived in another place or time or that you were another person? If it was too long ago to remember when, why did you quit?

9. When was the last time you shared a daydream with someone else? Have you ever had a conversation with someone in which you tossed a daydream back and forth? (e.g., what if we could take a trip anywhere we wanted for free—where would we go?) If not, why not?

10. When was the last time you played make-believe (e.g., imagining in the swimming pool that you were a shark sneaking up on someone)? If it was long ago, why did you give it up?

Comments on these questions:

1. Chances are that you made the decision long ago based on feedback from your environment. You made many important decisions about yourself as a toddler. Suppose you were the second child and you came along three years after your older sibling. The perception of the three-year-old is, "My sister can do *everything:* tie her shoes, answer the phone, ride a real bicycle, and go to school. I am not good at anything." A sense of inadequacy or incompetence becomes deeply lodged in the child's self-concept, and that self-concept, if unexamined, may never change. The adult's whole life may be unconsciously governed by decisions made decades before by the toddler. People, more often than not, underestimate their native creative abilities. The first step in enhancing creativity is to examine your self-concept as a creator, being willing to revise or abandon the old concept in favor of a more current and realistic picture.

2. People often start creative projects to relieve boredom; creating is inherently interesting. If the project takes longer than the time allotted for it, then the project doesn't get finished. When the next opportunity to work on the project comes around, it is more interesting to start a new project than to finish an old one. Of course, it is possible that the project isn't turning out as you originally envisioned it. Disappointment with the outcome is a frequent reason for abandoning a project.

3. People find different aspects of creativity satisfying in different ways. In some cases the work was a group project, such as a play or a fund-raiser, and the memories of feeling close to others in the group are most memorable. Some people say, "Whee! I finally proved I could do it." The project may have been a milestone in personal growth. For others the project was simply a release of some inner tension, a need to express something, or the sense of being in touch with an object of beauty.

4. The creative process does not proceed at a steady rate but lurches forward in fits and starts. Often an original idea goes through many revisions along the way. For people who are used to being rewarded by quick success and expect a tangible product in short order, the irregular rate of progress associated with creative work does not feel comfortable. Early efforts at creativity often look crude and childish and may evoke embarrassment. To enhance creativity requires

one to abandon perfectionism and substitute another value—free expression—which is more conducive to creativity.

5. Everyone's a critic! Maybe the person will say something cruel about your whistling. It is easier to give up what you feel than to risk upsetting others or being hurt by their criticism. But is it better?

6. You may have decided to put only your best foot forward in everything you do and withhold any effort that you suspect won't look good. If you were to fumble or produce something that is less than praiseworthy, in your own mind, you may risk a loss of status. Recall that as a child you probably weren't concerned much about protecting your status because you had little of it and weren't especially perceptive in knowing what other people thought about you anyway. However, as an adult, the desire for status and peer approval is a much greater inhibitor of creativity.

7. Children play make-believe games; adults seldom do. Such games are viewed as childish. But while the word *childish* has a negative connotation, *childlike* does not. For an adult to be childlike demonstrates psychological security and a willingness to be vulnerable. In a healthier world, adults would enjoy the freedom to be childlike without fear of ridicule and loss of status. Perhaps you grew up with killjoys who said things like "Don't be silly!" "Stop clowning around," or "An idle brain is the devil's playground." A family I know actually used the expression "Don't be glad" when children were laughing or singing. Perhaps this attitude is a holdover from our Puritan forefathers who viewed pleasure with suspicion.

8. Of course, after puberty, sexual thoughts take over what little is left of our fantasy life. But it can also be relaxing to take a nonsexual fantasy trip to another place, say the greatest fishing hole in the world or a trip to the south of France. Building up the details of the scenario is a very enjoyable pastime.

9. Finding someone to play imagination games with is not easy. If you have a loved one with whom you share yourself, why not share imagination games?

10. If you have preschool children, you may have played fantasy games or had tea parties with them. There is no scoring, no winner, and no prize. This kind of play is for the sheer joy it brings the believers. At an adult birthday party, you may have played nightclub singer or done a skit. But have you ever played elaborated charades in which small groups of people take turns miming various modes of travel such as riding in a balloon or a roller coaster while the others guess what they're doing? This form of noncompetitive adult play is, alas, too rare.

Keeping a Diary

In answering the above questions, you have the basis for keeping a diary. Of course, the content of your diary will depend on whether you believe that someone else will be reading it. It might be a good idea to keep to yourself the very fact that you are keeping a journal, lest you tempt someone's curiosity beyond what he or she can bear. If you are a teacher thinking about giving a journal-keeping assignment, make sure students are absolutely clear about who will read the journals and what the contents of the diary should include.

In your personal journal, you may wish to include your reflections about your childhood as in the questions above. Also, it's a good idea to elaborate at some length on your own past successes. Forget about past failures for now. You're probably more interested in finding new paths to follow than being weighted down by concerns over the ones that were dead ends.

Also include in your diary a record of new thoughts, no matter how impractical or strange. Record all your unusual ideas, your dreams, and strong feelings of all types. Write down what you wonder, questions you can't answer, decisions you have to make. Elaborate on your recurrent or compelling urges to say or do something. Make sketches or describe your raw ideas for inventions, cartoons, and other projects, whether you ever complete them or not. Upon re-reading your diary, you can reflect on the strong emotions you experienced. How well did you work through them? Are any feelings being repressed or denied, or have you processed your emotions fully? Are there emotional incidents you "forgot" to mention that may be causing selective forgetting and result in a blockage?

Having the Courage to Create

Any changes in your activities and your way of perceiving yourself will be noticed by the people who know you. People are used to you the way you are. Changing things about yourself will produce some resistance from those who want you to stay the same. Is that OK with you? What are you willing to risk to become more creative? Status? Approval? Free time?

There is no doubt that the greatest sources of creativity lie deep within the inner region of a person's psyche—a region not generally known to our conscious minds. In his book *The Undiscovered Self,* psychiatrist Carl Jung (1957) discusses the process of discovering the hidden side of the psyche. When the inner self is totally free, one's powers of creativity are unfathomable. But the joys of exploring the hidden treasures that lie in the inner self are not easily accessible. According to Jung, those very things desired—joy and a sense of inner power—lie beneath the deepest fears and the most uncomfortable admissions one could make.

Jung gave the name *shadow* to the unconscious side of the psyche, which accompanies the conscious mind and affects us at all times. The shadow is connected to the more primitive side of human nature. Becoming aware of the shadow side is not necessarily easy to do, for the shadow side contains energies and impulses that "decent folk" don't have, or so they believe. There is a natural tendency for people to ignore the shadow side, to deny its existence, and to repress its energies. But the process of repressing the shadow side, according to Jung, can result in serious maladjustments and even severe mental health problems. Furthermore, the shadow side is deeply involved in the creative process. To reach greater heights of creativity, one must overcome the fear of the inner bogey men who roam the corridors of the subconscious mind. Anyone who is serious about unlocking the full potential of the creative mind must become comfortable with, and, indeed, learn to embrace the shadow side. Although bringing these issues to light in the right manner at the right pace will ultimately result in greater happiness, inner freedom, and more zest for life, such a program of self-discovery requires considerable courage.

A Fable: *The Boy and the Unicorn*

Once upon a time near a great and unspoiled forest there lived a shy little boy who loved to spend his days walking in the woods, keeping an ear tuned to the sounds of the animals who lived in the forest. Whenever he saw one of the animals who lived there, he gave it a name. He knew many deer, birds, and badgers by name and even some foxes, and they grew to know him and trust him. One day as the boy came home from the forest, a thoughtless man in the town saw him and said, "Look, there's the scruffy little forest urchin who thinks he's a boy." He laughed and laughed at the boy, and the name "forest urchin" stuck because the boy spent so much time in the woods. After that incident, the boy spent even more time there because the animals did not tease him and mock the things he loved.

One day on his way deep into the woods, the little boy came to a secluded grove he'd never seen before, even though he'd been near it many times. The grove seemed to glow, and the boy moved deeper into the woods to find out why. To his great surprise, behind a large sycamore tree, he found a live unicorn. When the unicorn saw the boy, it was not alarmed, so the boy came slowly out of the trees toward it. The unicorn seemed to know the boy was trustworthy. The boy walked slowly around the unicorn, which glowed with a soft, wondrous light. The boy could not turn his eyes away because he was filled with the greatest amazement and joy he had ever felt. He petted the unicorn and let it lick his hand with its long, rough tongue. He thought of taking the unicorn back to the village. But then a little voice inside him said, "If you take the unicorn to the village, people will make cruel jokes, and you will be sorry." Yes, the boy thought, and straight away he set about building a shelter for the unicorn so it would be there in the forest when he came back to find it.

The boy piled up heaps of flat stones and laid branches over them. "This will make a fine shelter," the boy said and settled in with the unicorn until the sky was nearly dark. As the light faded, he promised to come back to feed it and comb its soft, fleecy coat every day. He sadly waved good-bye to the unicorn and set out down the path toward home.

That night the boy did not say a word to anyone about the unicorn, not even his little sister. He went to bed and fell fast asleep with thoughts of visiting the unicorn the next day. But when the boy woke up, he had a vague sense of dread, and he decided to wait a day before he went back into the forest to the unicorn shelter. The next day, the boy had chores to do, so he couldn't very well go to the woods that day. The next day, it looked like it might rain, so he

RAHAM

didn't go back into the woods then either, though he planned to go back to the unicorn shelter by the end of the week. But on Friday, he stubbed his toe and thought, "I'll wait till this wound heals; after all, it's a long walk to the unicorn shelter." Another day passed, then a week, and the boy found new interests that kept him from taking the long hike into the woods.

One night many months later, the boy went to sleep as usual, but all night long he dreamed about the unicorn, how hungry it was, how lonely it was, and how badly it needed him. He dreamed it was dying. At daybreak the boy sprang from his bed, put on his clothes, and dashed as fast as his legs would carry him into the woods toward the unicorn shelter. But now bramble bushes had grown over the path, and he got lost. Still, the lad's determination was strong, so he kept searching and searching till he found his way. He ran down the path and soon came to a pile of mossy rocks, which he recognized were the flat stones that had once been the unicorn shelter he had built all by himself so long ago. "What bad shape it is in now," he thought, "with stones all tumbled away by the rain and woodchucks." He wished that he had come back sooner. He called and called for the lovely unicorn, but it never came. Sadly, the boy turned and walked slowly out of the woods toward home. ♦

Growth Activity 2-3: Thinking About Blockages to Creativity

Write another ending to the fable *The Boy and the Unicorn.*

REFERENCES

Abra, Jock. 1988. *Assaulting Parnassus: Theoretical Views of Creativity.* Lanham, MD: University Press of America.

Arieti, Silvano. 1976. *The Magic Synthesis.* New York: Basic Books.

Crutchfield, Richard. 1973. The Creative Process. In *Creativity: Theory and Research.* Edited by Morton Bloomberg. New Haven, CT: College and University Press.

Jung, Carl G. 1957. *The Undiscovered Self.* New York: Mentor.

Lomboroso, Cesare. [1864]/1976. Genius and Insanity. In *The Creativity Question.* Edited by Albert Rothenburg and Carl R. Hausman. Durham, NC: Duke University Press.

May, Rollo. 1975. *The Courage to Create.* New York: Bantam Books.

Russ, Sandra. 1993. *Affect and Creativity: The Role of Affect and Play in the Creative Process.* Hinsdale, NJ: Lawrence Erlbaum.

Springer, Sally, and Georg Deutsch. 1981. *Left Brain, Right Brain.* San Francisco: W. H. Freeman.

Torrance, E. Paul. 1963. Creativity. In *What Research Says to the Classroom Teacher.* Washington, DC: National Education Association.

Vygotsky, Lev. 1978. *Mind in Society: The Development of Higher Psychological Processes.* Translated from the 1930 original. Cambridge, MA: Harvard University Press.

FURTHER READING

Adams, James L. 1974. *Conceptual Blockbusting: A Guide to Better Ideas.* San Francisco: W. H. Freeman.

Amabile, Teresa, and Beth Hennessey. 1988. The Conditions of Creativity. In *The Nature of Creativity: Contemporary Psychological Perspectives.* Edited by Robert J. Sternberg. New York: Press Syndicate of the University of Cambridge.

Barron, Frank. 1967. The Psychology of the Creative Writer. In *Explorations in Creativity.* Edited by R. L. Mooney and T.A. Razik. New York: Harper & Row.

———. 1976. The Psychology of Creativity. In *The Creativity Question.* Edited by Albert Rothenburg and Carl R. Hausman. Durham, NC: Duke University Press.

Crutchfield, Richard. 1967. Instructing the Individual in Creative Thinking. In *Explorations in Creativity.* Edited by R. L. Mooney and T. A. Razik. New York: Harper & Row.

Kubie, Lawrence. 1967. Blocks to Creativity. In *Explorations in Creativity.* Edited by R. L. Mooney and T. A. Razik. New York: Harper & Row.

Maslow, Abraham. 1964. *Religions, Values, and Peak Experiences.* New York: Penguin Books.

———. 1967. The Creative Attitude. In *Explorations in Creativity.* Edited by R. L. Mooney and T. A. Razik. New York: Harper and Row.

Starko, Alane Jordan. 1995. *Creativity in the Classroom: Schools of Curious Delight.* White Plains, NY: Longman.

Torrance, E. Paul. 1967. The Nurture of Creative Talents. In *Explorations in Creativity.* Edited by R. L. Mooney and T. A. Razik. New York: Harper & Row.

———. 1976. Education and Creativity. In *The Creativity Question.* Edited by Albert Rothenburg and Carl R. Hausman. Durham, NC: Duke University Press.

Module 3

The Creative Teacher at Work

In an attempt to combine sports and academics, officials at Culver High devised aerobic algebra.

CAN ANYONE WHO WANTS TO TEACH CREATIVELY, DO SO?

Like needlepoint or archery, teaching creatively depends on natural ability, self-perception, and commitment to practice. Of course, not everyone has the steady hand and keen eye it takes to become an expert at needlepoint or archery. But needlepoint and archery are only two of the many ways the creative process manifests itself. Detectives, architects, and government policymakers, too, exhibit the kind of divergent thinking that is central to the capacity to come up with something new. As we have already seen, creativity is not rare. The average person possesses hidden or suppressed creative abilities, which are capable of unfolding—even blossoming—given the right setting, training, and encouragement. Virtually any teacher already possesses sufficient creativity to do quite a good job of creative teaching.

In becoming good at something, it is often necessary to become "not bad" at it first. In other words, the first and immediate goal for improving performance is to avoid the pitfalls that subtract from performance. As political pollsters say, to have "low negatives" is positive.

Some Things Poor Teachers Do That Good Teachers Don't

According to student surveys, teachers are not good when they:

- lose their temper; are cross, crabby, or grouchy; never smile; nag; use sarcasm;
- do not provide help with schoolwork; do not explain lessons and assignments clearly;
- plan task sequences poorly;
- exhibit partiality; have "pets" and pick on others;
- maintain an air of superiority; are "snooty," overbearing; "do not know you outside of class";
- exhibit futility, impatience, and frustration, and verbalize this frustration in such ways as "Aren't you ever going to learn this?" and "No, wrong again!" (Hamachek 1968, 9-10)

There's no secret to being a "not bad" teacher: Simply don't be impatient, aloof, sarcastic, disorganized, unhelpful, or condescending, and you'll be a "not bad" teacher.

What Good Teachers Do That Poor Teachers Don't

Being a "not bad" teacher is a gigantic first step for a novice teacher, but it is clearly not enough. To become a good teacher, one must adopt gradually, through feedback and practice, new behaviors, skills, and attitudes. Having a pleasant appearance, a kindly nature, and a good deal of patience are personal prerequisites to good teaching, but these are not part of the craft of teaching. The craft of teaching focuses on teaching behavior, which is something a willing person can change if necessary. Research has identified some of the behavior patterns present in good teachers but lacking in poor teachers (Hamachek 1968, 10). Good teachers:

- exercise flexibility;
- see the world from students' viewpoint;
- personalize teaching;
- engender willingness to experiment, try out new things;
- ask questions skillfully;
- possess a broad knowledge of the subject;
- exhibit skill in definite, regular assessments;
- provide study helps;
- act in a manner appropriate to the situation, both on a verbal and nonverbal level;

- employ a conversational manner and a relaxed, informal attitude;
- maintain the belief that everyone can learn this subject;
- are genuinely concerned about the students' growth;
- use constructive, not critical feedback: "Aha! that's a new idea." "Do you suppose you could supply a better word?" "You're on a roll; expand on that thought." "Maybe my question wasn't phrased clearly. I'll ask it another way."

Concept Development Activity 3-1: Creating Super Teacher

From your own experience, pick out half a dozen qualities of the best teachers you've had from all levels of schooling. Describe the Super Teacher, who is a combination of all these qualities.

Six Skills for Creative Teaching

The foundation of creative teaching is a set of learnable skills, that is, the craft of creative teaching. As with needlepoint or archery, virtually everyone can learn the skills of creative teaching. Listed below are six skills necessary to teach creatively; these will be elaborated on in Module 4:

- Managing
- Presenting
- Questioning
- Designing
- Running Activities
- Relating

What Does Creative Teaching Look Like in Practice?

To become a creative teacher, you must combine creativity and good teaching. Based on her own research and that of others, Sandra Russ (1993) found certain traits more frequently in teachers who were identified as creative. Creative teachers were

more likable
more interested
more satisfied
more enthusiastic
more courteous
more business-like
more professional
more encouraging

Many of these traits are personality factors rather than classroom behaviors. In answering the question "What can teachers do to help students develop their own creativity?" psychologists Teresa Amabile and Beth Hennessey (1988) and E. Paul Torrance (1963, 1967) provide several guidelines.

1. Whenever possible, give students a choice of how to perform a task.
2. Use rewards to reinforce positive feelings about the project, not as the sole purpose of doing it.
3. Encourage play and fantasy in the right context.
4. Maintain sufficient emotional distance in relationships with students; be warm and supportive but allow the student to develop independence and initiative.
5. Help students make constructive evaluation of their work, and don't overuse evaluation.
6. Recognize and tolerate the unusual.
7. Help students resist peer pressure to conform for conformity's sake.

Putting all these factors together, here's an example of a skilled creative teacher in action.

A Creative Lesson in French

The room was set up almost like a ministage: a semicircle of six chairs at the front facing the audience, a stack of hats, colored markers, and an easel with blank paper. On the wall behind the semicircle hung a chart showing the verb forms of "to be" and "to live," and the words to the song "On the Bridge of Avignon" were posted in French. Nearby hung butcher paper posters containing lists of French words: colors, French cities, occupations, and first names (Jacques, Brigitte, Yvette, Pierre, and so on.)

After the class had settled in, the teacher, Pamela Rand, changed her voice, manner, and posture and spoke exclusively in French for nearly all of the next 90 minutes. She greeted us in French and with hand gestures, coaching us to repeat her words. We spoke the phrases several times, prompted by Pamela's gestures to listen to the sounds. We repeated the phrases, making attempts to improve them.

She called for six volunteers to take seats in the semicircle. Obeying Pamela's mimicry, the volunteers each chose a first name from the list of names. Pamela introduced herself and picked up a flower. She described the flower in French, then handed it to one of the members of the circle, gesturing him to introduce himself to a neighbor and present the flower. Likewise, the volunteers chose a city they were from and an occupation (artist, banker, doctor, builder) and took from the stack of hats the one appropriate to his or her occupation.

In the process of choosing hats, the group conjugated the irregular verbs *to live, to work,* and *to give.* The students then chose a color, made a name tag, gave their French names, told what city they came from, and what their occupations were. Counting to 10 was presented during this phase and practiced several times.

Pamela then pulled a hand puppet out of a grocery bag. The puppet introduced himself, and called on each volunteer student to tell his or her name, home city, and occupation. During the segment with the puppet, someone made a wisecrack and things got silly. Pamela broke into English and had all the students close their eyes and imagine themselves putting on a huge feathered hat which she described. As the class settled down, the students opened their eyes, and Pamela continued the description of the hat in French. She abandoned the hand puppet at this stage.

Pamela broke into the song "On the Bridge of Avignon." After singing it once, she pointed to the poster and brought the class in on the song. The song has slots in it for each person to insert his or her name, city, and occupation. The song was repeated over and over with each person filling in the slots with appropriate name, occupation, and city. During the singing of the song, Pamela joined hands with a volunteer and began a dance, then more and more people entered the dance until there was a circle that eventually included every class member. Finally, Pamela signaled the last verse. The class finished the song and everyone sat down.

In the course of the lesson, the teacher had spoken more than 500 French words and had drilled the class in more than 100 French words. She conjugated a dozen irregular verbs, counted to 10, gave the days of the week, months of the year, and major French cities. The class's attention did not wane even with the copious repetition and 90-minute format.

Some Observations of What Pamela Did

During the 90-minute French lesson Pamela did the following:

- Maintained a continuous outpouring of joy, a positive, partylike feeling
- Dispelled apprehension and self-consciousness with a soothing tone of voice and graceful body language
- Did not leave learning to chance
- Read students' readiness level by nonverbal cues and responded accordingly
- Let students know their responses had been heard
- Did not say "no," but stated the correct response
- Stood close to pupils; touched them appropriately, suggesting "if you trust, you'll learn"
- Maintained expectancy; was always ahead of students' expectations
- Involved everyone with eye contact, hand gestures, and proximity
- Used puppets to inject humor into the lesson and for practicing familiar forms of address not possible otherwise
- Suggested esteem for every student by individual help, eye contact, and smiles for everyone
- Allowed a rhythmic flow of activity but introduced "just imagine" to throttle back the pace
- Reduced self-consciousness by not verbalizing commands, using gestures in place of many verbal commands as in "Follow the Leader"

- Used her voice well, changing volume, pitch, and tone at various times, and even singing
- Moved to every section of the room
- Was very responsive to the class's moods and level of understanding

STAGES OF CREATIVE INSTRUCTION

Creative teaching is not really spontaneous though skilled teachers such as Pamela make it appear so. The creative teacher establishes an environment where creativity is a normal part of learning. Units of study unfold at a brisk pace with a great variety of learning activities designed to produce a higher level of understanding and personal appreciation of the topic. Generally, the organization of the instruction for a unit proceeds in four stages:

1. Designing the Unit of Instruction
2. Immersion
3. Construction of Knowledge
4. Culmination

Stage 1: Designing the Unit of Instruction

The teacher lays out a unified block of instruction that will last about three weeks or so. The teacher's goal is to engage every student fully in meaningful learning for the whole unit. This is accomplished by examining the material to be studied, identifying curiosities and interesting questions, and formulating a central problem to work on. In teaching the material, the teacher will employ a variety of formats such as role-playing, games, dramatic readings, fictional narratives, case studies, seminars, scripts and story writing, and performances by individuals, small groups, or the teacher. The tasks selected require that students use various forms of creativity: artistic, constructive, theatrical, inventive, and interpersonal.

A unit should be designed with the understanding that learning does not occur instantaneously. True learning occurs only when the student has constructed a meaningful network that ties together facts and ideas with personal interests and concerns of the student. A model called the Learning Cycle, proposed by Robert Karplus (1964) and Ed Labinowicz (1980) divides learning into three repeating stages: exploration, invention, and application. During a unit of study, the teacher should provide activities and materials that guide students through the three stages of the Learning Cycle, first on a simple, observational level, then on a more detailed and abstract level.

The atmosphere of the creative teacher's classroom is one of positive energy and success, of people respected for their individuality, yet able to work together for the common good. Tension is absent. The mood is light; if fun isn't happening right then, it may break out at any moment. Students enjoy their relationships with the teacher and each other. Learning is a joyful enterprise. The feeling is that students are eager to share what they've created because they believe that it will be respected. Students know what is expected of them and willingly produce a tangible product containing their own self-expression or original thinking, which is appreciated and encouraged.

Stage 2: Immersion

Immersion puts students in direct contact with exploration, the first and most often neglected stage of the Learning Cycle. The immersion phase may last a quarter hour to several days. The students are exposed to the central problem via a demonstration, a mystery, an observation, a photograph, a case study, a poem, or some other means of piquing students' interest. (This stage goes way beyond Madeline Hunter's anticipatory set because it is interactive and raises more questions than it can answer at that time. Also, the anticipatory set is a brief interlude in a teacher-driven process, whereas the immersion phase of the creative teaching process draws students into a topic to explore, investigate, analyze, and link to other knowledge.) The immersion stage presents the central question, mystery, or major issue that will serve to anchor the entire unit. The point of the immersion phase is to arouse curiosity, anticipation, and the personal need to know, and to provide a focus for primary data to be analyzed and extended later. If the immersion phase does its job, it will leave the students wanting to know more about the topic presented and eager to pursue solutions to the central problem.

Students must be given time to develop an interest in the material, not have it handed to them. The immersion phase of creative instruction ignites the creative process, which begins by *sensing dissonance* or a felt need. Without a discrepancy to resolve or a personal felt need, motivation will be less than 100 percent. Immersion also initiates the pooling stage. No conclusions are drawn; no overview is given yet.

Stage 3: Construction of Knowledge

Construction of knowledge is the heart of the learning process. This phase begins with the identification of learning goals and lesson objectives. Initially, these objectives may be chosen by the teacher, but after several units, students will participate in determining some of them. Once the learning goals and lesson objectives are determined and presented, an approximate timetable is established and notice is given in writing of the unit's written and reading assignments.

Right about now you may be questioning the need for such

a well-defined structure in a classroom focusing on creativity. After all, isn't creativity connected to freedom? Maybe so, but creative work demands a lot of concentration. The purpose of having a study guide containing the unit goals and lesson objectives is to free the students' minds from "housekeeping" chores and reduce one of the main sources of background anxiety: worry over "What am I supposed to do?" Maria Montessori found that when the structure of learning is managed efficiently by the teacher, the total energy of the students can be used for creative tasks. In Montessori's words,

> It is the perfect organization of work, permitting the possibility of self-development and giving outlet for the energies, which procures for each child the beneficial and calming satisfaction. And it is under such conditions of work that liberty leads to a perfecting of the activities, and to the attainment of a fine discipline which is in itself the result of that new quality of calmness that has been developed in the child (Montessori [1915] 1965, 187).

The creative teacher uses a broad selection of activities and assessments of learning on a continuous basis. Students are asked to reflect on their own learning and perhaps periodically record self-observations of their level of cooperation and contribution to the class's climate and progress.

During the construction of knowledge phase of the learning process, the creative teacher uses three overlapping and concurrent classroom skills: questioning on many levels, presenting tasks and material, and running activities.

Questioning

A creative teacher is most easily recognized by the manner in which he or she asks questions. The creative teacher

- asks more questions than a traditional teacher;
- inquires about students' suppositions and previous knowledge;
- follows through by asking students to elaborate on their reasoning after both correct and incorrect answers;
- asks open-ended questions such as "What is music?";
- asks students to link one bit of knowledge to another;
- asks more higher-order questions such as *classify, analyze, design,* and *rearrange* rather than just *who, what, when, where*; and
- inquires about students' feelings and calls for individual reactions to what is presented.

Presenting

The creative teacher's presentation of new material is clear and lively, maintaining a balance on the work-play continuum. Students and the teacher laugh occasionally, and between laughs, the mood is one of levity, the readiness to laugh. Laughter is never at anyone's expense unless the humor is self-deprecating. Tasks are presented clearly with sufficient instructions so there are few procedural questions. Tasks to be assessed or scored are explained clearly with written guidelines to refer to as the project proceeds. Sufficient guided and independent practice is provided before any scored assignment, graded test, or performance in front of the class. Students expect to be held accountable for all work they've done and realize that some type of assessment is part of all learning.

Running Activities

The creative teacher runs activities smoothly, always with an end purpose in mind. Rather than developing a capacity to parrot what the teacher or textbook says, activities should deepen the child's understanding, make connections to what is already known, identify suppositions and misconceptions, present the material from another viewpoint, and allow students to appreciate wonder and beauty contained in what is studied and build a meaningful personal understanding of the material.

Relating to Students

While interacting with students, the creative teacher's caring way of relating to them is evident. The teacher openly values individual uniqueness, makes eye contact generously and democratically, jokes with students, encourages and assures students, praises their efforts (not products) lavishly, and smiles a lot. When speaking to a student one to one, the teacher positions himself or herself at or below the student's eye level, listens attentively, and may call for a clarification of the question before giving an answer. The teacher might touch students lightly in the neutral zone from wrist to shoulder as he or she interacts with them.

The creative teacher uses a wide variety of work formats: large group, team, pair, and solo. The teacher engages students in dialogues about their learning and their feelings. To keep students on task, the creative teacher keeps an alert eye on the whole group and does not "write off" any student. Sometimes the creative teacher acts more like a shepherd or a coach, keeping the group working on the task at hand. When discipline is necessary, the creative teacher intervenes early. The interaction is private, calm, and corrective rather than punitive and judgmental. The teacher asks the student to reflect on the problem behavior as it affects the other students and himself or herself. The focus stays on behavior that needs to change and not on the many side issues in which the unwanted behavior is embedded.

Stage 4: Culmination

With the teacher's help, students in the culmination phase of learning will unify, consolidate, and reflect on the learning that has taken place. Students will

- review the central problem and list and compare the solutions found;
- look back over the unit to identify themes and large ideas it contained;
- review concepts and vocabulary;
- produce a tangible product to demonstrate that learning has taken place;

- reflect on what and how they learned; and
- possibly take a practice or scored exam.

Concept Development Activity 3-2: Watching Conrack, a Creative Teacher at Work

Pat Conroy, author of *Prince of Tides, Beach Music,* and other novels, taught in a public school for several years. *Conrack,* a movie based on his book *The Water Is Wide,* starred Jon Voight. Rent the video of *Conrack* (Ravetch and Frank 1974).

Part A: Look for several instances of creative teaching. Tell what teaching skill they relate to.

Part B: Were any of Mr. Conroy's methods counterproductive? Which ones? Why?

PUTTING CREATIVE ELEMENTS TOGETHER

Coaching Students in the Creative Process

Each of the various stages of the creative process requires specific skills. Developing these specific skills is the focus of the remainder of this book. To start, here is an overview of some ways to encourage habits for greater creative productivity.

Sensing Dissonance

Finding a fertile project requires a nose for contradiction, oddity, mystery, riddles, wondering, and questioning. Indeed, creativity has been defined as *problem-finding* ability (Getzels and Csikszentmihalyi 1975). The teacher should, on occasion, ask questions that he or she can't answer. The teacher should also ask open-ended questions with no predefined answer. Initially, some youngsters will think you are teasing them because they literally believe that you know every answer and must be withholding answers to torment them. Other children have lived under strong authoritarian rules at home and are too timid to question what they see as discrepancies. Children need permission to ask exploratory questions. The teacher should invite student questions and should honor every question a child comes up with.

Pooling Elements

The usual pattern at this stage is for a student to fire off two or three similar ideas, then want to move on to the next step in the lesson. This is where the teacher must direct the learning process. Not only are we looking for a large number of ideas, we are looking for diversity in ideas. The fifth or sixth item of the same type is less valuable than a new type of item. At this stage students need to go beyond their comfort zone.

A knowledge of the regulatory rules and constraints of the specific situation you're working in is vital here. The diversity of ideas is often limited by external constraints, for example, in a short-story contest, the guidelines for length, content, format, even type of paper may be specified. The whole project could turn out worthless if you inadvertently slip in an element that will later cause the solution or product to be disqualified.

Searching for a Synthesis

This stage takes time. Many students have been conditioned to seek quick results and will want to hurry this part of the learning process along. People who have not done much creative work do not respect the need for creative play with the elements. Playing with the elements helps people get to know and appreciate the subtle characteristics of the situation. The teacher must play brakeman to keep the train from running away toward the first possibility that comes along. As with the pooling stage, while searching for a synthesis, many people want to throw out one possibility and close down the process. Creativity's essence is finding alternatives. The teacher needs to get in the habit of asking, "What's another way to do this?" The list of possibilities should always include at least several, if not many, contrasting alternatives. What's called for here is high frustration tolerance and deliberate suspension of closure.

Once the students are moving in the right direction, they will need encouragement. Now the teacher is the midwife. Midwives coach women giving birth with phrases such as "Push, push, push, breathe, take a rest; you're doing fine." When children are giving birth to a creative idea, the creativity coach says, "You're off to a good start; let's spin that out. Yes, now give me another idea. Yes, and what else? Can you think of an alternative? Give me a different way to express that." No criticism is offered, only exhortations to continue, expand, alter, diversify, modify, or complete the original idea.

Incubation

To the novice, incubation looks like quitting. But this confusion grows out of the lack of appreciation for the unconscious processes of the mind. Creative ideas cannot be forced out. Creative projects need more lead time than routine projects because incubation is often needed in the middle of the project.

Inspiration

The inspiration stage, the time when you finally locate the solution or main idea, is a moment of relief of frustration, if not unbridled celebration. If you savor the moment of inspiration before returning to work, then finishing the project becomes a pleasure rather than a burden.

Verification

After the moment of celebration has run its course, it is time to get down to practical matters. Here is where honesty and flexibility are required. Honesty means being true to what a thing is. If a large investment of time and effort has been made, there is a tendency to want to be finished. Often students do not take the time to proofread, edit, or check their results. Some students may want to fudge the specifications of the project or overrate the product to protect the previous investment in it. But the truth will eventually get out. Better to face up to what a thing is—good, bad, or middling—than to pretend it's something it's not. Students need encouragement not to quit the project before this vital stage is completed.

A Summary of 30 Tools for Creative Teaching

To help students learn best, teachers need to develop a whole range of varied teaching tools—a veritable treasure chest of techniques—to choose from in planning and presenting lessons. Here is a brief rundown on some creative lesson formats that can be adapted to most subject areas and levels; formats will be explained or illustrated in the coming modules.

1. *Storytelling* may the oldest art form, and for good reason. The human mind seems particularly adept at comprehending information when it is presented in the story format. Effective storytelling can be learned by anyone willing to practice the craft.
2. *Seminars* provide students an opportunity to read a passage or examine a work critically, then engage in conversation to enrich their understanding of the work.
3. *Discussions* come in many varieties, from anecdote swapping to teacher-directed discussions. Students need opportunities to recite as well as receive or construct knowledge.
4. *Puzzles* contain discrepancies that both motivate and provide students the opportunity to burrow deeper into a subject.

5. *Problem Solving* involves more than doing math; it refers to open-ended problem solving, too. Teacher-designed problems can be used in groups or by individuals to polish problem-solving skills.

6. *Designing* requires a complete understanding of constraints and trade-offs. It requires innovation and divergent thinking. Designing involves collaboration and a thorough understanding of the content involved, providing excellent practice in three upper-tier activities on Bloom's (1956) taxonomy: analysis, synthesis, and evaluation.

7. *Ensemble Design* is a group project. Suppose a city is to be built in space. What economic, social, political, religious, educational, and physical mechanisms must be built in to make it work? Small groups design one aspect, then pool results for class discussion.

8. *Dramatic Reading* occurs when the teacher, a student, or several students prepare a special piece of written material (a poem, diary, narrative, speech, or other work worthy of oral reading) and present it to the class using vocal and theatrical technique.

9. *Question Stringing* is a technique in which the teacher, given a curio or stage prop such as an antique rifle or specimen from the sea floor, makes observations, asks questions, and reflects students' questions back to them without giving any information about the object until the end of the lesson.

10. *Story Writing* provides an alternative to a long report. Students instead research factual material and incorporate it into a story. A dramatic story needs four basic elements to be successful: vivid description, engaging characters, imagination, and dramatic structure.

11. *Creative Elaboration* develops the ability to imagine, empathize, and deduce particular consequences for characters in history or fiction.

12. *Description* can be either subjective or objective. Each requires close observation by students. Both scientific work and creative writing benefit from observation and description activities.

13. *Imagination*, unfortunately, is rarely used in the classroom. With some guidance and practice, a teacher can blend imagination activities into many learning situations.

14. *Readers Theater* involves a group of students reading orally from a prepared script derived from a literary work of enduring merit.

15. *Choice Mapping* helps students learn the basis of making sound choices. To choose wisely, one must first have a clear idea of the available choices. Choice Trees, Outcome Cascades, and Option Grids help students clarify and evaluate assignment choices as well as personal and societal options.

16. *Ethical Dilemmas* can be resolved by students in the classroom. Lawrence Kohlberg and others have found that discussions of scenarios involving a choice between two or more options facilitate the development of moral reasoning. (See pp. 137-43.)

17. *Collaborative Inquiry* puts the entire class to work on various aspects of a large investigation to which everyone contributes.

18. *Case Studies* are investigations of a hypothesis using data from a particular source. Case studies seek to uncover and understand cause-effect relationships, which are vital to true learning.

19. *Reconstructive Writing* involves putting new words to old songs or combining an historical document with a game show format; it adds interest to dry material.

20. *Fictional Narrative* involves students, after studying events in the past, devising a fictional character and constructing the event as seen through the character's eyes.

21. *Fictional Correspondence* allows students to write City Hall about recycling or any current topic or, after studying two sides of an historical debate, to invent characters who carry on a correspondence about the question. In a variation of fictional correspondence, *Fictional Diaries* can serve as the record of imaginary people who lived in various periods of history, or even colonists writing about their struggles in the early days of life in the first Mars colony.

22. *Simulations* re-create complex processes on a small scale: For example, after studying nineteenth century immigration, class members re-create and enact a series of stops at the processing center on Ellis Island. Some immigrants are allowed to pass through; others are sent back.[1]

23. *Discovery Labs* make use of common, safe phenomena such as soap bubbles and spinning tops so that students can explore the properties in an unstructured way. The teacher facilitates the learning by asking the right questions and focusing attention.

24. *Role-Playing* provides an opportunity for students to explore controversial issues in a fictional form, which evokes less defensiveness than direct confrontation.

25. *Scripts* can be as simple as an interview or as complex as a play. Nearly everyone can write short dialogues to convey a point because people engage in dialogues every day.

26. *Ensemble Biographies* allow students to play people in the life of a famous person, for example, Thomas Jefferson. Students must research their roles (e.g., the housekeeper at Monticello, a neighboring farmer, Jefferson's father-in law, a rival in the House of Burgesses). The teacher plays a TV interviewer and asks each character to come forward and tell what he or she knows about the famous person.

27. *Enactments* are the most engaging form of theatrical creativity. Learning to enact is a three-step process. Begin with script-writing, add performance, and you get to enactment.

28. *Schematizing* or creating a Schematic Drawing, Flow Chart, or Concept Web, requires a good understanding of both the factual content and the relationship of the pieces to the whole. By actively

constructing their own schematics or customizing stock diagrams, students build a deeper understanding of the material and its internal organization.

29. *Board Games* satisfy the deeply human urge to create games, an impulse that is apparently universal in humans and is a significant motivator in young people. To create a simulation game requires thinking completely through the game parameters. Designing strategies and rules for a game is equivalent to constructing knowledge about the material to be learned.

30. *Class Publications* provide an excellent opportunity for in-depth learning to take place. Students put together a scrapbook, catalog, or newspaper from another period or place: *The Renaissance Times*, *The Left Bank*, or *The Colonial Daily News*.

Choosing Activities That Fit Well Together

Activities vary in many important ways; for example, length, concentration level required, and size of the group involved. Generally speaking, the larger the group, the higher the energy level, meaning there will be more noise, spontaneous speaking, joking, and fun. Solo projects such as writing a story, drawing a schematic, or working on a Hypercard file usually produce intense concentration and an examlike quiet. In between the low-energy level of solo work and the high-energy level of performance activities lies small group work, which at best produces intense focus and such good peer interaction that it is hard to recapture the class's attention. Discovery labs, board games, collaborative inquiry, open-ended problem solving, and ensemble design usually fill the room with "good noise"—students interacting, asking each other questions, proposing hypotheses, or challenging each others' suppositions or beliefs. Small group activities, however, do require constant monitoring. If supervision is lacking, some students will likely drift off task into mischief. Performance and other large group activities such as readers theater, ensemble biography, simulations, dramatic reading, and seminars usually have the highest energy levels. The problem with these activities is managing the group dynamic: neither squelching positive energy nor letting childish chaos take over. High-energy activities are usually a good choice for the first thing in the morning or right after lunch, when energy levels need raising. On the other end of the spectrum, a large group activity on the Friday before a vacation, when students' energy levels are already high, may get out of hand.

In designing a unit, the teacher should choose activities for balance and rhythm, producing a smooth flow between levels of energy and avoiding sudden shifts up or down. The length and difficulty level of activities should be varied as well as the size of the group involved—solo work being mixed with large and small group work into a balanced blend. With experience, choosing a balanced variety of activities becomes second nature. For example, after an imaginary excursion, you will probably want to avoid any kind of performance activity such as readers theater, role-playing, ensemble reading, or student skits. These activities will not work well without a high-energy level, and students will probably want to savor the quiet mood brought on by the imaginary excursion. A better choice to go with the mellow mood of an imaginary excursion would be specimen drawing and other observation activities as well as solo projects such as individual research, fictional correspondence, or computer work such as a Hypercard file.

A Sample Unit for Creative Teaching: The Mysteries of Easter Island

Note: This unit is provided as an exemplar of what is possible rather than as an illustration of what a teacher would actually do. It is hard to imagine a school setting where a teacher had such an abundance of time and complete control over the curriculum as presented here. Still, this unit illustrates how to replace some traditional (and all but worthless) techniques such as lengthy silent reading, long-winded teacher talk, outlining the chapter, and defining lists of words with engaging methods of teaching.

Audience: Eighth-grade social studies class

Materials: A set of about two dozen slides have been prepared by rephotographing from library books. (See appendix 3: Preparing Slides and Transparencies from Books) The slides depict the landscape, beaches, and volcanic cones rising high above the islands. One slide depicts a tall ship anchored in the harbor. Many other slides show the famous elongated stone heads in various stages of completion, a few still on their backs in the quarry. Petroglyphs of birds and other figures are shown in one view and, finally, a high crag with large birds' nests in the foreground. In the background, a short way out to sea off a jagged point of rock, lies an even more rugged, volcanic island which lacks any beaches. Select a tape of music with a relaxing, slightly mysterious mood and no discernible melody. Have available copies of the *National Geographic* article, "Easter Island and Its Mysterious Monuments," by Howard La Fay (January 1962).

Day 1

At the beginning of the lesson, the students are told, "We are going to take a trip in our imaginations, a trip I think you'll like. I'm going to ask you to use your imagination, and it should be a lot of fun." The lights are dimmed, the music is turned on low, and the *imaginary excursion* begins.

For a minute or so, the only sound is that of soft music played to set the mood. The teacher models deep breathing relaxation, standing before the class with eyes closed and body relaxed. The teacher says nothing during this time. Students who want to follow the teacher's lead and take deep breaths, close their eyes, and relax their bodies will do so on their own. (Some students may be reluctant to participate, believing they are about to be hypnotized. Of course, that is far from the intent here. In any case this is not a relaxation activity, it does not involve any subliminal suggestions and the teacher is *not* guiding anyone through the use of second-person directive statements.) The teacher then turns on the slide projector, displaying the shot of the beach at twilight, and instructs those students who have closed their eyes to open them and focus their attention on the image.

Near the water a bonfire burns, and we see a row of natives, bodies painted, wearing tall straw headdresses. They appear to be dancing to a drumbeat, although no explanation of the scene is offered here or, for that matter, anywhere in the entire hour of this lesson. (This first lesson in the series is the day of discovery; the sense of mystery will be sustained for several days, and only during the unit itself will solutions to the many of the mysteries of Easter Island be revealed.)

The teacher begins to tell a story in the first person. The story is impromptu in the sense that it is not read from a script, although the main parts of the *fictional narrative* have been committed to paper and reviewed.

> Captain Roggeven thinks they will greet us with friendship, but with natives of these South Pacific islands, there's no predicting. We sighted this island two days ago, on the afternoon of Easter Sunday in the year 1722. For half that day and all the next, we circled the island, which is a triangle six miles on a side, with volcanic peaks jutting up on each point.

The story continues at a leisurely pace with moments of silence while slide after slide of the landscape is shown. The teacher intersperses statements of amazement and wonder such as "I wonder what . . ." "No one knows . . ." "That's curious," and "Will you look at that! I don't believe what my eyes are telling me." The imaginary excursion takes us all over the island. After perhaps 20 minutes the teacher finishes. Without making any mood-breaking statements, the teacher sits down or pauses to listen to the music for a moment more, then turns the lights back on and the music down.

There is no clear break to indicate when the imaginary excursion is over and the next phase of the lesson begins. The teacher asks students to review at random what they saw, making sure to steer clear of making interpretations and inferences about the scenes. A student is called on to make a list on the board of the things they saw. There is no effort yet to organize the items. The teacher frequently asks students to elaborate, "What else could you see?" The teacher asks question after question, and when students begin to ask "why" questions, the teacher says, "What do you think?" After acknowledging the answer, the teacher calls for more and more elaborated descriptions.

After about 20 minutes, the teacher looks at the board-filling list and says, "Let's put these things we saw into groups." Categories are proposed and given numbers or letters, then the items are classified with the teacher probing some answers, not because they're incorrect, but to encourage students to verbalize their reasoning. The teacher makes few suggestions as to what categories to list and which items belong where. Finally, the items are all categorized and the lists copied down by the students for future use. This concludes Day 1 of the lesson sequence.

Day 2

The list compiled by the students is again written on the board. This lesson, a *collaborate inquiry*, begins with the teacher asking, "What questions could we ask about the things we've seen so far?" Brainstorming questions continue for 20 minutes. When the board is full of questions, the teacher picks one of the categories of listed items and says, "Let's see if we can come up with any hypotheses as to what might have caused these things to come out the way they did." The class as a whole comes up with hypotheses. When several sample hypotheses are proposed, the students are divided into small groups and told to come up with at least three additional hypotheses for their group. A student from each group writes the group's hypotheses on the board, then each student is asked to copy the entire list of hypotheses from the board.

Day 3

The teacher distributes to the students copies of the article on Easter Island for a *case study*. Each student is asked to work alone for 20 minutes to find information bearing on the hypotheses, and to write down that information. Then the teacher reconvenes the groups that were formed during the Day 2 lesson and gives them the instruction to select one of their hypotheses for the following study. Each group will discuss the evidence and come to one of three conclusions: (1) We accept the hypothesis based on the evidence; (2) we reject the hypothesis based on the evidence; or (3) we do not have enough evidence to either accept or reject our hypothesis.

Day 4

The teacher gives the students a written assignment to do in class. Each person is to summarize what his or her group has done so far and how the group reached its conclusions. The summary will include what questions were originally asked, the various hypotheses offered, and the hypothesis chosen and why. The evidence will be reviewed and the conclusion summarized. Students will then meet in small groups with students who are investigating other hypotheses, to report what has been found so far.

Day 5

Groups report their findings to the whole class. The entire small group, not just a representative, goes to the front of the class in a show of support for each other and to strengthen the idea of the group working as a unit. Class members ask the small group members questions about their findings. The teacher then directs a discussion to identify the individual roles, social groups, sources of conflict on the island, and the ways in which these conflicts were resolved. The students are asked if Easter Island would be a good place to live. Students give *creative elaboration* of the life on the island. The teacher calls for students to speculate at length about what they think daily life would have been like there: how it would have felt, the food, the society, the dreams and the fears of the islanders. (Note that, while a full week into the unit, the teacher has not yet given any didactic instruction. In Karplus's (1964) Learning Cycle, exploration and investigation must precede verification and application.)

Day 6

Using a handout, the teacher summarizes what has been found out so far, then shows a video on Easter Island. Afterwards, the students are asked to specify what new information they learned from the video, what conclusions the video made, and what evidence it presented to support these conclusions.

Days 7 and 8

The teacher leads an exploratory discussion to analyze the island's institutions. Specifically, the structure of the island society is examined in its ways of providing goods and services (economic institutions), making decisions (political), having and raising children (familial), passing on traditions and knowledge to the next generation (educational), and practicing beliefs about the origin and purpose of the people in the group and possible afterlife (religious). After the discussion, students work in groups using colored markers and a large piece of butcher paper to construct a *concept web* illustrating the society's institutions and how these institutions work together and influence each other.

Day 9

The teacher provides a two-page handout summarizing the chronology of the important events that happened in the history of Easter Island. Included on the list are resource depletion, overpopulation, crop failure, waves of immigration, fires, intertribal war, and finally, the arrival of Europeans. The historical events are explicated orally by the teacher: The Easter Island civilization collapsed. The teacher leads an *exploratory discussion*, seeking cause-effect relationships. The students are assigned to write an interpretive essay on an aspect of the Easter Island civilization of their choosing, (e.g., sources of conflict and ways of dealing with them, the effectiveness of institutions, the influence of the lands and resources). The first draft is due on Day 12 of the unit.

Day 10

The task this day is to design a *board game* called "Island." It will use events typical of Easter Island as a point of departure but will not be an historical reconstruction. The teacher supplies a help sheet explaining the basic parameters of the game. The object of the game is to build the Sacred City. The island population is divided into three societies, each of which is subdivided into farmers, workers, and leaders. Each turn represents one year in the life of the island. The Sacred City has several separate projects to complete: road construction from the quarry, timber harvesting, and stone masonry.

Students may be able to go forward on their own from here, but if they need some guidelines, you might suggest that a game has elements of skill and chance, it might use squares directing players to roll dice and draw a card from one of several piles, Diplomatic Relations, Food Harvest, Population Changes, and Natural Events. All of the piles should have both positive and negative fortunes. For example, diplomatic relations cards can say,

> Neighboring society shares harvest, gain 100 worker days.
>
> Border raided by unknown marauders, lose 10 percent of this year's harvest.

Day 11

Students try playing their own game, then swap and play another group's game. Near the end of the session, students are asked to reflect on the game and also on the problems facing an island society.

Day 12

First drafts of the interpretive essays are exchanged for peer coaching in spelling, punctuation, and grammar. Students return to their groups. Groups discuss which words, facts, and concepts about Easter Island are important to know and retain. The teacher distributes index card to the groups. Each student will write down on a card at least one important word or fact to know, and two major concepts. The teacher then collects the cards (to be used for a review later). In examining the cards, the teacher may pause occasionally to ask the author of the card to explain his or her reasoning in choosing a particular word, factor concept, not because it's wrong, but because any thinking should be explainable. With the teacher as collaborator, the students are guided to finalize the learning objectives to be incorporated into their assessment. Students devise a list of vocabulary, concepts, and facts, as well as devise multiple choice, skill demonstration (such as pointing to places on the map), short answer, and essay questions for the unit assessment.

Day 13

Review session: The class breaks up into review groups to practice answering questions based on the index cards and identify the large ideas of the unit. The class reconvenes to hear a summary of the unit's main ideas. The review is turned into a game with only loose scorekeeping and no winning and losing teams.

Day 14

Unit Assessment: Students take an in-class exam or write an essay and turn in their completed interpretive essay.

CREATIVE TEACHING: THE PAYOFF

As you can see, materials for creative teaching will have to be adapted from materials on hand, or new materials will have to be custom made. This will require time and energy, as does any new teaching assignment in the first year. What is the incentive to invest extra time and care to teach creatively? What are the payoffs for improving instruction? What difference will it make if you take up the quest to rediscover your own creativity and make an effort to help others do likewise? From my own experience (and I do not exaggerate), if you make a committed effort to learn the habit of playful, creative expression, you will enjoy life more, you will carry joy with you wherever you go, and you will improve the lives of people around you. Not a bad day's work.

NOTES

1. I am indebted to Jennifer Brunetto for this example.

REFERENCES

Amabile, Teresa, and Beth Hennessey. 1988. The Conditions of Creativity. In *The Nature of Creativity: Contemporary Psychological Perspectives.* Edited by Robert J. Sternberg. New York: Press Syndicate of the University of Cambridge.

Bloom, Benjamin. 1956. *Taxonomy of Educational Objectives: Handbook I: Cognitive Domain.* New York: David McKay.

Getzels, J. V., and M. Csikszentmihalyi. 1975. From Problem-Solving to Problem-Finding. In *Perspectives in Creativity.* Edited by I. A. Taylor and J. V. Getzels. Chicago: Aldine.

Hamachek, Don E. 1968. *Motivation in Teaching and Learning.* Washington, DC: National Education Association.

Karplus, Robert. 1964. The Science Curriculum Improvement Study—Report to the Piaget Conference. *Journal of Research in Science Teaching* 2 (3):236-40.

La Fay, Howard. January 1962. Easter Island and Its Mysterious Monuments. *National Geographic* 121 (1).

Labinowitcz, Ed. 1980. *The Piaget Primer.* Menlo Park, CA: Addison-Wesley.

Montessori, Maria. 1965. *Dr. Montessori's Own Handbook.* [Written in 1915.] New York: Schocken Books.

Ravetch, Irving, and Harriet Frank Jr. 1974. *Conrack.* Produced by Martin Ritt and Harriet Frank Jr. 20th Century Fox. 111 minutes. Videotape.

Russ, Sandra. 1993. *Affect and Creativity: The Role of Affect and Play in the Creative Process.* Hillsdale, NJ: Lawrence Erlbaum.

Torrance, E. Paul. 1963. Creativity. In *What Research Says to the Classroom Teacher.* Washington, DC: National Education Association.

———. 1967. The Nurture of Creative Talents. In *Explorations in Creativity.* Edited by R. L. Mooney and T. A. Razik. New York: Harper & Row.

FURTHER READING

Brooks, Jacqueline Grennon, and Martin G. Brooks. 1993. *In Search of Understanding: The Case for Constructivist Classrooms.* Alexandria, VA: Association for Supervision and Curriculum Development.

Conroy, Pat. 1972. *The Water Is Wide.* New York: Dell.

Davis, Gary A., and Margaret A. Thomas. 1989. *Effective Schools and Effective Teachers.* Boston: Allyn & Bacon.

Lozanov, Gregorii. 1978. *Suggestology and Outlines of Suggestopedeia.* New York: Gordon and Breach.

McPherson, John. 1993. *High School Isn't Pretty.* Kansas City, MO: Andrews and McMeel.

Montessori, Maria. 1964. *The Montessori Method.* [Written in 1912.] New York: Schocken Books.

Papert, Seymour, and Idit Harel. 1991. *Constructionism: Research Reports and Essays, 1985-1990 by the Epistemology and Learning Research Group.* Norwood, NJ: Ablex.

Torrance, E. Paul. 1962. *Guiding Creative Talent.* Englewood Cliffs, NJ: Prentice-Hall.

Module
4

Building Skills for Creative Teaching

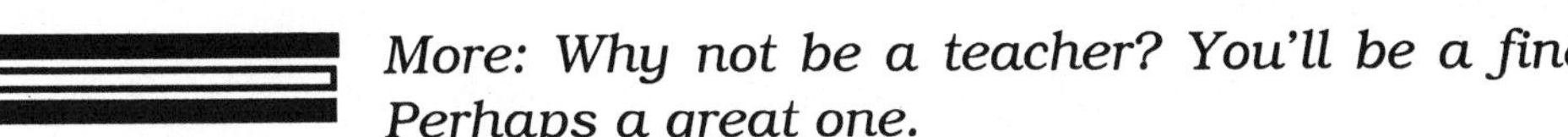

More: Why not be a teacher? You'll be a fine teacher. Perhaps a great one.

Rich: And if I was, who would know it?

More: You, your pupils, your friends, God. Not a bad public, that. . . .

—Thomas More in A Man for All Seasons *by Robert Bolt*

SIX SKILLS FOR CREATIVE TEACHING

1. *Managing.* Establish an orderly work environment that honors inquiry and creative expression.
2. *Presenting.* Present material in a lively, organized manner that calls for frequent responses from students.
3. *Questioning.* Ask questions that stimulate students to think about connections, alternatives, and new possibilities.
4. *Designing.* Design a wide variety of activities that allow the whole class to be fully engaged in constructive learning all the time.
5. *Running Activities.* Provide activities that lead students to develop creative initiative as well as mastery of skills.
6. *Relating.* Communicate caring and concern for students' progress in original thinking and creative expression.

MANAGING

> **Creative Teaching Skill 1:** Establish an orderly work environment that honors inquiry and creative expression.

Creativity requires proper nourishment. The hard truth is that creativity in children doesn't evaporate; it is driven out by specific behaviors either by thoughtless children who don't know better or by well-meaning parents, teachers, and other adults who don't realize how harmful their actions are. Creativity is a very delicate commodity. Some people are wrongly suspicious of it and are not really sorry to send it underground. I wonder how much of the violence of our society is perpetrated as subconscious acts of revenge for assaults on the spirit. Task number one is to focus on the creative environment and ways to improve it.

Physical Environment

Creativity can only flourish in a responsive environment; that is, a situation in which actions by the child evoke responses from the environment. For the most part, watching TV is passive and not growth producing because no response is required from the environment, and nothing the child does short of changing the channel has any effect. The lasting educational effects of TV in general are small, except that a large diet of violent programming has had the negative effect of establishing new norms of acceptability of violent behavior. Having students invent their own stories is far more enriching to the mind than hours of passive viewing.

The creative environment needs to provide the right level of sensory stimulation. A bland, totally quiet room which provides no sensory stimulus whatsoever has a dulling effect on creativity. The opposite environment, a sensory barrage such as a bustling marketplace or rock cafe, so dominates the mind that creative thoughts cannot get through. What is called for is a low to moderate level of nonspecific stimuli. Places such as empty beaches, mountain paths, stream banks, or even deserted cafes provide multiple sensory inputs at a low level: smell, sound, sight, touch, temperature, and taste. It is no surprise that people with hard thinking to do head for these settings: They provide a pleasant level of background stimuli for all the senses without invading the foreground of thinking space.

Social and Emotional Environment

Given that typical schoolchildren hide their creativity, the chief task of the teacher is to establish a classroom atmosphere in which creativity is valued. The first step in establishing such a climate is simply to acknowledge creative responses by children at the time they occur by saying things like, "That's a creative idea," "There's a lot of originality in this project," or "Wow! Anything more?"

It is vital to the climate of the classroom that students not be allowed to mock one another's ideas. A single comment, "You whack-o," or even a sarcastic tone by a classmate can cause a student with a creative thought to go permanently into hiding with it. The teacher needs to be alert to all signs of the creative process at work and enlist the students' participation in protecting the process of creating.

The routines and procedures that foster creativity go a step beyond efficient classroom practices. Creativity can flourish in a classroom only when certain obstacles are removed:

- pressure to conform
- competition in creative productivity
- high stakes for failure in creative areas
- implicit or explicit sanctions against questioning behavior
- divergence from convention seen as unhealthy

Removing these obstacles is an important first step toward fostering creativity in the classroom. In addition to removing negative attitudes, the teacher should encourage certain positive attributes. The classroom should be stimulating visually. If possible, exhibits such as an aquarium or terrarium, science toys, models, and maps to stimulate curiosity should be available for informal investigations. Following Montessori, ground rules for using and taking care of these exhibits should be part of the class's responsibility.

Teaching About Creativity and Modeling It

Present your students with creative role models from the past as well the present to help students form an image of the creative person at work. Doing so may help overturn some of the cultural bias against creativity and provide positive precedents for creative activity. Here are a few tips for valuing and modeling creativity.

- Provide adequate time and an appropriate setting for creative activity.
- Give approval of the act of creating rather than the quality of the product.
- Call attention to beauty and creative acts in your environment, such as a sunset, a piece of music, a landscape, an occasion, a day, an act of goodness, a talented performance. No "if only's" or "buts" allowed.
- Do visibly creative things. Make birthday cards or presents yourself. Create unusual gifts—for example, a balloon with a dollar bill inside for each year, ice cubes containing sayings inside like fortune cookies, or welcome-home banners. Sing out loud, write a poem, compose a piece of music, provide a surprise or treat for no reason, make something with your hands, develop a new skill or hobby, or dress in a more individual way according to your own feelings, rather than in a predetermined way.
- Teach your students about the creative process. The central process of creativity is generating alternatives. To help students develop and remember the ways to creative alternatives, use the acronym SCAMPER, proposed by A. F. Osborne (1953). The acronym letters stand for the verbs

Substitute

Combine

Associate or amplify

Magnify or minify

Put to other uses

Eliminate

Reverse or rearrange

- Wonder out loud. Be open about what puzzles you, what discrepancies you see, and what things don't fit together. Look for contradictions, but resist the urge to criticize or express any feelings of what you don't like.
- Talk about all creativity as a good thing. Express the joy you feel in creativity: yours, other people's, your child's. Tell stories of individual acts of creativity.

The psychological climate of acceptance of creativity is critical to fostering creative urges. The teacher's preliminary task in setting up an environment that fosters creativity is to do a self-inventory and ask the questions, "What attitudes do I hold toward creativity? Do I hold or promulgate any of the creativity-blocking attitudes and values? Am I suspicious of any of the forms of creativity? Do I believe divergent thinking is as important as convergent thinking?"

Skill Development Activity 4-1: Cartoon: Selling Creativity

A super salesperson would do the following: use the product, endorse it, display it, talk about it, be alert to examples of its use in his or her everyday life, and enjoy it.

Part A: Describe how a teacher and his or her classroom would look if he or she were a super salesperson for the product Creativity.

Part B: Draw a cartoon depicting the super salesperson promoting creativity in the classroom.

PRESENTING

Creative Teaching Skill 2: Present material in a lively, organized manner that calls for frequent responses from students.

Engaging Students Fully

Boredom occurs for two reasons: lack of cognitive interest and lack of affective stimulation. Higher student achievement levels in creative classrooms result when the creative teacher provides affective stimulation as well as cognitive interest, both of which help to capture and hold students' attention. (Maintaining students' attention is half the battle!) Creative teaching works on the principle that the right hemisphere must be activated to arouse the left hemisphere's readiness to learn. Developing a lively and playful presentation style will help students pay attention.

Skill Versus Style

A clear distinction must be made between teaching skill and teaching style. *Skill* refers to a body of related techniques that are implemented deliberately to bring about a given result. *Style*, on the other hand, is a pattern of individual choices. Being disorganized is not a style; it's the lack of skill or self-awareness. Dressing up in costume hats before holidays is a style, not a skill. All teachers need skill, whereas style is an individual matter.

Clarity and Vividness

After a teacher has mastered the basics of oral communication (speaking up, avoiding distracting mannerisms, etc.) the next task (one that never ends) is improving the presentation so that information is communicated in a clear and vivid manner. Clarity is audience specific; what is clear to a fourth grader is not clear to a first grader. In general, clarity is improved by stimulating both hemispheres of the brain at the same time, that is, giving both the verbal (left) hemisphere and pictorial (right) hemisphere something do. The creative teacher will monitor every presentation by asking, "I am telling, but what am I showing?"

A vivid presentation captures and holds attention through the skillful use of body movements, pictures and drawings, changes in voice, colorful descriptions, and fresh analogies. Vividness makes use of sensory saturation, which means employing color, sound, light and dark, temperature, movement, and voice that will engage the senses to a maximum degree. This capacity to capture and hold students' attention is one of the marks of an effective (as opposed to a "not bad") teacher.

Coherence: Using Knowledge Organizers to Unify Material into a Systematic Whole

The trouble with facts is that there are so many of them, and when learned in isolation, they are not very meaningful. Any teacher's goal should be to bring about true learning, not rote learning. Unfortunately, far too much school learning is superficial. Knowledge must be more than rote; it must be *meaningful*, that is, linked to other concepts, facts, and ideas. To be of value to the student, subject matter should be learned to the mastery level. *Mastery* means learning the content so well that it can be applied without external prompts to new situations to solve a problem or answer a question one generates on one's own. Mastery level learning requires that knowledge of content be organized into a structure that coordinates concepts and ideas systematically, making them accessible when needed (Joyce and Weil 1986). At the risk of oversimplification, I offer the analogy of shoes in a closet. A dozen pairs of shoes heaped into a pile on the closet floor are not very accessible; time is wasted every day searching for both shoes. If a shoe rack is used, however, pairs of shoes are easily accessed. Introducing a series of levels—a hierarchy—such as dress shoes, athletic shoes, and casual shoes makes the job of locating appropriate footwear even easier. It seems as if most courses of study have too many shoes and too few shoes racks.

Teachers can facilitate the development of meaningful knowledge by helping students mentally organize information into a unified, coherent body of material held together by cross-linkages and fit together into some meaningful whole. As the students proceed with their tasks, the teacher should reinforce the structure of the knowledge. This job is accomplished by five mini-techniques:

- *Previewing.* A short preview should be presented to show the location of the new material in relation to the old.
- *Embedded Repetition.* Normally frowned on in ordinary conversation, embedded repetition or redundancy is useful in aiding the novice in establishing the new material and fixing it in the mind.
- *Recapitulation.* Periodically during the presentation, a quick recapitulation—reviewing main points covered so far—is beneficial.
- *Cross-referencing.* An effort should be made by the teacher to cross-reference the new material with old new material.
- *Review.* At the conclusion of the presentation, a short review of what was presented helps the student comprehend the material at the time it is presented. If students don't comprehend the structure of the material at the time the material is presented, the presentation needs to change. The teacher should watch the students' body language and check for misconceptions by calling on students and asking them if they understand the material, or more importantly, asking questions that require demonstration of knowledge.

Using advance organizers and these five mini-techniques of presenting makes a substantial difference in retention rates, especially in children above elementary school age (Joyce and Weil 1986). These mini-techniques should be practiced by the teacher until they become second nature in all presentations.

Skill Development Activity 4-2: Presenting Material

The trio of effective presentation techniques consists of clarity, vividness, and coherence.

Part A: Create a one-page lesson plan on a subject that you know. Include what students are to learn, materials needed, procedure to teach the lesson, and a means to assess that learning has taken place. Practice teaching the lesson so that no confusion could possibly creep in.

Part B: Using the same material, teach the lesson again, exaggerating the embedded repetition, recapitulation, and cross-referencing. Choose vivid visual examples and use your voice and body to illustrate your meanings.

Modulating Smoothly Between High and Low Levels of Energy

To maximize learning, teachers should create a smooth flow of experiences that are absorbing, enjoyable, and challenging (Csikszentmihalyi 1990). Creative teaching skills may be learned in steps, but the act of creative teaching must blend elements together. To modulate means to flow back and forth between levels. The chemistry of the human brain is based on the alternate action of neurotransmitters. To wake up the mind and body and get ready for a day's action, the brain releases natural stimulants. To prepare the mind and body for a night's sleep, the brain releases natural sedatives. In fact, stimulants such as caffeine and sedatives such as phenobarbital simply enhance the effects of the natural neurotransmitters at some stage in the multistep process of generating, releasing, and breaking down the natural chemical. During the day, hour by hour, the brain's chemistry changes gradually from higher to lower levels of opposing neurotransmitters and back again, and the attention level and readiness to take action varies accordingly. The mind seems to work best and learning takes place most efficiently when a pleasing alternation of activity occurs. This means a natural rise and fall of activity level, with neither too much time spent on one activity nor an abrupt change in the tempo of the activity.

Creative teaching requires planning and presenting instruction that flows smoothly and naturally between the higher and lower levels of activity. With a conceptual understanding of the effects of various learning activities, especially the tools for creative teaching, a teacher will soon realize that imagination activities calm the mind and create a restful, soothing mood, whereas movement activities arouse the individual to action and raise the energy level. Too long a time spent in either of these modes begins to work against the brain's natural rhythm. There are no formulas to guide the teacher in deciding how long is too long, although the most common error by teachers is maintaining low activity levels for too long a period of time. The rate and degree of modulation between levels of activity depend on many factors, especially the age and maturity of the students. But any speaker or teacher should be aware of the necessity to modulate between more active and less active modes of learning.

Unleashing the Friendly Ghosts Levity, Expectancy, and Enthusiasm

Bored children turn their unused energy to creating mischief. The wise teacher senses children's need to play and turns it into learning energy. In this way you call out the friendly ghosts and enlist them as helpers. One of the best ways to do this is by creating a sense of levity—readiness to laugh. Levity is produced almost entirely by the teacher's nonverbal cues. Teachers who laugh easily and deeply, never at anyone's expense (except perhaps their own) will gather levity around them.

Another way to unleash friendly ghosts (rather than spooks that will haunt your room) is to create an air of expectancy—what's going to happen next? To establish an air of expectancy, engage the students' imagination with some form of "just imagine." Hint at a surprise you're planning, or let the class know you have a secret, but won't tell until later. When presenting new material, ask a string of questions that you don't answer. Offer mysteries, puzzles, and apparent contradictions to be explained later. Make frequent statements such as "I wonder. . ." "Expect a good surprise," "I think you'll be delighted to. . ." "I'm sure you'll enjoy. . . ." Use the holiday seasons to create special occasions or to invent your own tradition such as an Arbor Day festival or a celebration of a famous person's birthday. To build excitement, talk about the upcoming event as though no one outside your class is supposed to know about it. After the event, recall it, and review the fun you had. Cultivate an air of expectancy in your classroom, and you'll be on your way toward breaking down the barrier between work and play.

Enthusiasm is the application of positive energy. Although the expenditure of positive energy can be draining, it is not nearly as draining as a day of constant stress from trying to keep a room full of bored students from misbehaving. As with levity, enthusiasm is cued with body language and large vocal inflection. Enthusiasm exaggerates the excitement level but stops short of "hype." Sometimes mock enthusiasm or calling for excessive response from the students amuses them and raises their level of arousal. Enthusiasm is contagious. As Dale Carnegie put it (consistent with psychological experiments on affect): "If you act enthusiastic, you will be enthusiastic."

Maintaining a Balance on the Work-Play Spectrum

As we have already seen, creative teaching requires a trio of presentational skills: clarity, vividness, and coherence. But creative teaching has a playful side, too. Like the mischievous coyote of Navajo creation legend who grabbed the blanket on which the stars rested and flung them willy-nilly into the heavens, the teacher must prevent classroom activity from becoming so routine and predictable that there's no room for a surprise. If classroom procedures become humorless and regimented, children tune out, even if the content is worth knowing. As the old proverb states, "The wise teacher makes learning a joy."

Younger children don't distinguish between work and play until they are taught to do so. To a teacher, it may seem undignified to engage in playful behavior, but students see it the opposite way. If you can play with them, let down your hair, and really enjoy the moment, they will undoubtedly warm up to you. Mirth, a sense of fun and humor, releases tension.

Lest this concept of the work-play spectrum be misunderstood, I hasten to add counterexamples. Adding on play time as a reward for hard work is not the idea. Creative teaching is not an adult-to-child bargain: "I'll swap play time later in exchange for your hard work now." Such an arrangement may be OK at times, but it's not the point of the work-play spectrum. Readiness to play with the material does not mean hilarity, at least not too often. Also—and this is very important—you must not be seduced into giving up your actual authority or the rightful place to bring a lesson back to a lower level of activity. It's a bit extreme to be a killjoy and declare, "That's it, now let's go back to the lesson," but it may be necessary. The concept of playful work will not be understood right away. Some students will want to play, play, play, instead of work, play, work, play. The skill required here is the capacity to move freely back and forth between moments of play and moments of work. As with other behavior, the teacher must coach students toward the desired result. Levity does not mean chaos in which all the students do their own thing whenever they want or disrupt the flow of a lesson in the name of spontaneity.

The idea of the work-play spectrum is to break down the barrier between work and play and to stop seeing them as two different activities. The best learning takes place when you are not even aware that you're learning. Students know they are expected to get work done, and if you have a talk with them about working-play and playing-work, they generally will respond positively to your collaborative efforts. The important realization that they must reach is that they must not scuttle your efforts to get back on task after a moment of levity. Once they realize how much more fun learning can be when the teacher takes them freely into playful moments, then back to the task, students will almost surely cooperate.

QUESTIONING

> **Creative Teaching Skill 3:** Ask questions that stimulate students to think about connections, alternatives, and new possibilities.

The single best indicator of the instructor's level of teaching skill is his or her questioning technique. Good teachers

- ask many more questions;
- ask deeper questions that call for thought, not merely recall;
- often follow up a question with another question, rather than an answer;
- probe correct as well as incorrect answers; and
- ask open-ended questions that call for divergent thinking.

Bloom's Taxonomy

Long before *A Nation at Risk* appeared in the early 1980s, Benjamin Bloom, a professor at the University of Chicago, produced his now famous *Taxonomy of Educational Objectives: Handbook I: Cognitive Domain* (1956). In it, Bloom classified learning tasks by the level of mental complexity involved in doing them.

From most demanding to least demanding, Bloom's cognitive objectives are as follows:

- *Evaluation.* Making judgments or doing a critique.
- *Synthesis.* Putting information together; designing or proposing a hypothesis.
- *Analysis.* Examining a complex item by looking at its parts separately and diagramming, mapping, or outlining.
- *Application.* Using information in a new context; constructing, organizing, transferring, reworking, or completing an unfinished item.
- *Comprehension.* Grasping a concept; demonstrating, explaining drawing and labeling, describing, and summarizing or interpreting new items of a similar type.
- *Knowledge.* Learning factual content; recalling, listing, reciting, labeling, or naming.

In recent studies of United States classrooms, it was found that students are being asked to do mainly lower-tier tasks and seldom, if ever, being asked to do upper-tier tasks. As a result, students are learning only at the second level of mastery, the comprehension level. Teaching to the mastery level means including more upper-tier tasks. Guiding students through each of the six levels on Bloom's taxonomy requires the use of specialized questions incorporating the key words listed in Table 4.1.

Stimulating Divergent Thinking by Asking Open-Ended Questions

Questions that have a definite answer call for *convergent thinking.* Such questions limit student thinking. Students need to open up their thinking, to consider new possibilities, to devise ideas they have never thought of before. This widening process is *divergent thinking.* Questions that call for divergent thinking will give students a nudge toward discovering connections to tie together individual insights, past observations, facts of history, discoveries, current events, and their own subjective experience. Here are some prompts teachers can use to stimulate divergent thinking.

- What if. . . ?
- What would it be like to. . . ?
- What alternatives can you think of?
- What difference would it make if we changed. . . ?
- How could that have happened?
- Why do you suppose that. . . ?
- Could it occur that. . . ?
- How would you feel under those circumstances?
- What else is possible?

Table 4.1. Action Words for Tasks on Each Level of Bloom's Taxonomy.

Upper-Tier Tasks				
EVALUATION	rate judge select evaluate	justify debate conclude defend	assess rank appraise challenge	criticize estimate decide choose
SYNTHESIS	manage create design compose arrange	predict hypothesize write invent simulate	role-play propose collect formulate combine	extend devise construct develop flowchart
ANALYSIS	divide classify dissect distinguish break down	compare contrast diagram subdivide isolate	survey separate debate test examine	outline formulate survey investigate dismantle
Lower-Tier Tasks				
APPLICATION	organize construct use	practice illustrate operate revise	schedule translate compute infer	group relate manipulate teach
COMPREHENSION	compare express draw discuss summarize	review explain restate report contrast	locate recognize construct relate paraphrase	predict translate interpret generalize tell
KNOWLEDGE	list locate observe match fill in	label discover show repeat describe	name recall reproduce state tag	recognize who what when where how

Skill Development Activity 4-3: Questioning Effectively

Using the lesson you created for the last activity, construct several questions to illustrate each of the six levels of Bloom's taxonomy.

One function of asking a question is to get more information. But the other, more important, use of questioning is to elicit another question. A discussion can be thought of as a string of questions; each answered question triggers another question. *Shepherding a discussion* requires opening up a discussion that gets too specific or bringing a discussion that has drifted into the ozone back to Earth. The throttle on the discussion is Bloom's taxonomy. Generally speaking, asking questions from the bottom tier of the taxonomy will cool or slow down a discussion, whereas calling for analysis, speculative synthesis, or evaluation will fire up the discussion and propel it to higher philosophical planes. Ideally, the discussion will take on a life of its own with the teacher merely moderating or directing traffic. (The specific techniques of discussion and holding seminars is the topic of Module 5: Discussions and Seminars.)

Question Stringing

A good way to get an inquiry lesson going is to bring in a mystery object such as an antique kitchen tool, a swirled rock, a spiny specimen from the sea, or a mathematical model. When done effectively, it is possible for the skilled teacher to conduct an entire lesson without giving any factual content until the very end. For question stringing to work, three ground rules must be followed.

1. Only observations can be offered; no facts, information, or outside data can be used. This guideline is necessary, at least initially, to curtail the deeply ingrained habit of many novice teachers to conduct a dialogue with themselves which students are allowed to overhear.
2. "I wonder why" and "Do you suppose?" prompts are allowed.
3. Questions by the students are not answered but reflected back to them as new questions.

Question stringing is the tool of choice for the discovery stage of Karplus's Learning Cycle (see Module 3). Rather than being reserved for occasional use by the teacher, this device should become an established technique in every unit.

Skill Development Activity 4-4: Stringing Questions

Part A: Go back to the material you have chosen for the last two activities. Recast the lesson using questioning exclusively.

Part B: Find a willing audience and give the lesson using question stringing exclusively.

Encouraging Students to Identify Discrepancies and Define Problems

The creative process starts with the sense that something isn't quite right. Sensitivity to mystery, self-contradiction, ambiguity, discrepancies, antinomies, unusual occurrences, and oddities is a good indicator of inventive creativity. Be on the alert for ways to start a lesson with a mystery, a puzzle, or the unexplained. It is crucial for the teacher to acknowledge when a student has asked an unusual question. Teachers who listen well and don't start answering before the student completes the question encourage more questions. Be respectful and honor all questions, even the annoying ones. As Jean Piaget said, school failure is the result of telling too much and asking too little.

DESIGNING

Creative Teaching Skill 4: Design a wide variety of activities that allow the whole class to be fully engaged in constructive learning all the time.

The traditional teacher-driven classroom bores most children. You don't have to have the native creativity of Robin Williams or Bette Midler to teach creatively, but you will need to become skilled with the process of generating a wide variety of lesson plans and alternative tasks using creative teaching tools. Then, with a little time and ingenuity, the content of the lesson can be recast into a creative format.

Dimensions of Learning Activities

Students' motivation to learn increases when they are presented with a variety of different activities. Variety needs no justification. Two of the important dimensions of the learning structure to vary over the course of the year are (1) the size of working groups, which may be solo, pairs, small groups, and the whole class; and (2) the length of projects, which may last a portion of an hour, a full class period, several class periods, weeks, or even a whole semester. The length of projects can be gradually increased as students become familiar with the process of working on their own over time.

Learning Modes or Styles

No two people learn exactly alike. It has often been observed that schoolwork is saturated in verbal learning, which leaves out a large portion of students for whom verbal learning is not a strength. Activities should address the strengths and preferences of all students, with attention to building up strength in weaker areas. Some students need to learn how to listen critically, others to read or see critically.

Listening

Not counting teacher talk in giving instructions and information, do students have any opportunity to practice discrimination of sounds or to hear a passage of music or oral reading? If not, why not?

Seeing

Being observant does not come naturally to students. They will only improve their attention to visual details if they participate in activities that help them to isolate, identify, and name what passes through their visual field.

Movement

Sitting still was hard for me as a youngster, and I always appreciated teachers who would incorporate incidental movement, such as picking up a handout myself rather than having it passed back. Of course, allowing freedom of movement requires establishing limits and soliciting cooperation so time is not wasted. During the course of a lesson, activities that involve movement can be incorporated naturally. With a little ingenuity, games (such as science charades) involving movement can be devised to conduct necessary review sessions in a partylike atmosphere, avoiding the spirit-executing technique of question-and-answer drill.

Reading

Reading lends itself to variety by its very nature. Students can read silently, orally, in unison, dramatically, or in ensembles. They can read for content, read critically for connections, read for the sounds of the words, or read for the style and intent of the author. Students can read to entertain themselves, or they can be read to. Even in upper grade levels, reading should be varied for the sake of skill building as well to avoid monotony in the classroom.

Speaking

Students need to ask and respond to questions to learn, but they also need to verbalize their ideas to identify misconceptions. One effective way to do this that allows a large number of students to speak simultaneously is the small group process. Possible formats for small group activities are countless, but one effective way to help students build knowledge and root out misconceptions is the Triple-Consensus Discussion lesson. Students are given a list of a dozen or so statements which must be classified as belonging to category 1 alone, category 2 alone, both categories, or neither one (in a chemistry class these might be the First and Second Laws of Thermodynamics). Students work together in small groups until a consensus is reached. This phase will often proceed rather quickly as outspoken students convince others of their views, and the rest of the group, not having thought very hard, will go along. Groups are remixed and discussion resumed until the second set of groups comes to a consensus. This phase will take longer because, by now, some people have become committed to certain answers. Finally, after the second set of small groups reaches consensus, a representative from each group writes the group's results on the board, and the whole class discusses any discrepancies until there is a final consensus. This kind of small group activity produces more opportunities for students to present and defend their thinking than a large group process does.

Opportunities for Subjective Responses and Statements of Personal Significance

Much of school life is dominated by regimentation and requirements to do certain things whether students want to or not. When students feel like robots, they have less motivation. Perhaps this feeling is what led the Danish philosopher Kierkegaard to declare, "Truth is subjectivity." Students will spend more time on a project when they choose it themselves. If opportunities are provided in the course of a discussion or a written assignment for the students to express their personal feelings and preferences, the sting of conforming to "adult rules" is reduced. This is not to advocate the teacher's abdicating his or her rightful role as classroom manager, but in providing some opportunity for self-expression, the teacher shows respect for the child's sovereignty as a human being.

The Need for Variety in Learning

Although a certain amount of routine in the classroom provides students a measure of security and frees their energies for concentrating on the learning tasks, monotony is the enemy of student and teacher alike. Selecting for variety should not be difficult once the teacher becomes familiar with the 30 tools for creative teaching provided in Module 3 (pp. 44-47).

RUNNING ACTIVITIES

Creative Teaching Skill 5: Provide activities that lead students to develop creative initiative as well as mastery of skills.

For any material to be truly learned, rather than merely assimilated, it must be practiced. The type of practice depends on the type of content. After a solid questioning technique, the next most valuable skill that a teacher needs is the ability to select good practice activities. Teachers who just move from one topic to another without practice are not teaching for the long term. A student who says, "Yes, I've heard of that, but I can't remember much about it," probably had an instructor who did not assign good practice activities. Highly routine and repetitious activities are nearly worthless, not to mention unpopular, because students are not engaged mentally or emotionally; only their hands are busy, not their hearts and heads. Meaningful assignments and practice activities are accepted by the majority of students, but tedious, irrelevant repetition can dull the enthusiasm of even the most naturally curious students.

Skill Development Activity 4-5: Choosing Activities

Use the same lesson as before (unless you're getting tired of it, in which case choose another lesson).

Part A: Describe the instructions and a few relevant activities for your chosen audience.

Part B: Suggest assessments of the learning.

Encouraging Student Initiative in Creative Projects

Dissonance may produce an urge in students to capture an emotion in words or build a model to illustrate a concept. The question for the teacher is how to provide an opportunity for students to follow through on their own initiative. In social studies and science, students need to work toward the skill of developing their hypotheses and following through to find data that lead them to accept or reject their hypotheses. If a teacher chooses the creative project for students to do, or if the teacher provides the hypothesis to be investigated, students have not exercised their own initiative. On the opposite extreme, if the students are not given any direction, they will flounder. It seems apparent that a spectrum exists between the extremes of 100 percent teacher initiative and 100 percent student initiative. Table 4.2 presents details of this spectrum.

The spectrum represents four stages of turning over initiative to the students during the course of the year. During the first quarter the teacher directs the project, providing clarity and direction, leaving the students to concentrate their energies on the product. By the last quarter, the students should have learned how to do projects and should be capable of functioning on their own.

Table 4.2. Spectrum of Initiative in Classroom Projects.

100% Teacher Initiative			*100% Student Initiative*
Teacher assigns specific topic, sets standards, and chooses means of assessment.	Teacher provides list of topics to choose from and guidelines for standards and assessment.	Teacher suggests ideas for topics and collaborates with students on project parameters and assessments.	Students choose their own projects, seek help if needed, and participate in judging the merits of their product.
Advantage Sets standardization for grading process.	*Advantage* Provides guidance for low-initiative students.	*Advantage* Provides direction to project without determining the product.	*Advantage* Allows the greatest freedom for the creative process to work.
Disadvantage There is no student initiative and less student interest.	*Disadvantage* Product is only partly the student's.	*Disadvantage* Requires individual conferencing, a logistics problem if classes are large.	*Disadvantage* Requires unusually capable and independent students. Every project is unique; assessment is time-consuming.

Providing Support for Developing Student Independence

Developing student independence is a long-term project that can happen only if the process is gradual enough that students can easily take over. In developing independence in creative work, students need to have a clear idea of the product and practice the steps needed to produce that product. These steps are as follows:

Step 1: *Viewing Examples of the Product.* The main features of the product should be identified, along with the project's parameters and constraints, but to avoid inadvertently reducing the creativity of the product, the teacher should not supply a model that can be copied or even one whose structure or concept can be copied. Some students distrust their own creativity and, to reduce stress, will avoid trying to come up with a project of their own. A few understanding words about the difficulty of having to come up with an original idea will relieve some of their discomfort: "I know this doesn't look easy, but you guys can do it. You have already shown me that you are capable and can come up with your own ideas if you stick with it."

Step 2: *Guided Practice Activities.* The teacher asks students to apply what they have just been taught to work out misconceptions and fix the concepts and procedures in their minds. The structure of the practice is provided by the teacher so that the prerequisite skills for the task can be learned and applied. The teacher may make a suggestion and the student follows it through.

Step 3: *Nongraded Rehearsal.* In this step students actually perform some observable task related to the creative project, which usually involves many components or steps. Doing so provides students the opportunity to explore options and abandon attempts that don't work out without having to worry over the effect of the task on their grades. In the case of written work, this means the students hand in their rough drafts for comments but no grades.

Step 4: *Coached Practice.* This step allows for the practice of skills that require the students to initiate an action and the teacher to shape the behavior or performance to a higher level. Coached practice takes place in discussion, in feedback on written assignments, and as needed to develop the project to its fullest.

Step 5: *Presenting the Product.* Students will want to show off their products to classmates, friends, and parents. Of course, each student's project must be monitored along the way to ensure that it is something worthy of being shown off. It is important to acknowledge the students' initiative and to review the steps they went through to create the product. Before moving on to another topic, you might refer to a future project or ask how the students would go about doing a similar, hypothetical project.

Skill Development Activity 4-6: Designing a Large Group Project

Part A: From the list of 30 creative tools presented in Module 3 (pp. 44-47), select a class project such as an ensemble design. Choose a topic such as "The Seven Continents" for a geography class.

Part B: List the steps you would take your class through to produce a product such as a 70-slide show with appropriate music.

RELATING

Creative Teaching Skill 6: Communicate caring and concern for students' progress in original thinking and creative expression.

Acknowledging and Encouraging Creativity

The pattern of reactions a child receives in response to his or her attempts at creativity will determine the child's enthusiasm for future creative expression. In a survey of teachers who made a difference to highly creative children, psychologist E. Paul Torrance found that the common factor, and probably the most important one, was the teachers' capacity to form good relationships with their students (Torrance 1962). A big part of this relationship involved the genuine caring of teachers in the development of student talents.

Empathy and Manifest Caring

Empathy is the capacity to *feel with* someone. It is easy to empathize with people who have been genuine victims of misfortune or accidents. It is not so easy to feel empathy toward persons who have conspired with fate to bring on their own trouble. However, it is possible to have empathy for someone in trouble or pain without accepting the behavior that led to the predicament. Drawing this distinction is especially important in building relationships with students. Some students who have not done their work will expect the caring teacher to ignore this fact. For the teacher to do so would be to support counterproductive behavior. On the other hand, if the teacher withdraws all compassion toward the student who has not done what he or she is capable of doing, the student's anxiety level will rise and interfere with the process of working out a constructive solution.

It is important in building a rapport with students to *manifest* your caring, in other words to turn that concern into concrete expressions and actions. There is a big difference between the way adults and young people understand the verb "to care." Acts of caring must be made apparent to the child without conveying a sense of martyrdom or insincerity. If a teacher tells her class, "I'm interested in you," then shows indifference toward student projects, she has not manifested the interest she claimed. Each age group differs as to what constitutes being cared about, but most groups respond well to simple acts such as buying a book out of your own pocket and raffling it off for free, or buying a sympathy card for a youngster who has lost a loved one, or staying late at school to decorate the room for a party. Manifest caring may be as simple as postponing an assignment's due date because of a special event or telling some personal anecdotes from "the old days." Each year a new group of skeptical students walks in the door and challenges you to prove to them that you care.

Interpersonal Creativity

Many outstanding teachers have a gift of interpersonal creativity. Those who don't may have to work to acquire those behaviors that will help bring out students' creativity. If you are successful in doing this, your year will go much better than if you aren't. Here are a few suggestions to strengthen interpersonal creativity.

When presented with a creative project, the first thing a teacher should do is acknowledge the work and reflect the child's feelings back to him or her without judgment. The purpose of the creative act may be expressiveness and nothing more. In that case, the creative product or performance can be enjoyed for its own sake, without any evaluation or feedback. Use nonverbal signs of approval: Nod your head and smile with general comments of encouragement such as, "Boy, oh boy. Yes. You're heading in the right direction. I hope I see more." Point out how good a person feels when he or she creates. Respect the child's feelings, and let creativity be enjoyed for its own sake. Listen if the student volunteers comments about his or her own creative process, and ask open-ended, not leading, questions. The creative process is delicate; it has a life of its own that can't be rushed or forced.

Notice originality when it occurs. Acknowledge students' initiative and effort, rather than their products. Be careful about making any suggestions until the child indicates receptiveness. Avoid judging the child's ability and don't convey that you expect only showpiece quality products. Never compare one student with another or even one piece of creative work of the same student with another unless the student has produced a sizable portfolio of successful work. Sustaining growth in creativity by helping students have a good creative experience is the teacher's first priority, then when confidence and motivation are established, attention can be turned to improving the product.

The worst thing anyone could do is to mock the creative effort or embarrass the child. Surprisingly, high praise can also be detrimental to creative output. Providing large rewards for creative behavior has been shown to be destructive, not constructive to continued creative behavior (Amabile and Hennessey 1988). Therefore, it is important to emphasize the intrinsic rewards of the project versus the extrinsic rewards.

Giving Constructive Feedback

It has been shown that confident, high-self-esteem children eager to master an area of learning are the only ones to benefit from direct, fault-identifying criticism, and only if the criticism is couched in a supportive framework, not "putting the student down" (Amabile and Hennessey 1988). All other groups of children studied benefited from indirect identification of deficiencies in their creative work, that is, by taking note of the part that could be improved without stating the deficiency as such. Making a statement of the desired end contains within it the implication of what the fault is.

There is a time and a place for giving feedback, for coaching, and for assessing creative projects, but your first obligation is to do no harm to the child's creative instincts. Creative projects should not be graded like homework, giving A's for the best poems, B's for the next best, and so on; doing so dries up creative impulses. Likewise, requiring a performance in front of the class without prior rehearsal or grading a product without an opportunity to improve it produces an instantaneous dislike of creative work and may bring on an enduring creative block. (More will be said about assessing creative work in due course.)

Critical feedback says, "No, you're wrong. You should know that," or "Your project just doesn't measure up to other students'." What is conveyed by these and similar unhelpful teacher responses is more than what's lacking in the student's work. They degrade and devalue the student as a person. Students need to feel safe and secure from attack and ridicule. They need feedback, but it must be delivered in a constructive rather than a critical way. Constructive criticism says, "I see what you're saying. Have you tried X?" Giving constructive feedback aims at improving a piece of work by helping students find alternate ways to make it better rather than pointing out its faults or deficiencies.

Much of the time students can provide their own ideas for improving the product without suggestions from the teacher. Recall this module's earlier mention of the SCAMPER verbs to generate alternatives: *substitute, combine, associate or amplify, magnify or minify, put to other uses, eliminate*, and *reverse or rearrange*. Simple questions by the teacher such as "What about this part here?" or questions such as those listed below may be sufficient to trigger new ideas in the student's mind.

- You're pretty happy with this part. What about the other part?
- I wonder, is there another way to do this?
- If it had more ____ in this part, would you like it better?
- I wonder what else could work here.
- Pictures need balance. Do you like the balance in every part of your picture?
- Hmmm. Have you ever tried. . . ?

In the main, teacher support and encouragement to continue creative work is better for students' growth than specific suggestions of how to improve it. It is important that students focus on the inner rewards of doing the project, and not merely on how to win the teacher's or classmates' approval.

Skill Development Activity 4-7: Practicing Constructive Feedback

How would you respond with constructive feedback to each of these responses?

1. Earth is the planet closest to the sun.
2. The cause of the Civil War was British intervention.
3. All polygons are squares.
4. Apples are roots of plants.

Helping Students Complete Their Projects

Teachers and parents can help students to manage a creative project by

- pointing out in advance what is going to be required to finish it and providing suggestions of specific elements that the project should contain, rather than mandating the quality level or creative standard it should reach.
- setting up a reasonable timetable and planning creative tasks in small, doable steps.
- checking intermediate steps. It really helps motivation to tally mileage markers day to day. Even a small amount of progress is rewarding.
- requiring a finished product.

Sooner or later, creator's block will occur. To get past the blockage,

- reflect on steps already accomplished and point the way to completing a creative task; disregard the failures.
- break a trouble spot down into small, doable steps.
- encourage students onward with such feedback as "You can do it; only a small step to go. Keep at it. Way to go."

Keeping Creativity Going over Time

Children have short memories. To help students realize the extent of what they've done, the teacher or parent should help the student establish a portfolio of work. Of course, this portfolio should not be abused; it should not be shown to others without the child's permission. The purpose of the creative portfolio is for the child to see his or her own growth and make his or her own judgments. Again, care is needed here lest you inadvertently stifle the child's creativity. The urge for self-expression is weaker than the child's need for approval. If adult approval becomes the focus of keeping a portfolio, then creating may become directed toward obtaining approval rather than creating. Respect the growing talent in the child. Don't try to determine the direction the talent should take or the modes of its best application. Have faith that the talent will find its own best expression.

Role-Modeling

Role-modeling is a particularly powerful way for students who are hungry for norms and values to find some grounding, but role-modeling is very elusive. It is less a manner of teaching than a manner of being. Natural expressions of friendliness, compassion, kindness toward others, tolerance, and what Bertrand Russell calls "hypothetical sympathy for everyone" are noticed and, to a degree, imitated by students. Cynicism, intolerance, and all forms of dishonesty will also be noticed and copied to a degree. In the teaching profession there is no room for anyone who has a hateful or hostile nature.

Skill Development Activity 4-8: Identifying Fundamental Skills of Teaching

For each of the following descriptions, identify which of the six skills is missing:

Managing	Questioning	Running Activities
Presenting	Designing	Relating

MISS JONES

Miss Jones, a pert, nicely groomed math teacher in a suburban junior high school, always comes to class well prepared. She writes out math procedures and sample problems on overhead transparencies. Each day she opens the appropriate box of transparencies, places them in the proper sequence on the overhead projector, and allows students time to copy the material into their notebooks. She is never cross or sarcastic to the students and is always very efficient about checking homework. Sometimes while the children work, she files her nails or does crossword puzzles.

MR. BOWER

Mr. Bower, a 12-year veteran history teacher, is quite popular with students. He tells very animated stories and is well known around school for his ability to impersonate people. He arrives at school right before class but manages to get into something interesting after only a short delay. He loves kids. He never seems to have a discipline problem, and his assignments and exercises are creative and to the point. Students complain that they never can predict on what material they'll be tested; even Mr. Bower doesn't seem to have a clear idea about the test material. He shrugs it off and says, "Don't worry, you're all a bunch of geniuses anyway."

MRS. OLMSTEAD

Mrs. Olmstead's students always do well on the National French Exam because she knows how to take students to a high level of understanding. She's easygoing most of the time, but once in a while, she slams a book down or throws someone out of class rather arbitrarily. Students sometimes complain that they don't know where they stand, concerning grades, in her class. The photographs on Mrs. Olmstead's bulletin board are torn and out of date. When students bicker or tease someone, she turns her back. Mrs. Olmstead is slow to return exams and other student work, but she seems generally popular as indicated by the number of students in her office after school chatting and seeking advice on where to apply to college.

MRS. BLANCHARD

Mrs. Blanchard takes good care of her third graders and keeps in close touch with their parents. The principal brags about her beautiful classroom and the way the students have been taught to keep it tidy. Mrs. Blanchard keeps a file accessible for the students to place their incoming work and to get copies of the many sheets of supplements and instructional objectives for the units. Students' exam scores are surprisingly low. Mrs. Blanchard believes the students must learn to sit still and listen because life will not be just like you want it. She doesn't believe in bellowing or trying to entertain students. They're there to learn, and learn they shall.

MR. SAKARI

Mr. Sakari teaches his seventh-grade science class with enthusiasm. Unit by unit, he holds the students' interest with demonstrations, live animals, and slides galore. He's very knowledgeable. The basis of the course is the vocabulary, and he teaches a lot of it. There's little or no homework because he's so caught up in planning for the next unit or the next day; the only thing he assigns for a grade are crossword puzzles. Some of the better students pass notes during class or read thick novels and still get straight A's.

MS. ARLANSON

Ms. Arlanson is the best organized teacher at Whittier Elementary. Her room is spanking clean and tidy. She provides little treats for the students and takes them out to the park to tell them about the native flowers and trees, about which she is an expert. She is quite orderly and gets the students to mind well. When she calls on students, she expects answers. Students who respond incorrectly must write the question and correct answer in their notebook. Students are never idle because Ms. Arlanson keeps them busy doing projects and tasks and filling in their workbooks. Ms. Arlanson especially likes to teach reading, when she can explicate the stories for the children.

REFERENCES

Amabile, Teresa, and Beth Hennessey. 1988. The Conditions of Creativity. In *The Nature of Creativity: Contemporary Psychological Perspectives.* Edited by Robert J. Sternberg. New York: Press Syndicate of the University of Cambridge.

Bloom, Benjamin. 1956. *Taxonomy of Educational Objectives: Handbook I: Cognitive Domain.* New York: David McKay.

Csikszentmihalyi, M. 1990. *Flow: The Psychology of Optimum Experience.* Grand Rapids, MI: Harper & Row.

Joyce, Bruce, and Marsha Weil. 1986. *Models of Teaching.* 3d ed. Englewood Cliffs, NJ: Prentice-Hall.

Osborne, A. F. 1953. *Applied Imagination.* New York: Charles Scribner's Sons.

Torrance, E. Paul. 1962. *Guiding Creative Talent.* Englewood Cliffs, NJ: Prentice-Hall.

FURTHER READING

Ausubel, David. 1960. The Use of Advance Organizers in the Learning and Retention of Meaningful Verbal Material. *Journal of Educational Psychology.* 51:267-72.

Goleman, Daniel, P. Kaufman, and M. Ray. 1992. *The Creative Spirit.* New York: E. P. Dutton.

Kleinke, Chris L. 1978. *Self-Perception: The Psychology of Personal Awareness.* San Francisco: W. H. Freeman.

Torrance, E. Paul. 1967. The Nurture of Creative Talents. In *Explorations in Creativity.* Edited by R. L. Mooney and T. A. Razik. New York: Harper & Row.

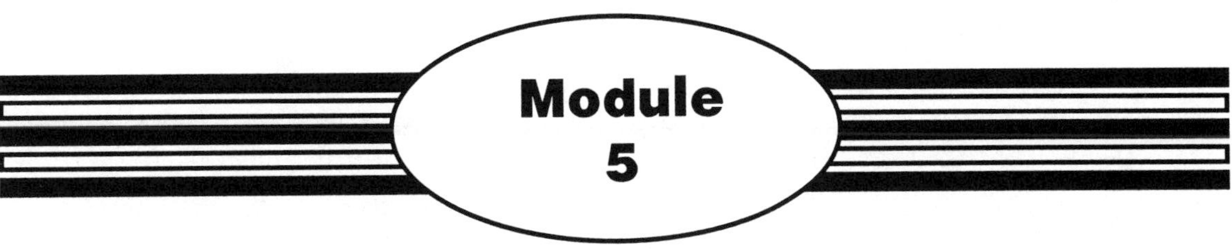

Module 5

Discussions and Seminars

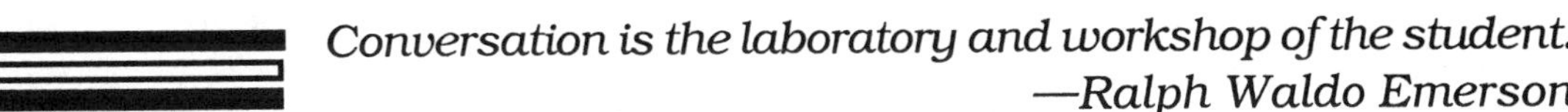

Conversation is the laboratory and workshop of the student.
—Ralph Waldo Emerson

For students to construct a field of knowledge, they must actively build a framework of concepts, facts, and emotional responses into a web of meaning. Few activities can make cross-linkages and expose groundless suppositions more effectively than an open discussion in which the teacher calls on students to elaborate on their own thinking. Discussion in the classroom can take many forms.

TYPES OF DISCUSSION LESSONS

A lesson with no contributions by students will usually flop. Generally speaking, *good noise* is preferable to *bored silence*. Of course, students can contribute their attention and energy nonverbally during an anecdote or block of exposition, but in the main, students should have opportunities to contribute. Here are a few kinds of lessons that call for students' oral response.

Tutorials are usually conducted for an individual or small group. The teacher provides a stream of exposition during which he or she observes the body language and expressions of the students to determine the right pace for presenting the material, and queries the students to determine if they understand the material. Often, the student has scheduled the tutorial and therefore maintains attention. Tutorials may focus on interests of the student but usually are unenriched, down-to-business training sessions.

Directed discussion is a probing technique that aims at getting the answer to a complex or ambiguous question, for example, "Was Hamlet a coward?" To answer this question, one would have to muster evidence to support his or her conclusion. Directed discussion has a specific purpose. If, in this example, the discussion wanders off into the romance between Ophelia and Hamlet, the teacher must refocus the attention of the class on the central question. In this manner the teacher does more than moderate the discussion; he or she guides or directs it toward a certain end.

Round robin recitation gives every student the chance to speak. The teacher asks questions, perhaps related to the previous day's lesson, adapting the difficulty level of the questions to the individual student. It is a shame that in some classrooms only the outspoken students have the opportunity to speak. Round-robin recitation prevents that.

Anecdotal discussion refers to sharing experiences on a given topic. Whether in a classroom or at lunch, people seem to have an endless appetite for swapping stories and tall tales. Sharing personal experiences creates a feeling of group solidarity and warmth.

Debates are, of course, structured conversations between people who stand on opposing sides of an issue. Formal debates specify the time allotted for each speaker, the order of speakers, and the sequence of exposition and rebuttal. The formal debating structure is a bit cumbersome for most classrooms. Also, depending on the topic, extensive library research must be completed before a debate will work. Despite the demands of preparation, however, the debate format can provide the opportunity for students to practice many process skills: researching, speaking, and listening.

Mini-debates are easier to manage. Toward the conclusion of a unit of study, questions are given to opposing teams of two or three students. The students collaborate for a few moments, then hold a short debate, marshaling evidence collected in previous sessions. The questions, which must be relatively simple, are handed out on index cards. Four or five mini-debates can be conducted in a one-hour class, giving everyone in class the opportunity to collaborate and discuss an issue with their classmates, then to recite and hear opposing viewpoints. Questions can include such provocative and pointed issues as the following:

- "Has science done more harm or good to our society?"
- "Is a manned space program really necessary, or should we use only unmanned probes?"
- "Is science in general responsible for creating nuclear weapons, or was it a case of individual responsibility?"
- "Should the government restrict human genetics experiments, or should the scientists restrict them themselves?"

Mock trials are court trials featuring characters from history or literature. Was Lady MacBeth guilty of any crime? Did President Truman have any other choice but to drop the atomic bomb? Did Henry II kill Thomas à Becket?

Arena discussion, a technique made popular in law schools, requires a panel of experts, or students playing the roles of experts, from different fields. The arena is something like a courtroom, with the discussion leader or teacher serving in the role of advocate, sometimes devil's advocate. A huge complex issue such as health care reform serves as the platform of the discussion. In this example, panelists would represent health insurance companies, hospitals, small employers, large corporations, ordinary citizens, unemployed workers, doctors, and state and federal governments.

Panelists must be well informed in their areas of expertise. The advocate's role is to bring out all points of view and uncover important factors such as economics and fairness. The advocate has developed fictitious anecdotes—stories of individual people—that evoke a whole range of questions, such as "Do people have a natural right to health care?" "Who should pay to provide health coverage?" "Who should decide on limits to health care?"

SOCRATIC SEMINARS

Even a classroom that provides many opportunities for discussion and recitation does not fulfill all important student learning needs. Each of the types of discussion mentioned so far is teacher directed. Socratic seminars, on the other hand, are more student focused. The seminar, a teaching method popularized by Mortimer Adler, prolific author and editor of *Great Books of the Western World*, provides the opportunity for students to hold an in-depth discussion of a reading. The rationale and statement of purpose of Professor Adler's curriculum reform effort are presented in *The Paideia Proposal: An Educational Manifesto* (1982). Two subsequent *Paideia* books—*Paideia: Problems and Possibilities* (1983) and *The Paideia Program: An Educational Syllabus* (1984)—provide details and suggestions. (The word *Paideia* is from the Greek meaning *upbringing of the child*, but connotes the notion of universal learning.)

The *Paideia* plan seeks to bring up the quality of the weakest schools to the level of the best and to engage children of all ages in a deep discourse with great ideas. To accomplish this aim, the plan proposes changes in the school curriculum. It would eliminate most of the once-over-lightly survey courses and replace them with in-depth studies meant to build sound habits of mind, a good group dynamic, and a capacity for critical thinking. To accomplish these goals, *Paideia* proposed three kinds of teaching and learning: (1) direct instruction in the traditional sense; (2) coaching of students in communication and a broad range of thinking skills; and (3) discussion of books other than textbooks, as well as works of art and music, and involvement in the performing arts. *The Paideia Program* recommends Socratic seminars for every student on a weekly basis no matter what the students' age, background, or plans for future schooling.

How Does a Socratic Seminar Differ from a Regular Discussion?

Differences between various types of discussions and Socratic seminars are evident in the new teacher role, student behavior, and the nature and length of the conversation. Table 5.1 on p. 82 compares the Socratic seminar with anecdotal conversation and guided discussion.

Table 5.1. A Comparison of Three Types of Discussion.

Type	ANECDOTAL CONVERSATION	GUIDED DISCUSSION	SOCRATIC SEMINAR
Description	There is a sharing of personal experience.	Leader sustains a dialogue with a group pursuing an answer to a question.	A group has a conversation centered on a text.
Effects	The conversation builds rapport and warmth and adds human element, fun.	Many speakers participate; a text is explored in an interesting manner.	The seminar builds positive group dynamic; deeply enriches participants' understanding of the material discussed.

What Does a Good Socratic Seminar Look Like?

In a full-blown Socratic seminar, students spend about an hour in conversation about an article, document, drawing, sculpture, painting, poem, short story, cartoon, or photograph. A mini-seminar may last half as long. The conversation continually refers to the specific lines or details of the text or work. It is not a bull session because participants try to build a greater understanding of the work, rather than just offer opinions and feelings about it. Opinions must be supported by specific references to the work. The seminar is self-moderating, that is, participants take turns speaking without raising their hands. If some individual is dominating the conversation, someone else might point that out. Students interact with each other, making statements and comments, perhaps even asking questions about the text or someone's comment; they refer to each other by name, show evidence of changing their minds, and are able to question assumptions in the text. Observing a good Socratic seminar is inspiring. Students are enthusiastically engaged in exploring the connections within the text and the relevance to their own lives, and do so with few teacher prompts.

What Is the Value of a Socratic Seminar?

Socratic seminars provide active practice in six major process areas. (See figure 5.1.) Students will

- learn productive habits of mind;
- read, speak, listen, think, and write more clearly;
- engage their minds in meaningful conversation about ideas;

- receive coaching in oral skills and small group processes;
- deepen their level of understanding by developing *knowledge* as well as *facts well understood*; and
- concentrate attention on a text.

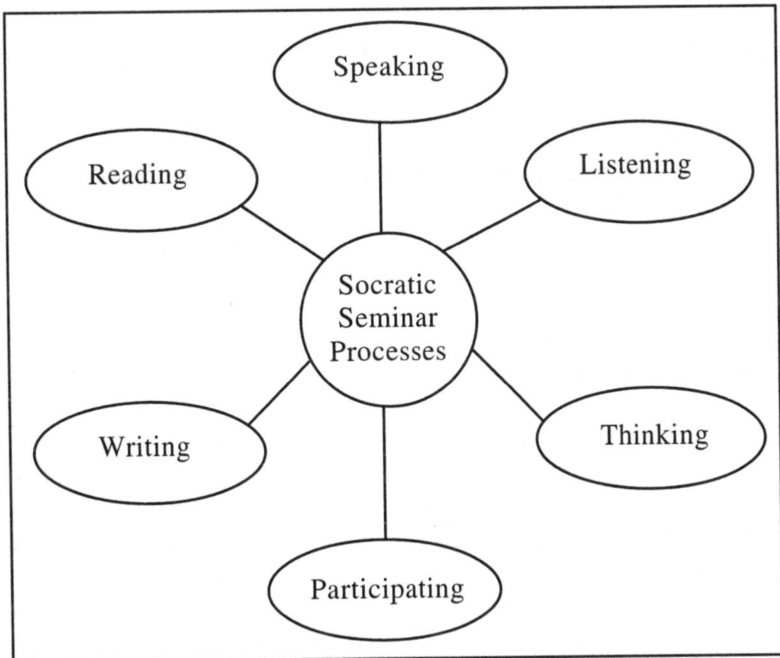

Fig. 5.1. Socratic Seminar Processes

Logistics of Conducting Socratic Seminars

Socratic seminars require preparation and practice. Here are a few pointers to help you get a good start on using them with your class.

Selecting a Reading

Texts for readings should be kept short, a page or two at first, depending on the age group of the students. In fact many a good seminar has come out of even shorter pieces: Euclid's Postulates, Newton's three laws of motion, or the Pledge of Allegiance. After the class has participated in a few seminars, short stories and longer articles can be used. The main selection criterion for any text is richness in ideas, values, and issues worthy of discussion. Essays that advance a single point of view or unusual slant on a familiar topic usually produce a good seminar because they spawn diverse opinions, and these opinions generate student interaction. Works that propose programs or discuss issues of universal importance—freedom, duty, security, characteristics of human nature, finding the best political system, etc.—generally make good candidates for seminar pieces. Also, op ed pages of daily newspapers stir up issues of local concern. The work chosen should be of genuine interest to the seminar leader. He or she should be able to answer questions about the author, the time period in which the text was written, and cultural influences surrounding the piece, if they are *relevant and helpful* to the deeper understanding of the text. Students should be expected and encouraged to ask for further information about the piece once they realize it has some bearing on their interpretation of the reading.

Bibliographies of Readings for Socratic Seminars

Readings will have to be custom tailored to the participants' reading and maturity levels. Fortunately, many lists of sources are widely available in school and community libraries.

The Paideia Program contains 53 pages of suggested readings for use in Socratic seminars with all grade levels from kindergarten through 12th grade. This is an excellent list with emphasis on classic works. (For some samples of this list, see Appendix 1).

The *Paideia* list, though put together specifically for Socratic seminars, was published in the early 1980s and thus contains only a smattering of culturally diverse selections. A valuable, annotated source book for selecting culturally diverse readings is *Teaching Multicultural Literature in Grades K-8* (1993) edited by Violet J. Harris. (For lists of readings for elementary students published in recent periodicals, and for a list of authors for primary grades who specialize in other cultures, see Appendix 2.) *Against Borders: Promoting Books for a Multicultural World* (1993), published by The American Library Association, contains more than 50 pages of annotated entries, including the grade level for which the reading is appropriate. It is divided into two parts: part 1 focuses on themes such as "The Perilous Journey," "Family Matters," "Friends and Enemies," and "Finding the Way Home"; and part 2 is a resource listing. The book also lists readings by country of the author's origin. Most of the readings are geared for middle school and up. (For a composite list from several sources containing only a small percentage of the books listed in these sources, see Appendix 2.)

Reading Deeply to Identify Major Issues

One of the keys to a good Socratic seminar is getting past flat spots in the conversation before all of the momentum and excitement dissipate. A few important moments can make or break your seminar. This is why the discussion leader must prepare for the discussion beforehand by reading the text material many times and getting a feel for the directions that the seminar could take. Although the teacher or seminar leader may be tempted to go as far as to prepare a list of possible questions to ask if the conversation stalls, preparing such a list carries with it the risk of forcing the questions into the discussion rather than letting the topic swing around to where the question is relevant. Instead of making a list of specific questions, you might want to identify half a dozen general areas of interest into which the conversation might travel. But don't be surprised if you end up using only a few of these. Typically, many perspectives and issues you had not thought of will come out during the conversation, and students will go after them in hot pursuit.

Preparing Students

A day before the seminar, introduce the material to the students and generate motivation. If the material is a written text, have the students read the text closely two or three times, then instruct them to read the text once more: "Read every line as you would a love letter." Before the seminar begins, have the students underline or list any word, phrase, or sentence they don't understand. These questions about unfamiliar words, references, or meanings can be answered in the course of the seminar by the students, with help from the teacher.

Setting Ground Rules

Before the seminar begins, the leader should go over a few ground rules.

- Take turns speaking.
- Don't insult or embarrass anyone.
- Tie your comments to the text and not to outside experience unless that outside experience is common to everyone.
- If someone has not read the material, he or she may participate as an observer but not as a speaker.

Asking the Opening Question

Generally, the leader offers an opening question, which is supposed to trigger the participants into examining the text, hunting for evidence, identifying assumptions, and formulating questions. The opening question should be broad enough to allow the conversation to take many turns, but not so vague that it dissipates interest. A good conversation is spoiled if the students try too hard to actually answer the question literally as they have been trained to do over the years. Keep in mind that sometimes the conversation may break out spontaneously during the preliminary discussion before the opening question is asked. By all means, if the conversation jump-starts itself, skip the opening question.

One leader, when kicking off a seminar based on the Chinese philosophers Confucius and Lao Tsu asked, "Which would you rather have as the headmaster of your school?" The question got students to ask what each philosopher said, what he meant, and what the applications of the philosophy were. A mini-seminar leader opening a discussion on the Declaration of Independence might ask, "Were the restrictions on the definition of *men* in the phrase *all men are created equal* justifiable?"

Facilitating

One of the highest goals of education is to help students acquire good judgment. To do this they must learn to examine assumptions and distinguish objective criticism from mere dislike. The seminar facilitator's task is to have students separate out hidden assumptions, evaluate someone's expertise, examine the structure of an argument, and judge the strength of a rationale given. At the same time he or she must recognize the basic premise of the Socratic seminar that the conversation belongs to the students. This makes the task of facilitator a delicate one: to help the conversation along without guiding it. The teacher's temptation is to interject the learned or historical perspective. Resist the urge to play expert as it really kills the discussion. Allow the students to initiate and direct the conversation; the special value of the seminar is wasted if it becomes just another reading with a teacher-directed question-and-respond session (with blocks of exposition about the meaning of the piece thrown in at no extra charge.)

The leader should have no special agenda, and there should be no particular goal governing which direction the conversation travels; in fact the unpredictability of the conversation is one of the Socratic seminar's most interesting features. A conversation that does not reach consensus is fine. In facilitating a Socratic seminar, two opposite poles must be avoided: "anything goes" and "here's the conclusion you need to understand." When the discussion gets rolling, typically, pairs of conversations will break out where two or more people return to the area of their interest while others go in a different direction. (I'm not referring to satellite conversations between two persons on the side but verbal Ping-Pong between speakers in the seminar.) This can all work out if the leader directs traffic. If the subject changes before a promising area has been fully explored, the leader might say, "OK, let's get back to what Jessica said, then go on to Alberto's question."

The leader should role-model the process of clarifying questions and calling on individuals to elaborate; "That's a fresh view; could you spin that out?" "OK, now where in the text did you see that?" "How did you come to that interpretation?" "Did everyone understand the question?" "What does that phrase mean?" It is important that the teacher remind students that they should direct their own traffic, ask their own questions, challenge each other's assumptions, and facilitate their own conversation. If the teacher talks too much or breaks the ground rules, the students should point this out to the teacher. It may be necessary to remind students to take turns. "Whoa, whoa, one at a time please." After several seminars, students learn to take turns and refer to the text. It takes longer for them to learn to follow up on each others' comments or pose a new question when the conversation begins to drag.

Observing Students' Body Language

Some students may become so involved with the discussion that they become overly emotional. Before any harsh words are exchanged or an outburst occurs, the leader should take control of the situation, perhaps by calling for a one-minute break. Conflict that arises naturally from human disagreement should be dealt with as normal, but highly emotionally arguments can be destructive to the group process. The teacher should provide a role model of good interpersonal problem-solving skills; otherwise, trust breaks down. The students are expected to be authentic in their comments, increasing their emotional exposure and vulnerability. Therefore it is necessary for the leader to be especially alert to the early nonverbal warning signs of trouble between students and forestall the problem behavior before it poisons the conversation.

Asking Follow-Through Questions

During the seminar, the leader must be ready to come up with questions that reignite a discussion when it starts to burn out. As already noted, it is important that these questions not be handed out in advance and that the leader does not force the discussion to go in a certain direction. As the seminar progresses, the questions should be of increasing specificity, following a progression that allows students to explore deeper and deeper layers of meaning, make more connections, and analyze specific parts of the reading more closely. The leader keeps the questions flowing. Facilitating a seminar is like sailing a small boat: You must keep your sails trimmed and heading somewhat against the flow of the wind but never head straight into the wind. Here are some specific techniques for keeping the conversation going.

- Point out a possible contradiction or discrepancy in the text.
- Propose a hypothetical situation illustrating a principle from the reading.
- Ask "Is X the same as or different from Y?"
- Provide relevant anecdotes from the newspaper.
- Call for clarification of a pair of similar terms.
- Suggest a bystander's role and ask for that bystander's feelings.
- Transpose the situation to a parallel situation and ask if this would make a difference.

Coaching

Leaders have important duties. They must coach in critical thinking, encourage reading for depth, exhibit open-mindedness, and function as a productive group member. "OK, now remember the ground rules; no insults or personally-directed comments." "That's good, Alisa, you're showing some original thinking." "Mareesha, I think what you're saying is worth hearing; can you speak up so everyone can hear you?" Of course, the teacher must be on guard not to suggest the "right" interpretation of the text.

Postseminar Follow-Up

Reflecting on the Group Dynamics and Individual Contributions

At the appropriate time, the leader stops the seminar. It is highly desirable to have students take a moment to reflect on their participation in the seminar.

Was I courteous?

Were my comments to the point of the text?

Did I listen well to others and process what they said, or did I just jump into the conversation with a comment of my own, unrelated to the previous comments?

Did I notice who didn't speak at all? Did I dominate or withdraw too much?

Did any of my ideas or opinions shift?

Did I speak clearly in a voice and phrasing that made me easy to understand?

Writing About Issues or Feelings That Surface in the Socratic Seminar

The Paideia Program recommends that every seminar be followed with some kind of writing assignment. Now that the students' minds have been filled with thoughts, they have done the hard part of writing: thinking about what to say. The same standard applied to the seminar applies to the written work: It should refer to the text. The value of the follow-up writing assignment goes beyond composition practice. It is an opportunity for students to become involved at the subjective level of "I thought," "I felt," and "I believe." Such an opportunity for genuine self-expression is not common and should be used to the maximum when it occurs.

The Participant's Role in a Socratic Seminar

Every student should read the text material closely at least twice before participating. If someone participates without having read the material, the conversation can be sidetracked by the unprepared person's opinions. Participants should try to listen well, speak clearly, and support a positive group dynamic. Students who, for whatever reason, have not read the text can be assigned the very useful role of observer.

The Observer's Role in a Socratic Seminar

It is good to assign a recording task to the observers, perhaps to tally the number of times each person spoke. Also, the observers could make use of a *sociogram*. A sociogram is a diagram that uses a circle to represent each speaker. A line connects any interaction between the speakers, for example, if Susan said, "Jenny had a cool idea," the observer would draw a line pointing from Susan to Jenny to show that they had interacted in the conversation.

Potential Problems Using Socratic Seminars

Old Habits

The first and greatest problem for the teacher seeking to adopt the Socratic seminar as a learning tool in the classroom is getting people to break out of old habits. It is a good idea to start the seminars at the beginning of the school year before bad habits can develop.

Generally, the students won't feel comfortable at first interacting directly with each other without teacher involvement. *The Paideia Program* maintains that 50-60 hours of coached practice are needed before a novice seminar leader is ready to fly solo. Although experienced teachers will find some crossover skills from ordinary discussions, Socratic seminars are much more difficult to master than other kinds of pedagogy. In learning to facilitate Socratic seminars, continuous progress is possible, and a continuous commitment must be made toward getting better.

Lack of Commitment to Doing a Series of Seminars

Although the first few seminars may drag for one reason or another, after several seminars, progress occurs rather rapidly. At least two seminars should be held per month, especially in courses for which reading is central. Although conducting a Socratic seminar may seem a formidable task, you just have to believe in eventual success and get through the first part, because it really does get easier.

Lack of Advance Preparation by Students

Some students will try to do the least possible work anytime, anyplace, even on a new and challenging project, but that is not the problem here. Students may be overwhelmed by a long reading and the new format. The Socratic seminar technique is worth the time it takes to develop, because students become its greatest fans and ask for more! To build some momentum, begin the seminar series by introducing a painting, a photograph, song lyrics, or a short article as the focus of the discussion. Lead at least a couple of mini-seminars before scheduling a full-blown seminar to iron out any "bugs." You may find that two classes will react to a piece in completely different ways. Eventually, students will be able to handle longer readings with the same enthusiasm as for shorter ones.

Not Scheduling Enough Class Time

Mini-seminars on short essays, poems, short works, artworks, and newspaper articles can be conducted in a single class period, but a full-blown seminar cannot. The best way to present a Socratic seminar within a limited time frame is to devote one session before the seminar to introducing and reading the piece closely, then a class period to the seminar itself, and another day to reflect on the seminar and do follow-up writing.

Getting the Conversation to Flow Smoothly

The facilitator will need to call for clarification and keep the questions coming. Sometimes the facilitator may press students to explain a rationale or search for a more fundamental principle, and students may show some discomfort. As Piaget (1958) tells us, learning requires disequilibrium before a new plateau of understanding can be reached. If you know your students, you will know how hard to press to achieve the right level of disequilibrium.

A rip-roaring discussion is great except when it becomes a forest fire. Sometimes when a comment sparks many students' interest, everyone has an urge to talk; group unity breaks down into multiple satellite conversations. The facilitator must step in and ask, "Who's next?" Students eventually must learn to take turns and assert themselves when interrupted.

The opposite problem is that what seemed like a fascinating piece to you bombs with the students. But beware, a teacher's idea of a seminar gone bust might be a student's idea of a good seminar. If there is a recipe for picking a good piece every time, I'll be first in line to learn it.

A Sample Reading for a Socratic Seminar in the Elementary Grades

An Aesop Fable: *The Grasshopper and the Ants*

One sunny day in winter, some ants were busy drying their store of corn, which had gotten rather damp during a long spell of rain. Presently, up came a grasshopper and begged them to spare her a few grains of corn, "For I'm simply starving," she said. The ants stopped work for a moment, though this was against their principles.

"May we ask," said they, "what you were doing with yourself all summer long? Why didn't you collect a store of food for the winter? After the grain cutters left, there were bushels of corn scattered over the field, yours for the taking if you had troubled yourself to pick them up as we did."

"The fact is," replied the grasshopper, "I was so busy singing that I hadn't the time."

"If you spent the summer singing," replied the ants, "you can't do better than spend the winter dancing." And they chuckled and went on with their work. ♦

Comments on *The Grasshopper and the Ants*

With any piece, it is important that everyone start with a literal understanding of the work. It may be appropriate to have students retell the story in their own words. An opening question might be something broad such as, "Were the ants too stingy with their grain?"

Here are some possible directions that the discussion might take:

Suppose the grasshopper was actually about to die of starvation. Would that make a difference to the ants?

If you were the grasshopper, would you feel entitled to receive help from the ants?

If the grasshopper and ants became children, who would you want in your class? Both? Neither?

Do you know any people like the grasshopper or the ants?

Did the ants have a right to make fun of the grasshopper? Couldn't they have been more polite?

How could you summarize the point of the fable in your own words?

A Sample Reading for a Socratic Seminar in the Middle School and Up

The Gentleman[1]

It is almost a definition of a gentleman to say he is one who never inflicts pain. This description is both refined and, as far as it goes, accurate. He is mainly occupied in removing obstacles that hinder the free and unembarrassed action of those about him, and he goes along with their decisions rather than take the initiative himself. His support is parallel to comforts or conveniences of the home, like an easy chair or a good fire, which do their part in relieving fatigue and cold, though nature provides us with the means of obtaining rest and body heat without them. The true gentlemen in like manner carefully avoids whatever may cause a jar or jolt in the minds of those he keeps company with—all clashing of opinion, or collision of feeling, or suspiciousness, or pessimism, or resentment—his great concern being to make everyone at their ease and at home. He has his eyes on everyone in his company; he is tender toward the bashful, gentle toward the distant, and merciful toward the ridiculous; he respects those to whom he is speaking; he is seldom prominent in conversation, never wearisome, and he guards against confusing or irritating topics. He makes light of favors while he does them and seems to be receiving when he is giving to others. He never speaks of himself except when really necessary, never defends himself by a mere insult; he has no ears for slander or gossip, is careful and honest about stating the motives of those who interfere with him, and interprets everything for the best. He is never mean or petty in his disputes, never takes unfair advantage of others, never degrades people to avoid answering to the point they are making, and never sneaks in accusations of wrongdoing which he dare not say out loud. By wisely looking to the future, he observes the maxim of the ancient sage, that we should always conduct ourselves toward our enemy as if he were one day to be our friend. He has too much good sense to be upset by insults; he has more important things to do than keep a list of all the hurtful things people have said or done to him; and he never carries a grudge. His philosophy of life is one of patience and resignation; he submits to pain because it is inevitable, to grief because there is nothing you can do about it, and to death because it is his destiny. If he engages in controversy of any kind, his disciplined mind prevents him from wasting his strength on matters of no importance, avoiding the mistake of others who may have better minds (though less education) than he has, who end up using their intelligence like a blunt weapon, tearing and hacking at an issue instead of cutting into it cleanly. Such people mistake the point of the argument, fail to see their opponent's strengths, and walk away from the conversation more unsettled on the issue than before. He may be right or wrong in his opinion, but he is too clearheaded to be unfair; he is as simple as he is forceful, and as brief as he is decisive. Nowhere shall we find more sincere honesty, consideration, and thoroughness; he projects himself into the minds of his opponents so he can identify their mistakes. He knows the weakness of human reason as well as its strength, its venue, and its limits. If he doesn't believe in God, he will be too profound and large-minded to ridicule religion or to act against it; he is too wise to be narrow and rigid or carry his disbelief to an extreme. He respects sincerity and devotion; he often supports organizations or groups as honorable, beautiful, or useful, even though he does not agree with them; he honors the ministers of religion, and he's happy to decline its mysteries without attacking them or starting arguments. He is a friend of religious toleration, not only because his philosophy has taught him to look on all forms of faith with an unprejudiced eye, but also because he values gentleness and womanly feelings which the finer things of civilization depend on. ♦

Comments on *The Gentleman*

Good readings will generate diverse opinions which can be discussed at some length. Nearly everyone will have some immediate reaction to this essay, but a good conversation needs more than immediate reactions. It needs a foundation upon which to build, and this requires a good understanding of the reading at the literal level. To establish this literal understanding, it may be a good idea to open the seminar with a round-robin recap of the traits in the essay: Each person picks out a trait, and a recorder compiles a list to which all can refer during the seminar. This is also a good opportunity to clarify unfamiliar words or phrases or to have students look them up in a dictionary.

Opening questions for this essay might include the following:

Would you like to have someone like the gentleman described here for a friend?

What would society be like if everyone acted like the gentleman?

If you changed every *he* to *she*, would this essay describe the ideal woman?

These questions call for a conclusion. When a student answers yes or no, the facilitator probes the response and asks for evidence from the text.

As so many traits are listed, there are bound to be some in opposition. You might ask students to look for contradictory traits. The entire middle portion of the essay describes behavior in conflicting situations. Present to the students some of these questions:

Is this behavior good? If the gentlemen is so kind and gentle, why does he get into so much conflict?

The gentleman doesn't volunteer information about his feelings, beliefs, or dreams. Is he boring, impersonal, and cold? However you answer, cite passages in the text that lead you to your conclusion.

We see how the gentleman acts, but does he stand for anything? Does he have any principles, or is he wishy-washy?

Would Martin Luther King Jr. be a gentleman according to this definition?

Would the gentleman make a good teacher, parent, or principal?

What jobs would the gentleman fail at, if any? What jobs would he succeed at?

How many of these traits does a person have control over anyway?

Can a person just become a gentleman (or woman) simply through willpower? How?

A Closing Note

Few teaching tools have as much to offer as Socratic seminars. They are engaging for students and usually provide a boost to class morale. Seminars provide opportunities for teaching the upper-tier skills on Bloom's taxonomy—analysis, synthesis, and evaluation—which are too seldom practiced in most classrooms. Teachers will find a positive crossover effect with other types of discussions after just a few seminars as students become more aware of the group dynamic and their contribution to it. Also, having reflected on their participation in the seminar, students will find that self-observation in other activities comes more naturally. When run skillfully, seminars allow students to follow through on their own initiative. The outcome is that students will be able to build a richer and broader understanding, a greater appreciation, and a deeper personal meaning of their world, themselves, and others. This is the essence of good education.

NOTE

1. This essay was adapted to make it accessible to younger readers from "The Gentleman" by John Henry Neuman (1801-1890), English scholar and clergyman.

REFERENCES

Adler, Mortimer. 1982. *The Paideia Proposal: An Educational Manifesto.* New York: Collier.

———. 1983. *Paideia: Problems and Possibilities.* New York: Collier.

———. 1984. *The Paideia Program: An Educational Syllabus.* New York: Collier.

FURTHER READING

Adler, Mortimer. 1981. *Six Great Ideas.* New York: Collier.

Eastman, Arthur E., ed. 1984. *The Norton Reader: An Anthology of Expository Prose.* 6th ed. New York: W. W. Norton.

Sommers, Christina, and Fred Sommers. 1993. *Vice and Virtue in Everyday Life: Introductory Readings in Ethics.* Fort Worth, TX: Harcourt Brace.

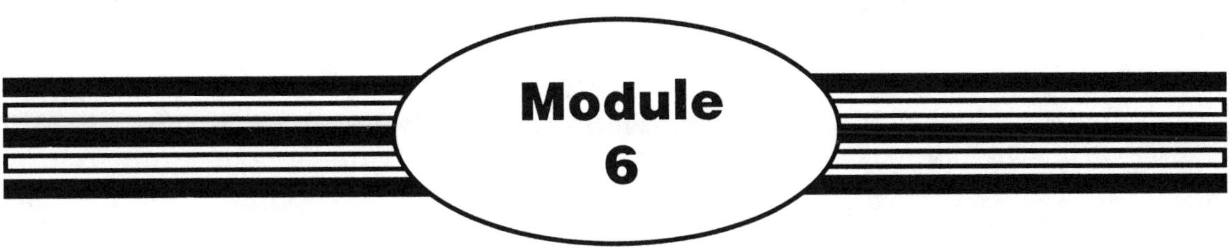

Module
6

Observing, Describing, and Imagining

To see a world in a grain of sand
And a heaven in a wild flower,
Hold infinity in the palm of your hand
And eternity in an hour.
—William Blake, Auguries of Innocence

SEEING WHAT YOU'RE LOOKING AT

The world around us is so complex that we cannot take in all the information that bombards our senses every moment. Psychologists have long known that the human perceptual process screens out and selects data from the stream of incoming sensations. We organize these selected sensations into perceptions without even being aware that such a process is going on.

However, certain activities as diverse as science, poetry, and storytelling require that we turn off the screening process and really see what we're looking at, in other words, observe more closely what is going on in the world around us. Hand a scientist a flower and ask for his or her observations and you'll probably get back a long list of precise and impartial statements, readily verified by your own scrutiny. Give the same flower to a poet, and you'll get back a collage of images and feelings about the flower. Each of these responses is appropriate in its place.

Certainly, for a person to be educated, he or she should have some knowledge of the laws of nature and how science goes about discovering those laws. Doing science requires attention to the details of phenomena, in other words, to observing. To be educated, a person also needs to be able to express his or her thoughts accurately and coherently, and in a manner that is pleasing to those with whom he or she is communicating. To be a good citizen, a person needs to be a fair judge, capable of distinguishing fact from feeling, what is actually there from one's impression of what is there. To be a complete human being, a person needs to be able to interact with other people fairly—not as mere figures in one's own mind, not as instruments to some egocentric purpose, but as sovereign human beings with feelings, rights, and value apart from the use they serve in meeting one's own needs. These developmental goals—knowing oneself in relation to the natural world and the social world—should be schoolwide goals to which all teachers contribute. To help students move out of their egocentrism, teachers can focus their attention on the world outside themselves. Although observation and description are vital to both science and language development, the greater goal behind classroom activities that focus on these skills is to teach the process of seeing and fully appreciating what is outside oneself.

Observing

Suppose you taught fifth grade and brought in a pumpkin a few days before Halloween and asked your students to make observations about it. You would probably hear a variety of statements: "It's round," "It's orange," or "It grows on a vine." Then you press your students to walk around the pumpkin and really look at it, touch it, and describe it. Now, sensing that you want more detail, students might offer things like, "A bird pecked two holes in it," "You would have room for one candle inside, but not two," or "The stuff inside is gooey and stringy." Note that none of these statements about the pumpkin qualify as actual observations. We can *guess* that a bird pecked two holes in it, and we can *judge* the size limit to be one candle. We can *remember* that last year's pumpkin had a gooey, stringy filling and reasonably *infer* that this pumpkin contains the same material.

Objective observations are simple reports of what the senses tell us. Good observations have a finer grain of detail than superficial ones. Yes, the pumpkin is orange, but what shade of orange? Orange juice? Tangerine? Setting sun? Carrots? Yes, it is round, but imperfectly so. Where does it bulge? Where is it flattened? Yes, it has freckles. What color are these? What size? Are they scattered evenly over the whole surface, or do they bunch up on one side? What is the size of the pumpkin in inches? What size are the holes? What does the material inside the holes look like? What does the pumpkin smell like? Like flowers? Dirt? Fallen autumn leaves? What is the surface texture like? Silky? Glassy? Leathery? How many grooves are there? How deep? What does the stem look like? Smell like? What is its exact color? What sound does the pumpkin make when hit with a knuckle? Does a tap sound the same everywhere?

Describing

The objective view concerns *what a thing is*, whereas the subjective view emphasizes one's *personal reaction to what a thing is*. To be fully educated, a student needs to be able to make both types of observation fluently. Table 6.1 delineates some characteristics of the two modes of description.

Table 6.1. Characteristics of Objective and Subjective Description.

Objective Description	Subjective Description
Purpose: to quantify and qualify	Purpose: to engage feelings and convey sensations
Uses as many senses as possible	Uses all senses, but does so selectively
Focuses on elements identical to everyone	Focuses on responses of the individual
Neutral in tone; detached	Engages feelings; evokes admiration or revulsion
Described object seen in isolation	Described object associated with other things
Sounds scientific	Sounds poetic
Makes no assumptions about past history of object	Can engender many possibilities of the object's past and future
Uses precise descriptors that bring accurate pictures to mind	Uses evocative descriptors that bring rich images to mind
Makes comparisons: close physical resemblance of comparison object to described object	Makes metaphorical comparisons: unusual, nonliteral linkage of comparison object to described object
Uses qualitative and quantitative descriptors for size, weight, time, etc.	Uses evocative and emotive descriptors for sensory impression and essence
Examples: botanical or medical reports	Examples: poetry, especially imagistic poetry and haiku; gourmet magazines; or fine art criticism

Concept Development Activity 6-1: Understanding Objective and Subjective Descriptors

For each item in the list, place a check mark in the column that best fits. The main criterion is, Would everyone agree (an objective observation) or is this a private experience (a subjective observation)?

Table 6.2. Description of a Pumpkin.

Objective?	Possible Description of a Pumpkin	Subjective?
	It is twice as big as a basketball.	
	It is like a giant ball of pizza dough before you smash it down.	
	It feels so smooth and cool, like it's wet.	
	It is smooth but also bumpy like my uncle's bald head.	
	The stem is yucky green and smells like my basement.	
	The hole in the stem is big enough to stick a pencil in.	
	It is puffing out like an angry man's face.	
	You can peel off the skin with your fingernail.	
	It is a lopsided, sad pumpkin.	
	The stem grabs the top like an eagle grasping a ball of cheese.	

Expanding Vocabulary and Range of Objective Description

Like muscles, vocabularies shrink unless used. Exercise is required to maintain a robust, diverse vocabulary.

Describing Color

- Set up a ground rule that no color-wheel words (red, blue, green, etc.) can be used without a modifier (brick red, sky blue, pea green).
- As a warm-up to descriptive thinking, brainstorm a lexicon (a specialized word list) of colors such as peach, cinnamon, burgundy, and coral.
- Describe the specimen's colors and pinpoint the location and extent of each color.

Describing Shape

- Set up a ground rule that no basic-shape words (round, square, long, short) can be used unless attached to a modifier. Instead, compare the specimen's shape to a familiar object, then suggest a modification of the object, for example, "bottle shaped, with a long neck," "egg-shaped, but with more tapering."
- As a warm-up, give one description of a specimen's shape and call for many more descriptions.
- Describe the specimen's body as a group of individual shapes, and tell how the shapes are arranged into the whole.

Describing Size and Texture

Repeat the process for *size* and *texture* of the specimen.

Literal Versus Figurative Comparisons

A rich description calls to mind both the specific physical characteristics of an object and the feelings it evokes. Literal comparison tries to match the characteristics of the object described with similar characteristics in familiar objects, for example, "The pumpkin is bigger than a basketball but smaller than a car tire. It smells like a flower but not as sweet as a rose. It is a darker orange than a carrot but not as dark as an apricot. It's smooth like cloth but not as flat as glass." Another type of literal description is quantitative, meaning a numerical answer is given to the questions "How big?" "How many?" "How heavy?" "How much?"

Figurative description, on the other hand, attempts to answer the question "How does it make you feel?" "Skin as cold and smooth as a dead frog's stomach." "Grooves like a weary old man's face." "A warm shade of orange like the friendly glow of a campfire." "A thunking sound like a ripe, sweet watermelon eager to give us its juice."

Tools for Observation and Description

A couple of classroom exercises will help get those descriptor muscles into shape.

Classroom Activity 6-1: Contrasting Observations of a Flower

Materials: A dozen or so flowers of the same type and color, perhaps leftovers from a florist.

Part A: Describe a flower.

1. Each student or student pair takes a flower, observes it closely, and describes it in writing. Once the students have completed their descriptions, the teacher collects all of the flowers. Next, each student retrieves his or her flower from the pile. Notice whether anyone took his or her description along as a reference. Ask why not.

2. Gather the flowers again. Have the students exchange their descriptions, read them, and try to find the flower described by the classmate. Discuss what descriptors made it easy or difficult to find the flower.

Part B: Write a wholly subjective description of the flower specimen.

Part C: Write another description of the flower, including both objective and subjective descriptors.

Classroom Activity 6-2: Expanding Descriptive Vocabulary

Materials: A live pet, a stuffed specimen, a large shell, or color photographs of tropical birds or other brightly colored animals.

Part A: Write a paragraph of wholly objective description mentioning size, color, texture, shape, and smell.

Part B: Write a wholly subjective description of the specimen, mentioning size, color, texture, shape, and smell.

Discovery Labs

Science involves laboratory activities. However, many classroom lab activities are "canned"; that is, they provide so much structure and even data sheets that the student is put into the passive role of data recorder, not inquirer. Discovery labs involve simple, safe experiments that allow students to engage in constructive play and make discoveries and observations by themselves. A discovery lab is one in which students improvise procedures themselves and are free to explore a range of phenomena (Labinowicz 1980). These are *process* labs, rather than opportunities to verify a predetermined conclusion. Discovery labs can be based on simple but interesting phenomena such as a toy top falling over, paper airplanes, or changes in colors on soap bubbles blown with a straw in a dish viewed in bright light. Play and individual initiative are to be encouraged, *but absolutely clear limits must be set beforehand.* Here are a few examples for middle school physical science discovery labs.

Lab 1: Chemical Properties of Household Chemicals

Purpose: To discover some properties of household chemicals

Materials: Droppers; bottles of safe acids and safe bases, labeled only as CHEMICAL 1, CHEMICAL 2, etc.; litmus paper; baking soda; solid acids such as tartaric acid and phenolphthalein, each labeled with its actual name

Directions: Find some kind of pattern to the way different chemicals interact.

Procedure: Obviously, safety guidelines such as no horseplay and no tasting of chemicals will have to be established beforehand. Students should devise their own testing procedure as independently as possible. Although there is no single best procedure, students will probably use drops of each chemical on each solid substance. They will make their own observations and maybe even write them down. Later, in a teacher-led discussion, the students can delineate similarities, differences, and patterns and perhaps even propose a system of classification.

Some possible outcomes (not to be given to students but to have them discover): Type "A" chemicals turn litmus paper red; turn red phenolphthalein clear; and cause baking soda to fizz, releasing carbon dioxide gas. Type "B" chemicals turns litmus blue and change clear phenolphthalein to red. After the students have come up with this generalization, the names are given: "A" chemicals are acids, "B" chemicals are bases.

Lab 2: Pendulum Relationships

Purpose: To find a pattern in the way a pendulum works

Materials: Thread or fishing line, a pencil or rod clamped firmly in place, large washers, paper clips

Procedure: Students should improvise a testing procedure as independently as possible. One possibility is to make a hook out of one paper clip (to hold the washers), tie it to a string like a fishhook, and attach the other end of the string to a paper clip bent into a circle and placed around a pencil or rod. Weights (washers) are changed systematically as is length of the string, and time for one round trip is recorded. (The longest length will need to be at least 10 times the shortest.)

Some possible outcomes (not to be given to students but to have them discover): The mass of the bob has no effect on the time for one swing of the bob, but the time for one round-trip swing is related to the square root of the distance from the washers to the pivot point. It is doubtful the square root relationship can be found. Students might find that the longer the string, the longer the time needed for one round trip, which does not vary much when small length changes are used.

Trait Grids

Descriptors can be used for any category of trait. Some of the most useful categories of traits to describe are

- form, which usually refers to shape;
- quantity, which is the amount or size;
- quality, which refers to permanent characteristics, including color;
- function, or the purpose or way the item is used; and
- essence, or what makes it uniquely what it is and not something else.

Classroom Activity 6-3: Using a Trait Grid for Practicing with Descriptors

PART A: Complete the following Trait Grid.

Table 6.3. Trait Grid.

	Categories				
Objects	**Form**	**Quantity**	**Quality**	**Function**	**Essence**
A bicycle					
An electric guitar					
A box of chocolates					
An orange					
A sunset					

Word Pictures

Reporters have to be good observers to describe events, places, and characters vividly and, in the case of print journalists, to provide written pictures of a scene or person. Novelists have to make their characters ring true, that is, to have the emotions and responses that make them seem like real people, not flat figures. To accomplish this, reporters and authors blend *objective* and *subjective* description into a warm and vivid balance.

Classroom Activity 6-4: Writing a Word Picture

Pick a setting where you can observe a sunset, moonrise, or simple occurrence such as striking a match, peeling and eating an orange, or mixing a cup of hot chocolate.

Part A: Make four columns headed with the words OBJECTIVE, SUBJECTIVE, LITERAL, and FIGURATIVE. As you observe, record impressions in each column, remembering to include as many different senses as possible.

Part B: Write a Word Picture, blending the information recorded in all four columns smoothly.

Classroom Activity 6-5: Contrasting Descriptions of a Nonphysical Object

Carl Sandburg (1970) in his poem "Good Morning, America" lists more than three dozen "tentative definitions of poetry." Here are a few samples:

- Poetry is a projection across silence of cadences arranged to break that silence with definitive intentions of echoes, syllables, and wavelengths.
- Poetry is an art practiced with the terribly plastic material of human language.
- Poetry is the tracing of the trajectories of a finite sound to the infinite points of its echoes.
- Poetry is a sequence of dots and dashes, spelling depths, crypts, cross-lights, and moon wisps.
- Poetry is an echo asking a shadow dancer to be a partner.
- Poetry is the journal of a sea animal living on land, wanting to fly in the air.
- Poetry is a series of explanations of life, fading off into the horizon too swift for explanations.
- Poetry is a sky dark with a wild duck migration.

Construct a list of contrasting definitions of

- the moon;
- computers;

- your favorite outdoor activity: hiking, sailing, camping, etc.;
- a setting in nature; and
- a person you know well.

IMAGINATION: THE ENGINE OF CREATIVITY

Stories or inventions need imagination to release them from the constraints of the ordinary world. Albert Einstein said that imagination was more important to him than knowledge. It seems that our culture has a divided attitude toward imagination, a mixed desire to both embrace its potential and reject the apparent idleness or self-absorption that it supposedly fosters. Fantasy and daydreaming are as important to the adolescent as make-believe play is to the child. Besides being a means to rehearse certain cognitive processes, fantasy is the source of innovation. "It is with the help of fantasy that not just literary works, but all the scientific inventions and mechanical achievements are created" (Vygotsky 1994, 285).

Imagination, whatever it really is, seems to run by an inner toggle switch that one can turn on or off. Freeing the imagination rather than getting more of it, is the goal here. The problem is that imagination is rooted in the unconscious mind, that realm of inner mystery few really dare explore fully. Shortcuts into the imagination such as those achieved through the use of psychoactive drugs are fraught with peril. In the main, techniques for exploring the imagination are tied closely with depth psychology and even philosophy, subjects beyond the scope of this book. OK, so there's no easy 1, 2, 3 method for discovering the core of truth about imagination. Does this mean what you have is what you get? Not exactly.

How to Uncork the Imagination

One of the main modes of imagination is modification. Let's say you're an inventor and you handle a widget, wondering what it does. You can't really see any use for it, so you forget about it. Later, while thinking about another design altogether, you have a breakthrough and realize that your breakthrough was an unconscious modification of the widget you could see no use for. (For an amusing version of this process see the short story "A Report on the Barnhouse Effect" by Kurt Vonnegut Jr.) Imagination is image-making. New images are usually combinations of old images.

Brain waves indicate the level of activity in the brain during the course of different activities. Beta waves indicate mental concentration such as that involved in doing math problems. Alpha waves indicate a state of alert relaxation. Delta waves occur during sleep. Imagination, a state between sleep and concentration, requires alpha waves. Brain wave patterns change in response to demands on the brain made by different activities, but the response is not instantaneous; it takes about 10 to 15 minutes to make a switch. Athletes and ballerinas warm up before performing not just to stretch out their muscles but to increase the blood flow and electrical activity to the part of the brain that controls muscle action. In like manner, actors before going on stage often use mental imagery to get the creative juices flowing.

To produce the necessary alpha brain wave state for imagination requires some changes in the stimuli in the surroundings. Reducing the level of light and playing soft, meandering music produces changes in brain waves, usually within five minutes. Even changing your manner of speaking by lowering volume, slowing the rate, and stretching the vowels can have a similar effect. As we saw in Module 1, the incubation period which is so often essential to the creative process works better when the stimulation level is reduced after concentrating on a problem for a several hours.

Imagination, however, requires more than the right setting. As with any activity that involves the creative process, elements must be available for modification and combination. In other words, to create images, you have to seed the imagination beforehand so images can grow and blossom. For example, looking at pictures or models of a foreign location provides the raw material for your imagination to take you there.

One of the tamest modes of teasing out imagination for classroom use is the imaginary excursion which involves traveling to another place or time. In effect this is what happens during the telling of a good story: The reader/listener/viewer is taken by his or her imagination to another time and place. An imaginary excursion resembles a story but lacks the narrative structure and characters. Here's an example:

A Sample Imaginary Excursion: *The Aztecs' New Fire Ceremony*

In the cool dusky twilight, I can see firelight far off. Blazing torches cast their orange light onto the white walls of the sacred precinct of our city, Tenochtitlan (TAY-**NOESH**-TEET-LAN). The procession to the Hill of the Star will soon begin, and the priests will carry out the sacred rite; they will bind together the years and the worlds.

Darkness has settled over all the city now, still and quiet as a tomb. Delicate starlight now flickers on the mirrored surface of Lake Texcoco. Orange bands in the western sky silhouette the peaks of the distant range. All day long canoes and boats have paddled up the

canals to marketplaces in our island city, bearing their mangos, corn, red beans, bunches of decorative feathers, clay pots, and woven reed mats. But now the canoes stand tied at the docks, and all hearth fires and lamps have been put out as the priests instructed us. No one dares venture out into the silent streets on this sacred night.

Our people, the Aztecs, have two calendars. One records a year of 260 days, which marks the coming of sacred times. Ceremonies must be performed on schedule by the priests or we risk dishonoring the gods. The other calendar of 365 days informs farmers when to plant and harvest corn crops and beans. Only once in 52 years do the days of these two calendars meet, and on the night of this one day, high priests will perform the New Fire Ceremony that binds together the years into a cycle of the new age. On this sacred day, the world of the gods and the world of the mortals are bound up and tied together in one fate.

From my rooftop, I smell the sweet scent of incense and hear the thrumming chirp of crickets. The cool November air rises from the water, and the breeze tosses back my husband's long black hair. He and my children have joined me here on the rooftop. All day long, I have brought in stores of food and water, for we will not be allowed to go out of our house until the ceremony is complete. The children have been told they must stay awake and not go to sleep all night, for children who sleep through the New Fire ceremony will be turned into mice.

All the thousand houses of the city are dark. On the night of new fire, all flames are extinguished, and with the dying flames go forces of decay and pestilence and evil spirits. This night, new fire will be given to the people from our protector god, who lives in the seven sister stars we call Tonactecuhtli (TON-AK-TEK-**OOCHT**-LEE). The stillness and deathly darkness have upset the children, and they huddle close to me. My husband speaks to them to quiet their fears. "Look," he says as he points to the temple, "the procession has begun." Out of the sacred precinct dance the priests in dark robes, their long, wild hair matted with dung and their own blood. They cry out to Tonactecuhtli to hear their prayer and accept the offering they are preparing to make. Behind them, in white starched robes, high priests walk forth, swinging incense burners and singing loud chants to rouse the gods. In the center of the procession walks the handsome, strong captive chosen to give his life to bind the years together, sustaining the life of the sun and continuing the Fifth Age of the Aztec people.

Now the torch-lit procession has wound through the city and onto the causeway that connects our island to the mainland. Slowly, the procession moves to the thunder of large drums. Away they move toward the high mountain peak across the lake, to the sacred place where the altar of Quetzalcoatl (KAY-**ET**-SAL-COE-**OTT**-UL) lies on the Hill of the Star. The procession has become a tiny line of torches flickering across the causeway. Wailing voices and the beating of drums have faded now to silence. Stillness grips the night so deeply that I too feel a chill. Above our heads, the stars blaze in unmatched glory. In the eastern sky above the high peaks, I see two rows of stars making the fire sticks, which other tribes call "The Hunter." To the north I see the seven stars of the Great Dipper. Near it stands the Star Which Never Moves. This star is the center of the Aztec night, marking the doorway to the unknown universe, the dwelling place of the Creator God. Near the center of the Aztec night resides Tezcatlipoca (**TES**-CAAT-LEE-**PO**-KA), the evil, trickster god who comes and goes like smoke. It must be he who sends the mysterious smoking stars upon us, bringing omens of misfortune.

Now across the lake on the Hill of the Star, the priests have begun the New Fire ceremony. The obsidian knife has been raised, the chosen youth is sacrificed. His soul will fly to heaven and enjoy the sweetest and highest pleasures there. Bundles of cut wood on the altar of Quetzalcoatl are touched with the sacred torch. Flames leap up toward heaven. Glowing smoke and flickering sparks carry the soul of the youth straight up to the top of the sky, where our protector god dwells in the seven sister stars we call Tonactecuhtli, which passes overhead on this one night and no other.

By morning we will know if our protector god has accepted our sacrifice. The fire must remain untended all night. If Quetzalcoatl accepts our people's sacrifice, he will spark new fire out of the ashes on the altar. This new fire will rekindle our hearths and fill our homes with love, and he will bless our fields with renewed rain and protect us from our enemies. Then all shall be well, and the years will be bound together again for another age.

(Music: [played as background to reading of imaginary excursion] *AZTEC: The World of Moctezuma* by Victor Spiegel. Music from the audio tour, copyright 1992, by Antenna and The Denver Museum of Natural History.) ♦

Contrasting the Imaginary Excursion with Guided Imagery

Guided imagery is an activity very different from an imaginary excursion. Guided imagery was popularized by Gregorii Lozanov. (Although the name of Lozanov, a Bulgarian physician turned creative teacher, is not familiar to most Americans, some aspects of his highly creative model for teaching foreign language may be. The lesson in French in Module 3, pp. 36-38, was an example of the Lozanov method.) Guided imagery is written in the second person and sounds to some ears like hypnotic suggestion, which is indeed what Lozanov intended. The expressed purpose of guided imagery is to promote relaxation so that the mind is more receptive to learning. Also, direct suggestions of well-being, contentment, and self-esteem are often woven into the piece of guided imagery.

Guided Imagery for a Gymnastics Team

Here is how a coach might use guided imagery with her gymnastics team. The athletes lie down and close their eyes. They are told to relax and clear their minds, then to think about a lovely day and their many well-wishers. The athletes are told how positive they feel and how good it will be to perform at the highest level. After some minutes of soothing words and attractive images, the coach describes the athlete doing a vault: "You are now standing at the end of the runway leading to the vaulting horse." Then the coach guides the girls step by step through all the sensations and complex movements for a perfect vault. After the vault, the judges smile and award wonderful marks. After perhaps two more minutes the coach says, "We'll be coming back to our gym and you will be getting ready for a good practice today." The team sits up and begins practice.

The Use of Guided Imagery

Guided imagery has its place but not in a state-regulated classroom. Regardless of their good intentions to help their students or the psychological need for improving student self-concepts, teachers ought to be aware of the perils of the semi-hypnotic aspects of guided imagery. The technique of guided imagery has proven to be quite powerful for athletes or adults learning a foreign language; however, guided imagery is not as easy to use as it appears. More than good intentions are required. Guided imagery demands a properly trained, sensitive leader who will not introduce negative feelings when students have their guard down. Guided imagery requires a mature, trustworthy leader who has established and deserves a bond of trust with the students. Because guided imagery requires specialized conditions to work, it is not a tool recommended for a public school classroom unless students and parents agree to the activity, with full knowledge of its deliberately suggestive character.

In contrast to guided imagery, an imaginary excursion

- ties the content of the piece closely to the *course content* and *unit of study*;
- is written in the *first person singular*, not second person;
- contains only *indirect* cues to relax, not overt suggestions;

- is *under 15 minutes long* when read aloud;
- contains *no shocks or surprises*, no interruptions, nothing negative; and
- although relaxing, this piece is *not used for the purpose of relaxing.*

How to Get Started Using Imaginary Excursions in Your Classroom

Imaginary excursions, like most creative projects, can be built up layer by layer. Of course, you'll need some pictures to look at, and from these you'll make your four-column list as in the Word Picture activity (Classroom Activity 6-4 on p. 103). But, instead of starting to write right away, you are going to actively daydream your way through the whole excursion, and go over it several times in your mind. Then you write it all down. Here's a breakdown of the individual steps in writing an imaginary excursion.

Source Material

Imaginary excursions are easier to write than stories, but like stories, they require pre-writing to be successful. Imagination needs a point of departure. Suppose you were about to begin a unit on the Pacific Ocean and wanted a fresh approach as opposed to a video or handout. Let's say you decided to write an imaginary excursion involving a scuba diving trip around a coral reef in the South Pacific. You might begin by perusing a coffee table book on coral reefs or a *National Geographic* article. You would probably proceed in a manner similar to that outlined the exercises in the last section.

Prewriting

At this stage you will want to load up your memory with images, and you'll need lexicons of descriptors of all kinds: quantitative, sensory, objective, subjective. You'll need a list of the sensations and emotions for each phase of the trip: diving, swimming, turning, exploring, returning to the surface. You'll need to describe specific underwater sites both objectively and subjectively, sites that you've probably seen in the photographs of your inspiration material. Finally, you'll choose a route to connect the various sites.

Writing Rehearsal

Now picture the journey in your mind, location by location. Repeat this journey several times. This *writing rehearsal* saves rewriting time later. When you can sit down without notes and visualize the entire excursion route, you're ready to write an imaginary excursion. After you're happy with your piece, you may want to tape record it and play it back. A few revisions later, you're there.

Adding a Music Selection

Next, you may want to choose some music (e.g., a noninvasive instrumental) to softly accompany your reading. Remember, though, that music changes the listener's alertness level drastically; you don't want people sinking into a pleasant stupor as there will be work to do after the imaginary excursion. Keep in mind that the imaginary excursion is not a reward, not a gimmick, and not an invitation to party; it's just another way of getting work done. After only 10 minutes of the imaginary excursion, you may find the students in a quiet mood that lasts an hour or more. As we have already seen in Module 3, you probably won't want to follow this activity with a high-energy activity such as a debate, performance, or group movement activity; the clash of moods will be too great. The students will probably want to write a fictional narrative or immerse themselves into books (or onto the Internet) and learn more about the curious things they have beheld in their own imaginations.

A Closing Word on Trying out Innovative Creative Projects in Your Classroom

There's a first time for everything, and to implement a new creative teaching technique, you will have to get ready and just go for it. To write successful imaginary excursions, as with any form of creative activity, a person needs three things:

- skill with the tools of the trade;
- relaxed confidence; and
- courage to take risks in presenting something that has never been seen before in the form you're presenting it.

Once you're properly prepared, try the activity. Chances are that if you have planned adequately, most of your experiments will work out, and the ones that don't can be turned into valuable learning experiences.

REFERENCES

Labinowicz, Ed. 1980. *The Piaget Primer.* Menlo Park, CA: Addison-Wesley.

Vygotsky, Lev. 1994. Imagination and Creativity in the Adolescent. In *The Vygotsky Reader.* Edited by Rene van der Veer and Jaan Valsiner. Cambridge, MA: Blackwell.

FURTHER READING

Abra, Jock. 1988. *Assaulting Parnassus: Theoretical Views of Creativity.* Lanham, MD: University Press of America.

Franck, Frederick. 1973. *The Zen of Seeing.* New York: Random House.

Freud, Sigmund. 1958. *On Creativity and the Unconscious: Papers on the Psychology of Art, Literature, Love, Religion.* New York: Harper & Row.

———. 1960. Wit and Its Relation to the Unconscious. In *The Comic in Theory and Practice.* Edited by John C. Enck and others. Englewood Cliffs, NJ: Prentice-Hall.

Sandburg, Carl. 1970. Good Morning, America. In *The Collected Poems of Carl Sandburg.* New York: Harcourt Brace Jovanovich.

Vygotsky, Lev. 1978. *Mind in Society: The Development of Higher Psychological Processes.* From the 1930 original. Cambridge, MA: Harvard University Press.

Module 7

Writing and Telling Stories

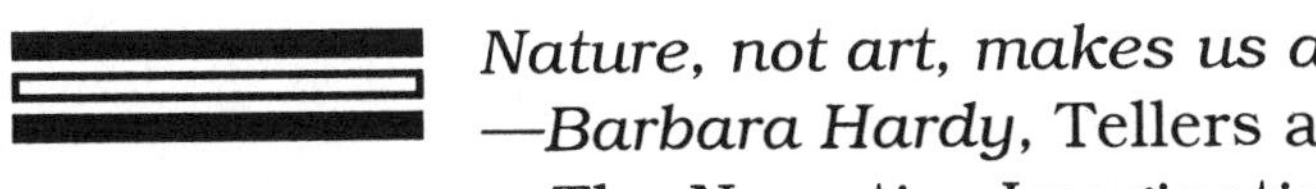

Nature, not art, makes us all story-tellers.
—*Barbara Hardy,* Tellers and Listeners: The Narrative Imagination

THE POWER OF STORIES

Long before there were bows and arrows, early humans undoubtedly sat under the stars beside flickering fires and told each other their dreams. We still do something like this, except the flickering light and storytellers are electronic. Journalists take the events of the day and reformat them into stories with an angle, because the human mind understands events better in the form of stories. Political candidates and preachers know that the quickest way to bring an abstract concept home to an audience is to personalize it with a story about a single individual or family. Likewise, stories have great potential for instructional use in the classroom.

The Value of Stories as a Teaching Tool

Over and above their value as vehicles to arouse interest in subject matter and pull diverse issues together, stories facilitate the growth of mental and moral capacities. One of the teacher's chief roles is to facilitate growth by presenting students with challenging material to explore, material in which discoveries and connections can be made. Research by Sandra Russ and others indicates the critical importance of affective integration in healthy development. Students who did not integrate affect well in play situations had more physical complaints such as headaches, stomachaches and chest pain (Grossman-McKee cited in Russ 1993). In a democratic society, schools are important agents in producing productive, happy citizens capable of getting along with and caring about each other. By coming to understand the characters in a given situation and generating feelings about, say, the conditions on a slave ship, one cannot help becoming involved in history and feeling empathy for the less fortunate. By verbalizing his or her feelings about the baby's death in *The Pearl* by John Steinbeck, a student helps form cause-effect connections between inner sensations and external events, a crucial process in affective integration. It seems apparent then that stories of all kinds can be used to draw students into more meaningful contact with course material and provide the starting point for discussions that help foster growth in several developmental areas: cognitive, emotional, and social. (More will be said about the use of stories as opportunities to stimulate the development of ethical reasoning in Module 8: Choice Mapping.)

Elements of a Good Story

Memorable stories contain

- vivid, evocative *description* that puts the listener or reader in the place and time of the story;
- *imagination* that makes the familiar seem fresh;
- *characters* with whom we can empathize; and
- *dramatic action*, a sustained flow of events that moves the story forward to a climax of intensity.

Stories as Alternatives to Lecture

Lectures at their worst are barely explained lists of facts recited in public, a poor way to teach. On the other hand, lectures at their best present an engaging, comprehensible, and memorable package of information. Good lectures have much in common with good stories. Broadly speaking, a good story is any narrative that ties people, events, and ideas together into a comfortable, engaging account that is easy to listen to and easy to remember. News stories must have an angle, that is, a point of emphasis that has some universal appeal. A good lecture must have a structure and an angle as well. For example, the key elements in historical narrative are political and military forces, powerful personalities and human drives, universal ideas, and the fickle element of chance. These elements should be combined in a unique and irresistible way to explain an outcome we know has happened. As storyteller, the lecturer's task is to provide organization and emphasis to shape key elements of the historical record into a structure that propels the narrative forward with intriguing questions, each leading to a deeper level of understanding. As though weaving a plot, the narrative lecturer suggests a certain outcome, then with plot twists or irony supplies the listener with a different outcome. The political fortunes of the historical figures in the narrative rise and fall unexpectedly. "The race is not to the swift, nor the battle to the strong . . . for time and chance encounters them all," wrote the prophetic author of Ecclesiastes. Since teachers inevitably instruct by narration at times, it seems most appropriate that they develop a level of expertise in the basic elements of story writing and telling.

Developing Skills for Dramatic Story Writing

Making up stories appears easier than it is. Each of the four elements listed above—description, imagination, characters, and dramatic action—can be taught separately, and in fact each has considerable value in itself (e.g., learning to observe and describe teaches young people to pay attention to detail and to distinguish between what the senses tell them and what the mind judges or infers based on observation). Students generally like to write stories and will show much greater enthusiasm for learning to observe and describe if it is directed toward writing better stories.

Creating Characters We Care About

Learning a subject should include what motivated people to pursue certain ends and how they felt about the events of their lives. This information adds a human dimension and more meaning to any subject matter. Moments of great scientific discovery and pivotal events of history carried great emotional impact for the people involved. Reading about an historical event, discovery, or situation does not always shed light on the actual feelings of the persons involved. What were the struggles, hopes, fears, dreads, and sorrows of the persons who lived through those events? When available, letters or diaries can offer insight. Take the case of President Teddy Roosevelt. Long before his political career began, he was apparently aware that his personal journal might be published one day because in that journal he discussed some of his career aspirations in detail (though he says nothing about falling in love). Armed with a diary, a teacher can turn a dry event of the past into a living drama.

Expert writers weave factual material together with emotional reactions. Observe how economically Nobel prize-winning author John Steinbeck creates a character in only a paragraph in *Of Mice and Men.*

> A tall man stood in the doorway. He held a crushed Stetson hat while he combed his long, black, damp hair straight back. Like others he wore blue jeans and a short denim jacket. When he had finished combing his hair, he moved into the room, and he moved with a majesty only achieved by royalty and master craftsmen. He was a jerkline skinner, the prince of the ranch, capable of driving ten, sixteen even twenty mules with a single line to the leaders. He was capable of killing a fly on the wheeler's butt with a bull whip without touching the mule. There was a gravity in his manner and a quiet so profound that all talk stopped when he spoke. His authority was so great that his word was taken on any subject, be it politics or love. This was Slim, the jerkline skinner. (Steinbeck 1965).

Creative Elaboration

Opportunities to engage empathic emotions arise when considering a part of history or an astonishing mathematical or scientific discovery. *Creative elaboration* is the name for a set of classroom behaviors that good teachers practice intuitively. In creative elaboration the teacher first has students consider objective facts then use legitimate inferences to complete a portrait in emotional and affective terms that gives us a feel for a character in history or literature the way Steinbeck gave us a feel for Slim, the jerkline skinner.

To elaborate on a subject in an affective way requires creative inference. Students can find out what an historical person did and sometimes his or her personal reflections on it. Once students have this information, they can project how they might have felt in that situation, or a similar situation. When the affective tie-in is established and students feel more personally connected to the individual, it is easier to motivate them to dig into the details of the historical record. Of course, a clear distinction must always be made between the historical record and the inferences drawn from the record.

To get a creative elaboration discussion started, certain "might have" and "what would you feel?" questions can be especially useful. For example:

- We have seen the circumstances here. How would you have felt if. . . ?
- What would it feel like to. . . ?
- Have you ever been in parallel circumstances. . . ?
- I wonder how I would feel if. . . .

It is important to allow adequate time to process these feelings. The teacher could give students a focusing question the day before reading a story or learning about a historical event. Afterwards, perhaps small groups could meet to collaborate on a list of some answers to the question "How did these people probably feel about their situation?" Later, when a discussion gets under way, questions can be asked to differentiate various emotions. Was the person eager or apprehensive? Enthusiastic or acquiescent? Brave or reckless? Timid or cautious? Sad or disappointed? In the process of contrasting similar emotions, the student learns the vocabulary of emotions, which is a necessary part of processing and integrating these emotions. Being "sad" is not the same as being "depressed." Feeling "concerned" is not the same as feeling "distressed." Also, by participating in discussions that call for creative affective elaboration, students can hear how other students respond with greater or lesser intensity or with different emotions. This kind of understanding provides the students with opportunities to empathize with others and to understand themselves better. Table 7.1 lists descriptive words and feelings.

Dramatic Story Structure

Although creative elaboration makes characters come to life, and imaginary excursions contain vivid descriptive and narrative movement from one location to another, neither necessarily qualifies as a story. A story is more than a list of events; it is a dramatic account. Figure 7.1 examines three types of narrative.

Report	Chronology	Dramatic Story
Facts presented telling about events and people	Flow of events in characters' lives over a span of time	Vivid account telling how a person driven by intense desire attempts to secure an objective, eventually succeeding or failing

Fig. 7.1. A Comparison of Three Types of Narrative

Table 7.1. Descriptive Words for Feelings.

"UP" FEELINGS			
lighthearted	overjoyed	relieved	thrilled
merry	pleased	satisfied	
AFFECTIONATE			
grateful	moved	sensitive	tender
intimate	passionate	sexy	warm
loving	romantic		
ANGRY			
annoyed	grouchy	peeved	sulky
enraged	grumpy	seething	touchy
furious	irritated		
HIGH ENERGY			
alert	enthusiastic	lively	revived
all alive	excited	peppy	spirited
awake	exhilarated	playful	spry
eager	fidgety	refreshed	talkative
empowered	frisky	rejuvenated	vivacious
energetic	hyper		
UNEASY			
awkward	discombobulated	frustrated	rattled
baffled	embarrassed	nauseated	restless
AFRAID			
aghast	fearful	nervous	tense
anxious	fluttery	overwhelmed	terrified
apprehensive	frightened	panicky	timid
boxed-in	guarded	queasy	trembly
burdened	hard-pressed	quivery	uptight
confused	horrified	shaky	weak
dismayed	horror-stricken	shocked	wilted
distressed	jittery	squeamish	
CONFIDENT			
adventurous	dashing	heroic	serene
assured	determined	loose	snug
at ease	easygoing	peaceful	spontaneous
bold	fearless	poised	strong
calm	free and easy	relaxed	unrestrained
courageous			
AMAZED			
astonished	expectant	intrigued	spellbound
awestruck	fascinated	surprised	stunned
dazzled			
"DOWN" FEELINGS			
aching	crushed	dismal	pained
agonizing	dejected	gloomy	pensive
ashamed	depressed	glum	sad
beaten down	desperate	grief-stricken	weepy
blue	despondent	heartbroken	whiny
chagrined	devastated	joyless	wistful
cheerless	disconcerted	lonely	zonked
cold	discouraged	mournful	

Of the three types of narrative listed in figure 7.1, only the dramatic story has any dramatic structure. Story writing, as opposed to rambling on about events that occurred, requires two major steps: (1) establishing *a time*, *setting*, and *main character*, or protagonist, the central figure whose action we will follow throughout the story; and (2) taking the main character through a series of challenging or threatening events (the dramatic structure).

Without proper attention to the story setup, the time and setting of the story, and the vivid description of the events of the story, a narrative will become pale and uninteresting because the lack of details will make it impossible for the reader to respond to the character and to feel what the character does. Without dramatic structure, the story seems to drift along without any point.

The G-O-D-O Story Plan

A simple plan for a "well-made" story, one with all the dramatic elements in traditional form, is a five-step sequence called the G-O-D-O story plan: Just set up and GO DO the story. Table 7.2 encapsulates the G-O-D-O story plan.

Table 7.2. Steps in the G-O-D-O Story Plan.

An interesting	*Character*	SETUP
at a specified	*Time*	
in a richly vivid	*Place*	
gets a worthy and understandable		GOAL
then has to work through a series of various		OBSTACLES
which lead to an unavoidable high-stakes		DECISION
which produces a logical if unexpected		OUTCOME

Following is an elaboration of steps in the G-O-D-O story plan.

1. At a certain time and in a certain place there lived a character, the *protagonist*, whose fortunes and misfortunes we will begin to follow.
2. An incident, the inciting incident, occurred just before we joined the story. This incident has upset the balance that existed before.
3. The protagonist decides, perhaps after meeting an *ally*, to do something to return to the previous state of balance. We learn the protagonist's main motive and general *goal*.
4. The protagonist begins to move toward obtaining the goal but discovers an obstacle blocking his or her way.
5. The obstacle was put in place by the protagonist's competitor for the goal, the *antagonist*, a person or force that tries to erect more and more *obstacles* so the antagonist can claim the goal for selfish reasons.
6. The *stakes* for the protagonist's success increase, as do the negative consequences of the protagonist's failure.

7. The protagonist encounters more obstacles of various kinds—people, circumstances, and inner conflicts—and gets beyond them with various means, but comes to an apparent dead end.
8. To break out of the dead end, the protagonist must make a *decision* to face and fight the antagonist. This decision reveals the depths of the protagonist's character.
9. The protagonist–antagonist *battle* takes place and results in clear victory for one or the other.
10. In a tragedy, the protagonist loses the objective, usually due to some character flaw such as pride or disloyalty. In happier stories, the protagonist prevails, and the *outcome* is a new, richer balance.

Writing a Story with the G-O-D-O Story Plan

Authors are fond of saying "Writing is rewriting." However, I would modify that statement to say "Writing is prewriting and rewriting." The story setting as well as the protagonist's quirks and virtues should all be spelled out on paper before the actual writing begins. Also, the specific frames of the action, the steps in the G-O-D-O story plan, should be thought through and made clear before the writing phase begins. Once the writing process itself begins, the story can take on momentum all its own, overpowering the original concept. Almost all student stories that fail do so because of lack of structure; that is, the story has insufficient obstacles or skips through the obstacles rapidly with no moments of conflict or confrontation in which the protagonist faces the unpleasant but inevitable realities that the antagonist has erected.

Students can, however, write marvelous and interesting stories when they are given preliminary instruction in story craft and are taken through the proper steps of story writing, namely, description exercises, research, prewriting, and practice with story structure.

Classroom Activity 7-1: The Improvisational Story

Materials: A photograph, slide, or poster of an exotic or interesting landscape such as the Amazon rain forest, an ancient Buddhist shrine, or a Jurassic landscape.

Procedure: The leader asks questions and guides the class through the story creation process. "OK, we have a hero. Male or female?" "How old?" "Describe him or her." "Here's the setting." Calling on individuals, the leader gets lots of good descriptors for such categories as size, shape, form, and color. The leader continues to intersperse questions about progress of the protagonist with on-the-spot invention of motives and unexpected obstacles and calls for more vivid and evocative descriptors. The leader takes the class through the steps in the G-O-D-O story plan and eventually brings the story to a timely end.

Classroom Activity 7-2: Composing a G-O-D-O Story

Procedure: Students break out into *rehearsal circles* of two or three people. Individuals take turns inventing brief G-O-D-O stories from scratch. Set a ground rule: The story must be made up; it cannot be something that actually happened to the storyteller or some other real person. After telling the story, each person receives constructive feedback to identify which G-O-D-O elements came across easily and which didn't.

If students get stuck, provide them with a menu such as this:

Protagonist	Goal	Obstacles
rodeo cowboy	win first prize in bronco event	injury, fear
football player	win a scholarship	bad weather, illness
student volunteer	buy gift for terminally ill child	car in shop; unable to get to store
hippie	complete the unfulfilled quest	self-doubt
hell's angel	find his father	police harassment

HOW TO GET STARTED USING STORIES IN YOUR CLASSROOM

Opportunities abound for using both written and oral stories in the classroom. A story writing project involves as much research as a term paper but generally evokes from the students more positive feelings and more commitment than yet another report. In biology, the story of the discovery of DNA makes a great tale. A student might summarize a unit on the Spanish American War by creating a fictional character who joins the army. His life story could be told against the factual, historical background as autobiography; as third-person narrative; or in letter or diary form. Discoveries always contain stories: a new planet, gold in California, or the dramatic glow of the element phosphorus, so stunning that the medieval chemist fell to his knees in prayer at the sight of the miraculous glowing element. The completion of grand tasks—writing the U.S. Constitution, building the transcontinental railroad, proving the first geometric theorem by the ancient Greek Thales, circumnavigating the globe—all have stories begging to be told.

Both teacher- and student-created stories should spring from a genuine context in the unit of study. Before tackling a big story project, students will need to learn the basics of story structure and the elements of a good story. If the story is to be graded, the parameters of the story need to be spelled out on an assignment sheet. Figure 7.2 presents an example; figure 7.3 presents an accompanying grading rubric. Both are from a geology class.

GEOLOGY

I. Project assignment: Volcanoes

Due Monday, Oct. 23, 60 points. Spelling, grammar, neatness, and other composition requirements will be counted. See below for details.

Option #1

Write a short story with the premise that the major character has been near an explosive volcano. Choose an actual volcanic eruption from history and incorporate as many facts as possible. The main character could be, for example, a farmer in his field near Mount Vesuvius. He struggles to rescue his family in the nearby village. Another possibility is a group of campers on a mountain near Mount St. Helens. The story should have careful observations woven into it. For example, the farmer might hear distant explosions that boom like thunder but crackle longer and come one upon another. He would notice the stink of gas like that of rotten eggs and the hot wind coming from the mountain. The ash might reach him, and he would have to figure out a way to keep the ash from suffocating him. He might notice the unusual peach color of the sky. When he comes to a river of molten lava, he would first observe its texture and sound before trying to get around it. He could observe the lava's effect on trees, the way it flows, its force, and its color. He could feel the glowing heat from its surface and notice the way it cools and forms a crust.

Option #2

Imagine you are a reporter carried back in time to a volcano that erupted explosively in the past. Tell what you see, hear, smell, etc. Interview people and tell their individual stories. Incorporate as much geologic fact as possible.

Option #3

Do a video version of Option #2. This option requires teacher approval first so you realize what you're getting into. Also, the same language standards that apply in the classroom apply in the tape. NO FOUL LANGUAGE on tape.

Points	Requirement
12	one-page project proposal. Graded for accuracy of historical facts of eruption, timeliness, clarity of concept, and completeness in stating details of what the project will include.
20	Incorporation and description of physical phenomena of volcanic eruptions. (See pp. 57-60 in textbook for list.)
10	Mechanics of written work.
5	Use description involving all five senses.
8	Use eight or more descriptors, at least two each of these: subjective, objective, literal (including quantitative), and figurative.
5	Use G-O-D-O story plan in the project.
5	Bonus points possible for ingenuity, creativity, or originality.

Fig. 7.2. Sample Story Assignment Sheet

Evaluation of Volcano Story

Geology

Name ____________________

Reviewer's Comments

I. Project proposal
_____ timeliness
_____ clarity
_____ completeness

_____ subtotal (10)

II. Historical data
_____ name
_____ time
_____ place

_____ subtotal (2)

III. Volcano phenomena
_____ earth tremors
_____ pyroclastic material
_____ tephra
_____ lahars
_____ lava plateaus
_____ sonic blasts
_____ steam jets
_____ gas clouds
_____ lava displays
_____ aa or pohoehoe

_____ subtotal (20)

IV. Descriptors
five senses:
_____ hearing _____ sight _____ smell _____ temperature _____ touch or taste

two each of these:
_____ _____ subjective _____ _____ objective _____ _____ literal _____ _____ figurative

_____ subtotal (13)

V. Using the G-O-D-O story plan
_____ status quo disturbed
_____ protagonist gets *goal*
_____ antagonist sets up *obstacles*
_____ protagonist surmounts obstacles, confronts or *decides*
_____ *outcome*: new status quo established

_____ subtotal (5)

VI. Composition
_____ spelling
_____ mechanics: proper use of commas, capitals, and other punctuation
_____ sentences, paragraphing, usage, grammar

_____ subtotal (10)

BONUS: Originality, novelty, ingenuity

_____ subtotal (5)

_____ grand total (60), with bonus (65)

Fig. 7.3. Sample Grading Rubric for Volcano Story

Classroom Activity 7-3: Writing a Story from a Photograph

Materials: Civil War or other historical photographs, current event photos, or photographs from prize-winning collections such as *The Family of Man* or *Fifty Years of Life* (Steichen 1955).

Procedure: Choose one photograph that you find particularly striking. Using the technique of objective and subjective description, create a description of the people and places shown. Create a G-O-D-O story using the event depicted in the photograph as the centerpiece of the story.

Notice that the geology assignment sheet provides categories and topics that should be included in the G-O-D-O story. Without such a list, students will leave out important elements (even *with* the list, some students will still leave out elements). It is not easy for anyone, especially young students, to create and plan at the same time. Thus, it is best to have students complete a preliminary outline and check to see that it contains all the right elements, then have students elaborate it into a full-blown story. This, by the way, is how many professionals write. The more mature the writer, the more time is spent on prewriting rather than rewriting.

Although it may be tempting to hand out to students the entire grading rubric as a guide to the project, you will find that the quality of the stories will not be as good. Students with the rubric in hand tend to write the story line by line, so the story lacks integration and unity. Giving too many guidelines and instructions can be as deadly to creativity as giving none at all. The assignment sheet should strike a happy medium between extremes: It should give enough information to reduce writer's block and lower grade anxiety but not so much as to infringe the student's initiative and creativity. In general, full disclosure of criteria and standards is the best policy for grading students on any type of assignment.

Note that the rubric in figure 7.3 gives just a few points in many small categories. Through the simple check-off procedure, the story can be scored in a fair and consistent manner. If the assignment sheet calls for five descriptors and the student's story contains only three, then three of five points are given. Students often worry that they'll be graded down because the teacher doesn't like their characters or story incidents. Making the scoring as objective and clear as possible will reduce student anxiety levels and prevent haggling over points when the papers are returned.

Biographical Stories

There is no course taught that does not have room for a biography. Teacher-written biographical G-O-D-O stories can be woven seamlessly into a lesson. Not only do they provide information in an easy-to-remember format, they are pleasant to listen to and when presented skillfully, command the attention of the class. Students can be assigned to write a story in place of a long report, provided they are given the time and support required. Given a choice of a standard report versus a story on a given topic, the overwhelming majority of students will choose to write a story. Just as with other G-O-D-O assignments, it is essential to design and hand out an assignment sheet as well as design a grading rubric at the beginning of the project.

Skill Development Activity 7-1: Recognizing the Basic Elements of Story Structure

For the following biographical story of Louis Pasteur, identify the steps in the expanded G-O-D-O story plan.

Setup: time, place, and the protagonist's identity
Inciting incident
Protagonist's goal
Obstacles
Antagonist (may be a force or situation, not just a person)
Stakes for success and failure
Apparent dead end for the protagonist
Protagonist's crucial decision to face antagonist
Protagonist-antagonist struggle
Outcome

A Sample Biographical Story

Note: This story is an exemplar of what an experienced teacher or advanced student might write rather than a typical example of student work.

The Story of Louis Pasteur (1822-1895)

In the 1830s, a tanner moved his family to the village of Arbois in France and set up shop. He enrolled his son Louis in school, but the boy was indifferent to his studies, preferring to romp in the forest, go fishing, or look for treasure in the village dump. Whenever he sat still for a moment, it was to take up a piece of charcoal and draw. He showed no extraordinary abilities in schoolwork, although he was a first-rate artist. His father insisted that if the boy wanted a better life than that of a tanner, he had better buckle down and get an education. The boy reluctantly agreed and improved his study habits. Eventually, he qualified for high school, then college, a rare accomplishment in the 1830s.

At age 19, Pasteur entered college and plugged along without attracting much attention. But even as a young man, he began to show the attention to detail that so marked his career. In his college chemistry class, he became intrigued by crystals of tartaric acid. Two types were known. When dissolved in water, one type caused a beam of polarized light to rotate; the other had no effect on the beam of polarized light. Pasteur intuitively knew that there was something different about these two sets of crystals—one from the chemist's shelf, the other from natural juices—and he had a hunch that the difference was caused by the action of microbes. He examined the crystals under a magnifying lens and noticed that the points on the crystals were oddly different: Some crystals had faces that leaned toward the right; other crystals had faces that leaned to the left. The rotation of polarized light was related to this property. The nonrotating crystal batch had an equal number of right- and left-leaning crystals, whereas the crystals that caused rotation were all right-leaning. (Noticing this peculiarity is like noticing that one bin in a clothing store contains all right-handed gloves whereas the other bin has equal numbers of right- and left-handed gloves.) Many chemists had known about the polarization of the two types of crystals, yet Louis Pasteur as an undergraduate was the first person to explain it using the concept of crystal shape. Was this discovery an accident? Not exactly. "Chance favors the prepared mind," he later said.

Pasteur graduated with a degree in chemistry, finished his doctorate, and obtained a position as an assistant professor. His first project was to find a way to prevent wine and beer from going sour during fermentation. The prevailing idea of the day was that air or chemicals alone caused fermentation, and that microbes came into being spontaneously. He proved once and for all that fermentation is the work not merely of chemicals, as most scientists believed at the time, but of living agents. Sterilizing the wine barrels with steam before filling them prevented spoilage.

Pasteur soon married and became a father. Life for Louis and Marie Pasteur was full in the decade of the 1850s; they were blessed with five children, and although not well-to-do, they had enough money to live on. As a result of his successes in the area of fermentation, Pasteur received an attractive offer to work in Paris, and he moved his family there. Less than a year after arriving in Paris in 1859, Pasteur's oldest daughter, Jeanne, became ill with typhus fever and died at age 12. Death was no stranger to people then, but do you think their grief was felt any less? Pasteur, a man whose life revolved around his family as much as his work, was devastated. After a period of mourning, he went back to work, now turning his attention to curing human diseases. But shortly after his new line of research began, he was stricken with a stroke that left his left arm paralyzed. How would you cope with two such catastrophes within a year? Pasteur's response was to continue his work with the aid of a few very dedicated assistants who kept pace with the long hours Pasteur put in.

The 1860s in Paris were a risky time for a mother to give birth, for an epidemic had swept the city. Three out of ten new mothers contracted a disease called childbed fever, caused by bacteria related to streptococcus. Blood vessels in the uterus provide easy access to germs, and many of the new mothers died. Although the French Academy of Medicine had officially maintained that this disease was caused by heredity and therefore no cure was possible, Pasteur had studied diseases in animals and was convinced that childbed fever was caused by a germ. Earlier in his career, Pasteur had developed a vaccine for chicken cholera, a disease that had threatened the entire poultry industry of France at a time when food was in short supply. He believed a vaccine could also be developed for childbed fever.

Pasteur wrote and circulated a pamphlet in Paris explaining childbed fever and recommending that doctors and midwives sterilize their instruments and wash thoroughly before touching any patient. You might think the public and the medical establishment would welcome any idea that could help prevent suffering and death. But the surgeons were insulted that a man—not even a physician, but a mere *chemist*—would insinuate that they used unclean practices and unknowingly did harm to their patients. A comparable case today might be a veterinarian from a rural town out west coming to Boston and circulating a pamphlet saying that anesthesia caused cancer. To make matters worse, a man whose wife had died of childbed fever read Pasteur's pamphlet and became so angry with the doctor who had delivered his wife's baby that he took pistol in hand and killed the physician. At the murder trial, some of Pasteur's critics went so far as to say Pasteur was an accessory to murder, because he had written the pamphlet that incited the grieving man to use the pistol.

Pasteur was deeply discouraged. Put yourself in his situation—knowing you were right, having a burning commitment to help parents avoid the death of their children and loved ones, yet being opposed by the highest medical authorities in the land. Pasteur was obedient and respectful toward authority, yet he was treated as though he had committed murder. Did the medical establishment reject his findings for other reasons? Pasteur, a lowly tanner's son from the provinces, spoke with a country accent. Marie and Louis enjoyed family life and kept away from the fast social scene of Paris. Perhaps his lowly social status helps explain why Pasteur was scorned and mocked and even threatened physically. Eventually, the Emperor Napoleon III forbade Pasteur to speak or write about the germ theory of disease. Pasteur realized he could not stay in Paris. He packed up his family and his laboratory and returned to his boyhood home in Arbois.

The Pasteurs settled in and became comfortable with the simpler life of the village. It would have been easy for Pasteur to just keep quiet and devote himself to teaching and raising his family, but Pasteur didn't quit his crusade against disease; he simply changed arenas. Pasteur taught at the local college and continued to research the problem of animal diseases in his own laboratory. Not long after Pasteur arrived in Arbois, some of his neighbors reported that an anthrax epidemic had swept through their cattle and sheep flocks. Animal mortality climbed to half the sheep in some villages. Pasteur went to work on the anthrax problem and painstakingly isolated the anthrax germ. In time he developed an anthrax vaccine which virtually eliminated the disease throughout the county.

Pasteur would have preferred staying out of the limelight, but that was not to be. Officials from the Paris government, knowing nothing of Pasteur's whereabouts, noticed the fantastic agricultural yields that farmers in Arbois were able to sustain, levels two and three times greater than those of the surrounding counties. Investigators from the Ministry of Agriculture arrived in Arbois to learn the reason for the high output and were sent to Pasteur, who explained the process of inoculation. Skeptical, they insisted on proof. Pasteur realized the value of this challenge and staged a dramatic experiment he knew would convince even the most determined skeptic. He gathered about 50 healthy sheep and had the visitors from Paris inspect them. Then Pasteur vaccinated two dozen of the sheep, leaving the other two dozen unvaccinated. Several days later, he infected the entire flock with live anthrax germs. In three days 100 percent of the nonvaccinated sheep were dead, whereas 100 percent of the vaccinated sheep lived. Word of this triumph spread throughout Europe. The French government gave Pasteur a cash prize and convinced him to move back to Paris. Once again, Pasteur loaded up his family and laboratory and moved to Paris, where he obtained a house large enough to accommodate his family and a complete laboratory in the basement.

Having conquered anthrax and cholera, Pasteur now faced the critical decision of whether to continue agricultural research or spend his modest income on seeking a cure for one of the most feared diseases on Earth: rabies. As a boy, Pasteur had witnessed a mad dog attack on a neighbor. In a matter of weeks the man came down with rabies and died an ugly death. Pasteur had been deeply affected by this incident. People bitten by rabid dogs did not even turn to doctors; they went to blacksmiths, who would gouge the wound with a red hot iron, cauterizing the tissue and killing the germ carried in the mad dog's saliva. Pasteur, a sensitive and kind man, could hardly stand to see such suffering, but conducting research on rabies presented serious problems. Rabid dogs would have to be captured and kept in cages in his basement laboratory. Successfully finding a cure for rabies would mean saving thousands of lives a year, but what would happen to his reputation if he could not find a cure? What if a rabid dog bit one of his assistants or escaped from its cage? Can you imagine Marie Pasteur's reaction when Louis announced that he planned to keep rabid dogs in the basement? The risks of rabies research were not only financial and professional, but personal as well.

Despite the risks, Pasteur decided to try to find a rabies cure. The problem of isolating the rabies germs turned out to be the most difficult one he had yet faced. For months, then years, he and his staff toiled with little progress. The rabies microbe turned out to be a virus, the smallest form of living thing, visible only with the aid of the electron microscope, which did not come along for another 70 years. Eventually, years of patient research began to yield results. Pasteur found that when the rabies microbe was allowed to stand in a flask for a few weeks, it lost its ability to cause disease, although the dead germ still triggered the body's immune system to fight the disease. Using this principle of passive antigenicity, Pasteur tried out a vaccine on dogs and found that it prevented them from contracting rabies.

One hot summer evening in 1885, a frantic mother arrived at Pasteur's house in Paris with her son, Joseph. The boy had been bitten a dozen times by a rabid dog. She pleaded with Pasteur to give the treatment to her boy. Pasteur told her that the procedure had never been tried on humans. The woman argued that the boy would surely die if left untreated. Seeing that the distraught mother and her boy had no place else to go, Pasteur took them into his own house. Pasteur, who was not a medical doctor, went for help from a physician friend. The doctor recommended that Pasteur not try the procedure until further tests proved its safety. Pasteur argued that doing nothing was the same as imposing a death sentence on the boy. The physician warned Pasteur that his fame was not sufficient to avoid serious penalties if anything went wrong. Pasteur could go to prison for practicing medicine without a license. If the boy died, he could even be convicted of murder and be sentenced to the guillotine!

Pasteur's wife, Marie, who had always been supportive, now begged Louis not to take this chance. He suffered terrible anxiety that evening in July 1885. What should he do? He had been run out of Paris once before and didn't know if he could face that kind of humiliation again. Until now, his wife had always supported his decisions. Was it right to go against her judgment? But there in his own house lay a terrified, sick, 12-year-old boy. Chills and tremors were already racking his body. Pasteur couldn't stand seeing the child suffer. By this time, not only had his eldest daughter died of disease, but two of his younger ones had died too. The picture of his own suffering children must have come to Pasteur's mind and stiffened his resolve. There was no longer any question; the world should not wait any longer for a rabies cure. Pasteur began the boy's first of 14 treatments that same evening.

Pasteur could not sleep that night. Twelve hours passed with little result. A day later, the boy was no worse, but still not better. Had something gone wrong with the vaccine? Or was his theory of rabies entirely wrong? *It couldn't be wrong; it worked on the dogs. Just be patient.* Finally, after two intense days and nights, the boy's chills and tremors ceased. In another day the boy was up and around. Pasteur continued the treatments but skipped the last five days of vaccination because the boy had recovered fully.

Pasteur's personal dedication, patience, and careful work saved little Joseph. Had Pasteur been less courageous, the boy and thousands of others would have died needlessly. But because of Pasteur's dedication to humanity, we all have a better life. Louis Pasteur was a great scientist, but in addition, his courage and saintly dedication to helping others place him among the greatest humanitarians who have ever lived. ♦

STORYTELLING

Telling stories is a different art from writing them. Anyone can learn to spin a pretty good yarn with the following: (1) a good story script, (2) attention to performance, and (3) rehearsal.

A Good Story Script

Good story scripts for oral stories must be short, not more than a few thousand words. If the story-telling time goes beyond 15 or 20 minutes, audience interest drops off quickly. Story material for classroom use should be connected to the goals and objectives of the instructional unit. If the story is in print, it should be read aloud to determine if it sounds like spoken speech or written language. If the teacher authors the story, it should be written out but not read. A story read aloud lacks the elements of immediacy and spontaneity. At this stage, bits of dialogue and creative elaboration should be added: "Imagine what. . . " or "Can you picture what that was like?" can be interjected at key moments in the story to expand the story to make room for more exploration into the emotional aspects of the characters. Falsification is not what's needed but a logical extension of the facts. The biographical material used to write the story of Pasteur did not mention what Marie Pasteur said when Louis told her he was planning to keep rabid dogs in the basement of their home, but the record does indicate that this was the only time she ever opposed one of Louis's experiments. It is a fair inference that he, being devoted to her, made his decision with great reluctance. The record says nothing about how the death of his own three children affected his decision to save little Joseph, but it is reasonable to assume that a devoted father such as Pasteur would remember his own children's suffering at that moment.

Once you have written the script, read it aloud to identify the passages that read smoothly and modify those that don't. Smooth these passages out but don't twiddle too much with the exact phrasing because you're not going to read them aloud anyway, and memorizing the wording is not desirable.

The Story-Telling Performance

During the performance of the story, as you change your voice, you should use your eyes, not just for eye contact with the audience, but also to define space in the imaginary setting with your gaze. Like a written story, a told story should have dramatic structure. In addition, an oral story should be embellished with

- alternative voices;
- sound effects;
- specific illustrative gestures;
- facial expressions;
- vivid word paintings;
- pauses to imagine emotions; and
- a frame that opens and closes the story.

The story frame is the illustration of a single unifying moral or theme. Suppose, for example, you want to tell a story about your fall into an irrigation canal as a child and how you were rescued by your older brother. Let's say he's the same brother who used to tease you unmercifully or hide your favorite storybook from you. To frame the story, you make a reference to the big brother at the beginning and the end of the story, and how the narrated incident changed his attitude toward you. The story might start off with, "When I was eight years old, my brother, who was twelve, used to tease me." You narrate the story, then close with, "After that incident, my brother never teased me again."

Rehearsal

The storyteller must be familiar with the material, so familiar that improvisation is possible. The storyteller doesn't read the story or tell it exactly the same way twice. It is helpful to record the story on audiotape and play it back without looking at the script. When you have rehearsed (but not memorized) the whole story and can tell it without notes several times in a row, you are ready to try it on a live audience.

Skill Development Activity 7-2: Reading and Telling a Story

Part A: Choose a short book or short story with which you are familiar. Read it aloud, building in the elements of storytelling mentioned above one at a time.

Part B: After you know the entire story by heart, close the book and tell the story without it. Improvise elements in the story, expanding parts here and there for interest and narrative color.

How to Get Started Using Storytelling in Your Classroom

To tell stories that have been previously scripted involves practice. Having students tell stories requires three things:

- Providing resource materials or guidance in locating the right kind of material on which to base a story
- Guiding students through the techniques of dramatic reading
- Providing time for safe rehearsal of the story before it is presented

With adequate planning time and some coached practice, children make wonderful storytellers.

STORYLIKE TEACHING TOOLS

Storyboarding

Besides providing direct instruction in story-writing techniques, teachers can incorporate *parallel practice* with students. Parallel practice involves activities that are similar enough to story writing that mastering them produces a positive carryover of skills. *Storyboarding* is the term used in the movie industry to describe the process of making drawings or frames of each scene in a film to aid in making script adjustments before the costly shooting phase begins. The end product looks like a comic book of the movie. The storyboard can be adapted to the classroom. All that is needed is a long string like a clothesline strung across the room; some paper clips or clothespins, a set of content-related photographs, pictures cut from magazines, or handmade drawings; and some ingenuity.

Storyboarding can be used for any situation where the goal is to organize many diverse elements into a meaningful whole.

Classroom Activity 7-4: Storyboarding in a German Class

Materials: A set of photographs of people, sights, and landscapes of Germany, Switzerland, or Austria cut from travel magazines.

Procedure: Each student is given a photograph and asked to prepare a short comment on it. A student leader or the teacher creates an improvisational story to which each student contributes. The students in turn hang their pictures on the clothesline as the story unfolds.

Story Scrapbook

A variation of the storyboard format is a *story scrapbook*, which contains one page per student, but is presented in print form rather than on a clothesline.

Class Publication

Students put together a scrapbook, catalog, or newspaper from another period or place: for example, *The Renaissance Times* or *The Left Bank Literary Magazine*. A class publication provides an opportunity for students to collaborate, to choose the contents within a framework of options, and to adapt material. Also, the activity forces them to get the "flavor" of the time and place where the publication appears, which requires reading and discussion. In *The Renaissance Times*, sections could include politics, the arts, even sports such as bear baiting. The class is divided into groups to produce each section. To design advertisements to include in the publication, students will have to research the technology, daily life, and economics of the period, and use some ingenuity to come up with an ad layout. Work is peer-coached by each group.

Ensemble Biography

Ensemble biography is a group project. The idea is for the class to choose a subject for a biography, for example Thomas Jefferson, and then have each student choose a person involved in the individual's life in some way: in the case of Thomas Jefferson, his wife, neighbors, parents, children, fellow statesman, slaves, and enemies. Next, each person develops a short presentation to give about his or her researched person when the "TV reporter" calls on him or her. This lesson plan format requires that the teacher provide adequate source material. Biographies selected as reference sources for this project need to contain anecdotes from the person's life and a sufficient number of people to give everyone a part. Parts can be stretched—for example, the number of neighbors—to accommodate everyone, with one anecdote allowed per neighbor. Making a video version of the biography works well, because in watching the video playback, student contact time with the material doubles.

Storytelling is such a natural part of everyday experience that students often will not notice that they are receiving factual information in a story format. When a teacher becomes skilled at intertwining stories with other teaching techniques, lessons are more joyful. You will know when you've mastered this technique because students will say "that was a great lesson on Pasteur" and never mention that you told them a story.

REFERENCES

Hardy, Barbara N. 1975. *Tellers and Listeners: The Narrative Imagination.* London: Althone Press.

Russ, Sandra. 1993. *Affect and Creativity: The Role of Affect and Play in the Creative Process.* Hillsdale, NJ: Lawrence Erlbaum.

Stechen, Edward. 1955. *The Family of Man.* New York: The Museum of Modern Art.

FURTHER READING

Dubrovin, Vivian. 1994. *Storytelling for the Fun of It: A Handbook for Children.* Masonville, CO: Storycraft.

Field, Syd. 1982. *Screenplay: The Foundations of Screenwriting.* New York: Dell.

Lajos, Egri. 1960. *The Art of Dramatic Writing.* New York: Simon & Schuster.

Seger, Linda. 1987. *Making a Good Script Great.* New York: Henry Holt.

——. 1990. *Creating Unforgettable Characters.* New York: Henry Holt.

Smiley, Sam. 1971. *Playwriting: The Structure of Action.* Englewood Cliffs, NJ: Prentice-Hall.

Module 8

Choice Mapping

Living is a constant process of deciding what we are going to do.

—José Ortega y Gasset

WHAT WE TEACH BESIDES SUBJECT MATTER

No one would dispute the need for learning content knowledge in school. But in addition to learning the three Rs, students who spend a year in a class together are learning many other things of a subjective and affective nature. In a course of study students learn important things about people, society, and life. For the purposes of establishing a stable, just, and prosperous society, teaching young people nothing but academics is insufficient. A recent survey by Public Agenda, a nonpartisan institute that gathers information on public opinion, found that 71 percent of all Americans believe that teaching values is more important than teaching academics ("First Things First" 1994). This opinion is not new. Sixty years ago, America's most famous educator, John Dewey (1859-1952), affirmed that the true purpose of education should be to provide conditions that foster the growth of democratic values and strong character.

> The aim of education is growth or development, both intellectual and moral. Ethical and psychological principles can aid the school in the greatest of all constructions—the building of a free and powerful character. Only knowledge of the order and connection of the stages in psychological development can insure this. Education is the work of supplying the conditions which will enable the psychological functions to mature in the freest and fullest manner (Dewey, cited in Kohlberg 1978a, 49).

Providing *collateral learning* may be as important an outcome of formal education as academic achievement. Some important aspects of social and personal growth involve learning the meaning and practice of:

- democratic values;
- collaboration;
- productive attitudes;
- self-concept; and
- character.

Democratic Values

Democracy is more than a political system that operates by majority rule. It is a living arrangement in which members are free to participate in forming their own end purposes. It does not mean unrestricted liberty, nor does it mean pressuring the individual to conform to group norms. Dewey championed the idea that democracy is a collaborative effort toward a common aim. Surely, if democracy is to work on the large scale, it must work first on the small scale. Democracy means inclusiveness and fairness. It means individual responsibility and respect for others. The teacher has an obligation (often explicitly included in teachers' contracts) to uphold and teach democratic values and processes in the classroom, including equal opportunity, inclusiveness of all groups and individuals in the classroom, and freedom from criticism related to religious beliefs, race, or ethnic origin.

Collaboration

Democracy requires collaboration. If democracy is a better living arrangement than the alternatives, it should be possible to incorporate the collaborative process at all levels, including the classroom. Teachers should set up at least a few group projects each year so that students can learn to work collaboratively. Ground rules must be established so that work in a group is truly collaborative rather than just in parallel. Given enough coached practice, eventually most students will become capable of voluntary self-restraint, one of the important milestones of maturation.

Besides building positive social interaction, collaboration has important cognitive value.

As Piaget (Piaget and Inhelder 1958, 346) put it, "It is most often in discussions between friends, when the promoter of a theory has to test it against the theories of the others, that he discovers its fragility."

Productive Attitudes

An attitude is a disposition to act in a certain way. Attitudes are learned indirectly, mainly by nonverbal cues and reinforcement of behavior. Thus, attitudes can be taught. Suppose the attitude of fairness toward classmates is to be taught. Impromptu coaching after an instance of fair play by one classmate toward another is the best way to do it. In teaching attitudes, it is preferable to identify positive examples of fair play when they occur rather than negative examples. Although occasional verbalizations such as "fairness is best" are appropriate, attitudes must be shaped over time by coaching. To provide the right occasions for coaching in a nonthreatening, planned setting, role-playing of scripted examples of fairness and unfairness can be used. A discussion follows each enacted scenario with coaching comments supplied by peers and, if needed, by the teacher. (Module 9: Role-Playing and Enactments will provide some useful guidelines to using role-playing activities.)

Self-Concept

The teacher may not be able to alter deeply rooted judgments young people have already made about themselves. As it is the physician's first duty to do no harm; so it is also the teacher's prime responsibility. A person's self-concept, whatever it is—high, medium, or low—is generally stable. People usually cling to it and defend it even when it is negative, apparently because it is very stressful to change one's self-concept. Any dramatic change in self-concept means that the terms of the individual's life must be renegotiated. New demands will be made, and different opportunities and different dreams will be the result. A radical shift in self-concept can be upsetting; most people choose to opt out of such a change.

Still, a person's self-concept can be influenced for the better. When an adult with authority over students treats them with fairness and dignity, really listens to them, makes generous eye contact with them, sincerely enjoys their company, and encourages them to be all they can be, students feel valued and internalize this feeling to a degree. Of course, teachers—especially those who see a student for less than an hour a day—may believe they have no influence in the student's life. Keep in mind, however, that the amount of contact is less important than the quality. When the collective impact of all the nonverbal cues has been tallied, the message that "You're OK" or "You are a person of great worth" might well be the turning point for that young person to accept a new self-concept, which in turn might lead toward a whole new life. To minimize the importance of the teacher's role in helping to develop a student's self-concept is a mistake.

Citizenship and Character

All people need self-discipline and empathy to become productive, happy adults and responsible citizens functioning in a free society. Institutions of the past that organized community life and passed on essential values—for instance, the community church of rural America, the extended family, and the small town—have virtually been bulldozed by the massive urbanization of the United States in the twentieth century. In 1900, about 80 percent of the population lived in rural settings or in small towns. By 1990, the reverse was true, with 80 percent of the population living in large cities. Institutions that pass on important social values are lacking, and consequently, acts of indifference, brutality, and criminality have become tragically common. Schools alone cannot restore a sense of decency to society, but it is important that they do whatever they can, not as a substitute for the family, church, or synagogue, but as a means of supporting them. Parents want schools to help them teach their young people to behave with decency, respect, and responsibility. In helping to shape pro-social behavior, sound character, and common decency, teachers are not usurping moral authority from parents but reinforcing the messages that parents are (or should be) teaching young people so that they grow up as happy adults capable of building a stable, just, and decent society in which to live.

EDUCATING FOR GOOD CITIZENSHIP

In his book *Educating for Character: How Our Schools Can Teach Respect and Responsibility*, Thomas Lickona (1991) identifies many ways that teachers, parents, and communities can support the formation of good character in our young people. Good character contains three dimensions of ethical behavior: ethical knowing, ethical feeling, and ethical action. A teacher can foster the growth of sound character by

- setting a positive example when it comes to fairness and mature human problem solving;
- demonstrating a concern for the development of caring and courtesy by verbalizing their value and acknowledging local and national events that promote positive values; and
- providing stories and ethical dilemmas—exercises to illuminate the occurrence of ethical decision-making all around us.

Other Things Teachers Can Do to Foster Strong Character

Besides providing opportunities for reading about and discussing ethical decision making, a teacher can also influence the formation of good character by coaching students when the opportunity presents itself. It is possible and desirable for teachers to incorporate instruction in character "incidentally" into classroom interactions. Every conversation with a student is an opportunity to promote growth. It is especially important that students learn to take another's point of view.

Dr. Scott Peck, psychiatrist and author of the best-seller *The Road Less Traveled* (1978), puts discipline as the first priority in establishing sound character. Discipline here does not mean forced compliance with a set of arbitrary rules. Discipline is a set of techniques for dealing with life. An Olympic athlete sets certain goals and adjusts his or her behavior to accomplish those goals. Likewise, a person who aims for good mental health and sound relationships employs self-discipline to bring these things about. Four essential tools to building solid character are

- delaying gratification;
- accepting responsibility;
- dedication to reality; and
- balancing.

Delaying Gratification

The first principle of self-discipline is postponing gratification. Classroom routines should be established in which students must complete work before participating in purely fun activities. Although it is not generally desirable to dichotomize the classroom schedule into work and play, there are tasks requiring hard work that must be done, and done first.

Accepting Responsibility

Individuals cannot solve a problem until they take ownership of it. It is easier to get a young person to accept that his or her behavior is causing a problem if that problem can be seen as a specific habit or correctable behavior, rather than a deeply rooted personality trait or character flaw.

Dedication to Reality

Telling the truth is the easier part of dedication to reality. Living the truth is harder but essential to good mental health. Dedication to the truth is the equivalent of dedication to good mental health and freedom from short-term solutions that have nasty pay backs in the long run.

Balancing

Balancing essentially means flexibility. It is possible to become so dedicated to a goal, especially a worthwhile one, that excessive sacrifice is made to achieve that goal. This can be true of making good grades, saving money, or sticking to a regimen of diet and exercise. Balancing means knowing when such dedication interferes with an even greater good such as affirming a relationship or accepting higher responsibility.

Does Character Training Really Work?

It is natural for skeptics to question the effectiveness of ethical training, particularly because it can be difficult to measure. Ethical behavior involves more than ethical judgment (the capacity to know which of the alternatives available is preferred and why). It also involves empathy (feeling what someone else feels) and ethical action (the courage and willpower to carry out a choice). Although scientific research in this important area is incomplete, one study conducted by the California Child Development Project showed statistically significant results (Lickona 1991). Six schools in San Ramon participated in the program from 1984 to 1989. Differences between the schools providing character training and the control group emerged in four areas:

1. **Classroom behavior**. Students in the schools with ethical education showed more spontaneous acts of cooperation, affection, helpfulness, and encouragement in classroom interactions.
2. **Playground behavior**. Children in the participating schools demonstrated more concern about others but no change in level of assertiveness.
3. **Social problem-solving skills**. In resolving hypothetical conflicts, students who received character training paid more attention to the needs of everyone involved in the dispute, were less likely to propose aggressive responses, and came up with more alternatives.
4. **Commitment to democratic values**. Children in the training group were more committed to beliefs such as *all members have a right to participate in the group's activities and decisions.*

Skill Development Activity 8-1: Practicing Collateral Teaching

Draw two columns on a sheet of paper and for each of the following scenarios tell what teacher behavior would *strengthen* and what behavior would *weaken* the process of collateral learning by the student.

1. A student insists that working in a group is not his style. He prefers to do the entire project alone.

2. After getting back a test with a low grade on it, a student runs from the room sobbing, "It's no use. I'm no good at anything."

3. A student insists that it is the teacher's job to tell the students what to learn and how to learn it. It is the students' job to listen and follow directions.

FACILITATING ETHICAL REASONING

Young people today face hard choices in a complex world. They have a wide range of adult options available to them, yet their thinking is immature and inexperienced. Even if young people do not have to make hard choices now, they almost certainly will in the future, at work, with friends, or at home. As Albert Einstein put it, "The development of general ability for independent thinking and judgment should be placed foremost [in education], not the acquisition of specialized knowledge" (Einstein, 1954, 71). Choice mapping activities provide some tools to help students illuminate alternatives and make better choices.

Lawrence Kohlberg's Research

In the middle of the twentieth century, behaviorism had a large impact on both educational theories and the social sciences: "Moral values are evaluations of actions believed by members of a society to be right" (Berkowitz 1964, 44). Cultural relativism holds that all values are arbitrary beliefs instilled in people by the culture in which they live; these values are not based on any logic of the inherent rightness of some actions over others. The assumptions of cultural relativism, like the parallel assumptions of behaviorism, have been gradually eroded by actual research: "The common assumption of the cultural relativity of ethics upon which almost all contemporary social scientific theorizing about morality is based, is in error" (Kohlberg 1971, 155). Lawrence Kohlberg, a Harvard professor, spent more than 20 years studying the growth of ethical judgment in children and adolescents. Kohlberg's data came from three areas of study:

- The same 75 boys, interviewed every third year for 15 years. The boys were 8-14 years old when the study began and 22-28 years old when it concluded.
- Children of middle-class parents as well as children of lower-class parents in the United States.
- Children in Taiwan, Turkey, and Yucatan, Mexico (and later several other countries)

The results of Kohlberg's studies were quite consistent. Young people from all the various cultures and socioeconomic levels developed a form of making ethical judgments that converged on universal ethical principles of justice, grounded in reciprocity and equality, whether their own societies were democratic or not. Instead of cultural relativism (the idea that every culture differs according to arbitrary factors), Kohlberg found that the capacity for ethical judgments develops in stages parallel to the development of cognitive capacities. Actual value statements of right and wrong were not found to be the same in all four cultures and across socio-economic groups, but the form of their reasoning was remarkably the same. "Judgment is neither the expression of, nor the description of emotional or volitional states; it is a different kind of function with a distinct cognitive structure" (Kohlberg 1971, 185).

Kohlberg's Stages of Ethical Development in the Child

Across all groups in his study, Kohlberg found that ethical reasoning developed in five stages. These clearly delineated stages or stable patterns of ethical judgment

- occurred in the same order in all cultures;
- were qualitatively distinct modes of response, that is, the separation in the stages came at definite break points connected to age and cognitive level; and
- were developmental, that is, the lower stages were reintegrated into the upper stages, and subjects in the study recognized a preference for higher over lower stages.

Stage 1: Punishment Avoidance

At this level the child has learned rules of conduct and uses them to make judgments of right and wrong behavior. But "right" and "wrong" are merely labels signifying either the physical displeasure or the hedonistic pleasure that follows an act. Rules are seen as the rather arbitrary exercise of the physical power of those who enunciate the rules and labels. Avoidance of punishment is the primary motivation for behaving one way or another. Authority is not seen in terms of a rightful system of equal enforcement, as in stage 4, but as an insurmountable power structure. Unquestioning deference to power may be necessary but is not valued in itself. A child makes choices based on a calculation of what brings the greatest net pleasure. If the pain is greater than the pleasure, the act is avoided.

Stage 2: Reciprocal Self-Interest

At this level of ethical development, right action consists of that which advances one's broader self-interest. Gratification can be delayed, and cooperation is possible, but only when these controls lead to some greater benefit. Human relations are viewed as transactions in a commodities market: "I'll scratch your back if you scratch mine." Elements of fairness and equality are respected, not on ethical grounds but for strictly pragmatic reasons—they're necessary to keep the system working.

Stage 3: Social Harmony

Meeting the expectations of one's family, class, community, or nation is perceived as valuable in its own right, and sacrifice of personal happiness or pleasure is acceptable if it advances social harmony. At this level, the person's attitude is more than mere conformity to the demands of a more powerful establishment as in stage 1. A person feels like he or she belongs to the group. Doing what is necessary to maintain membership in good standing takes precedence over hedonistic self-indulgence. Good behavior is anything that brings approval or caring from others. A person at this level wins approval by being "nice."

At stage 3, a person understands the rules of the group and abides by them voluntarily because doing so meets his or her needs. Conformity to social correctness within the framework of one's own group is the standard used to judge conduct—one's own or others—rather than conformity to universal ethical principles such as human rights or equal justice. The group's beliefs, behavioral norms, and social hierarchy must be mastered to acquire status within the group. In a negative case such as a youth gang, members gain status by committing acts of violence against nonmembers. At stage 3, incorrect behavior may be excused by reference to intent. "He means well" can soften the sting of inadvertently violating the group's norms.

Stage 4: Social Contract

At this stage a person reasons using the concepts of broad human or legal rights agreed upon by a society. Rules of the group are embraced as the means to maintaining a good system, the best living arrangement for all the society's members. The basis of authority is the greatest good for the greatest number, the central doctrine of utilitarianism. The U.S. Constitution is a stage 4 document.

Stage 5: Ethical Principles

At this stage, guiding principles are not concrete ethical rules like the Ten Commandments. Right is defined by the decision of conscience according to individually chosen ethical principles that are grounded in logical completeness, universality, and possibly a greater metaphysical system. Often these guiding principles are abstract and ethical (the Golden Rule or the categorical imperative argument: "What if everyone in the same situation behaved that way?"). At heart, these are universal principles of respect and responsibility, establishing a sense of justice based in equity, equality of human rights, and acceptance of the worth of human beings as individual persons.

At this level, a person may be guided by inner principles that conflict with established authority. Civil disobedience is possible on this level. For example, Antigone, the main character in Sophocles's play, is forbidden by civil authorities from burying her father, King Creon, because of his alleged treason. Believing that her father's soul could not rest for eternity unless she buries him, Antigone breaks the civil law and buries him. Antigone's act of conscience is a crime in the eyes of the law, but in her own belief system, not to bury Creon would have been a greater wrong than burying him. Civil disobedience, of course, is not a defense; anyone who knowingly breaks the law is still culpable under the law. The point of civil disobedience (versus ordinary disobedience) is that some higher principle is upheld even though it brings unpleasant consequences, and the unhappiness caused by the punishment is smaller than that of disobeying one's conscience. In civil disobedience one explicitly accepts responsibility for one's actions.

Skill Development Activity 8-2: Practicing with the Kohlberg System

Complete the following summary chart for Kohlberg's five stages of ethical development.

Table 8.1. Kohlberg's Stages of Ethical Development.

Stage	Description	Nickname	Person modeling this	Symbol or icon
1	Pleasure/pain orientation	reward/ punishment	toddler	a carrot and stick
2				
3				
4				
5				

Skill Development Activity 8-3: Recognizing Kohlberg's Five Stages of Ethical Development

Stage 1: Punishment Avoidance
Stage 2: Reciprocal Self-Interest
Stage 3: Social Harmony
Stage 4: Social Contract
Stage 5: Ethical Principles

Suppose you asked the question, "Why go to school?" and students responded with the following answers. Assign each response to one of Kohlberg's stages of ethical development.

_______ A. Because it would upset my parents and friends if I didn't go.

_______ B. Because school is a place to learn and become a whole human being. I want to reach the highest potential I can, and school will help me do that.

_______ C. My parents will ground me forever if I miss any more school.

_______ D. It's a reasonable deal. The community pays for my schooling now, so I'll pay for some other child's school in the future.

_______ E. Education is a natural right in this country, and it is my responsibility as a citizen to take full advantage of it.

Skill Development Activity 8-4: Applying the Kohlberg System

Write a script for a conversation among five students discussing the proposed honor code which states: "I will not cheat and will not tolerate those who do." Place each of the five students at a different level of ethical development.

Contrasting Views of Ethical Development

Questions have been raised about Kohlberg's scheme. Carol Gilligan (1982) argued against the universality of Kohlberg's stages. She maintained that the fifth stage is not universal but gender related. (Kohlberg's subjects were all male.) In other words, girls make legitimate ethical choices in a different way from boys, placing more emphasis on preserving interpersonal relationships than on abstract ethical principles. Given an ethical problem, such as whether a poor person with a sick loved one should steal medicine to cure that loved one, Gilligan would argue that females choose outcomes based less on the ethical wrongness of stealing than on the value of preserving a viable social unit.

Jack Fraenkel (1978) expressed several reservations about Kohlberg's approach. He questioned generalizing from a handful of cultures to humanity at large. For example, how would Kohlberg account for societies such as the Spartans of ancient Greece, who valued loyalty and self-sacrifice above justice and universal liberty? Fraenkel also challenged Kohlberg's methodology. In some of Kohlberg's studies, the agreement of scorers who classified the responses was as low as 66 percent. This undermines confidence in the conclusions. Fraenkel also questioned Kohlberg's transition from describing how people think to prescribing how people *should* think. Kohlberg seems to endorse the Socratic postulate that to fully use one's highest capacities is best. Such fidelity to one's own nature is called integrity, a value that needs no justification. (A horse *can* run, so a horse *should* run; a human *can* think, so a human *should* think; a person who *can* reason on a level of principles *should* reason on a level of principles.) Fraenkel would like to see a full philosophic analysis of Kohlberg's justification of *should.*

On a practical level, another objection to the implementation of the moral reasoning approach could be that certain institutions, such as schools, must take the lead in establishing a certain core of dogma. Shouldn't schools promote certain values over others, such as "Students who bring weapons to school will be expelled" and "Martin Luther's King Jr.'s values were superior to Adolph Hitler's"?

Kohlberg replies that the school and classroom can justly establish rules, codes of conduct, and explicit value systems as long as they are fully explained on the basis of higher levels of ethical reasoning ("Everyone will benefit by a small sacrifice of a few." "A safer, cleaner school is a better place to learn") not as an arbitrary edict ("You do that, and I'll clobber you" or "Because I said so, and I'm in charge" "That's the way we have always done it.") Racism violates the democratic principle of equal justice. Genocide is wrong because it fails both the reciprocity principle (*Act as you would have others act in the same situation)* and a fundamental democratic principle *(Respect the intrinsic worth of every individual).*

The *collateral curriculum*—the ethical atmosphere and social climate of a school—may teach more about establishing a just society than the formal curriculum. Children in despotic, regimented schools cannot progress through the stages of ethical growth "on schedule," that is, in conjunction with their cognitive developmental stage. Although rules may certainly be made and enforced, it is better that students have input in making or changing them and that rules be seen as benefiting the whole group, are well explained, and are justified on higher grounds rather than the exercise of arbitrary authority or sheer momentum.

Research on Stimulating the Growth of Ethical Development

Kohlberg and his student Moshe Blatt conducted a huge research project to test whether the discussion of ethical dilemmas—situations that call for making a difficult choice between two or more desirable alternatives—might have any effect on the growth of ethical reasoning. Kohlberg and Blatt found that within a single semester involving such discussion at least a quarter of the students tested progressed up a partial or whole stage of ethical development. However, three characteristics were necessary for progress to occur: the content of the ethical dilemmas had to be controversial, the students had to be on different levels of ethical reasoning, and the teacher must use Socratic probing techniques—relentlessly asking why—not didactic instruction (Kohlberg 1978a).

CREATING ENVIRONMENTS THAT SUPPORT THE GROWTH OF ETHICAL JUDGMENT

Although the order of the distinct stages was the same across groups in Kohlberg's study, lower class children in each of the four cultures studied lagged behind middle-class children. The conclusion: Ethical development can be slowed down by environmental conditions, or to it put differently, certain environmental conditions must be present for the growth of ethical judgments to occur "on schedule." These necessary environmental conditions are:

- Role-taking, a process in which children are asked to imagine themselves in another person's role; this activity stimulates the growth of the ideas of reciprocity and equality
- Family involvement
- Open communication with parents and other adults
- Emotional warmth
- The taking on of meaningful responsibilities
- Input from adults concerning the consequences of actions
- Encouragement by parents to participate in discussions of ethical conflict
- Exposure to examples of ethical reasoning of persons at stages higher than that of the child (Kohlberg 1971, 190)

Discussing Values in Context

Choice mapping activities have a strongly cognitive component, which should be emphasized. For example, working through a dilemma caused by new technology is like doing a math problem. It requires identifying elements and placing them in the right slots and manipulating them under certain logical rules. Language or literature classes require interpretation of meaning and the writer's intent. These are the same skills that a teacher is aiming to develop in choice mapping activities.

The best way to present values and ethical issues is within the context of normal classroom business and the regular curriculum. Conflict between two students can be an occasion to have a class meeting about resolving conflicts. Content areas present their own contexts. History and literature are loaded with conflicts between people and with questions of the value of individuality versus the well-being of the society. In biology classes, genetic counseling for future parents, death and dying, availability of health care, artificial insemination, test-tube babies, DNA testing, and genetic engineering can blossom easily into values discussions. In other sciences we can ask about the responsibility for and regulation of technologies such as electronic surveillance, body vest piercing bullets, designer drugs, compact plastic explosives, and other inventions that can do much harm. What about the millions of dollars that are spent on space exploration while inner-city toddlers go without inoculations? Who should regulate technology? Who should have access to the Internet?

Using Classroom Activities That Foster Ethical Growth

It seems apparent from Kohlberg's research that for students to reach their full potential to make ethical judgments, parents, schools, and teachers must provide the right support structures. Socratic seminars, role-playing, choice mapping activities, and discussions of ethical dilemmas in the classroom can help provide the cognitive nourishment needed to stimulate students to reach their highest ethical potential.

Option Grids

Impulsiveness rather than defiance of rules is the more frequent means by which children get themselves into trouble. When a young girl is faced with an urge, say, to take a pair of earrings from a store, it is important for her to be able to recognize, before the deed is done, that she is on the threshold of making a choice: Taking the earrings without paying is called shoplifting and creates all sorts of unpleasant consequences or (it is hoped) a bad conscience. Choice mapping is largely a matter of identifying alternatives and unwanted outcomes before taking action.

To identify the various outcomes available for a given decision, an *option grid* can be used. An option grid is a chart that lists the options available and the various outcomes of each. Each option will have more than one outcome, some of which will be positive and some of which will be negative. For example, suppose your sixth-grade class has collected aluminum cans all year. The price of aluminum goes up unexpectedly, and you now have an extra $87 to spend by next week when school lets out for the summer. Options for the money could be (1) give it to a fund for buying a big screen TV for the library, (2) give it to a local group that takes care of injured and orphaned wildlife, or (3) have a pizza party on the last day of school. Donating the $87 to the TV fund would not make the purchase possible until the full amount of the money needed is raised. However, the eventual positive outcome would be receiving a plaque with the class's name on it. Also, students coming into the library would be able to use the gift they gave and feel good about it.

Once the outcomes of an action are determined, each is scored for desirability on a scale from -5 (very undesirable) to +5 (very desirable). Using the options grid, the rating for each given outcome is recorded in each box below the outcome. The combined outcome score is found by adding the scores horizontally. With numerical scores in the right-hand column, ranking the options is simple. Table 8.2 presents such an option grid for the scenarios discussed.

Table 8.2. Option Grid.

	Outcome A Score	Outcome B Score	Outcome C Score	TOTAL
Option #1 library TV fund				
Option #2 wildlife hospital				
Option #3 pizza party				

Outcome Cascades

The ripple effect of a single act is not usually clear to students, or to many adults for that matter. A tool to illuminate these longer-range outcomes is an outcome cascade. It is so named because, like a stream of water going over a waterfall, it illustrates the far-reaching effects of a single action over time. A complete outcome cascade resembles a reversed tournament bracket, with increasing, rather than decreasing branches.

Classroom Activity 8-1: Using an Outcome Cascade

Scenario: A careless person tosses a burning cigarette out a car window, and it starts a huge brush fire that burns 31 homes and 1,500 acres of woodlands.

Using a reversed tournament bracket, identify and diagram the various consequences that accrue to the people directly affected, their loved ones, neighbors, wildlife, the ecosystem, the human community, the taxpayers, and the state.

Decision Trees

A decision tree is a schematic drawing or flowchart using Y junctions or yes/no triangles at all points in a given situation where a decision could be made. The decision tree does not identify which choice is morally preferred, only that a decision is possible at that point. When the diagram is completed, you have an inverted tree or pyramid. A discussion of which option is best and why can then take place.

Ethical Dilemmas

Case studies of situations that call for ethical judgments must be very age-specific, chosen or written with the age and cognitive level of the student in mind. These scenarios can be something as simple as "Angelina found a bank bag with checks and quite a lot of cash in it lying on the sidewalk. What should she do with it?" Other ethical dilemmas can involve playground events or broad social issues such as those presented below.

Whose Fight?

Chad and two of his friends, Mary and Phil, were spending Saturday afternoon playing in the park. They came upon two boys about their age who were fighting. Phil suggested that they break up the fight. He felt people shouldn't fight because there are better ways to settle problems. Chad disagreed. He thought they should stay out of the fight, that it was none of their business. As one boy finally started to get the better of the other and began kicking him, Mary sided with Phil, saying that they should break up the fight. She said someone might get hurt if they didn't. Chad still maintained that they should mind their own business, and he managed to convince his two friends. They left the two fighters to themselves and walked off to another part of the park. Is this what the children should have done? (adapted from Scharf 1978)

Caught in the Middle

During the war, a woman married a man from a foreign country. She had known him only a short time and did not know much about his past. She did know that, during the war, he worked as a scientist in a factory testing new kinds of weapons. Now he was working on another project in the same factory. After a few months, the woman noticed that several strange men were visiting her husband and that her husband was out late several nights that week. Something strange was going on! Today at home, she found a blueprint of one of the weapons her husband was working on in the factory. He had told her many times that everything he worked on was "top secret" and that he could not bring anything home. She confronted him with what she had found, and he broke down in tears. Some secret agents had contacted him. They offered him money for the plans, but he refused. But then they threatened to kill his parents and brothers and sisters, who still lived overseas. The scientist put them off for 48 hours, and now the time was almost up. The scientist was afraid that if the enemy got the secrets to the weapons, they would use them to plan for terrorist attacks with unbelievable loss of life, or they might even use the weapons to attack their neighbors and draw this country into a war. On the other hand, he loved his family overseas and could never forgive himself if he let any harm come to them. What should the scientist do? (adapted from Scharf 1978)

Nowhere in the curriculum is the teacher's role as facilitator more crucial than in the discussion of ethical issues. The teacher must not preach; that would undermine the value of the activity. Instead, the teacher must use Socratic techniques to develop a list of choices and the relative merits and demerits of each. As has been seen, students seem to progress through the sequence of ethical stages at their own rate on their own schedule. For older students, ethical dilemmas can spring from a newspaper story, medical or genetic counseling scenarios, or hypothetical new discoveries. Here is an example of an ethical dilemma for discussion in a high school biology or chemistry class.

Classroom Activity 8-2: Considering an Ethical Dilemma—New Medication

Tian and a fellow chemist in his laboratory have accidentally stumbled across a new drug they believe will relieve migraine headaches. In some people, it generates wonderfully vivid dreams. It can also cause brain damage when given in large doses, and it will be expensive to produce. Tian has a contract with his company to pass on any research findings, and so far he has done so. Jokingly, Tian's colleague says there's money to be made off this stuff on the black market. Tian has been a friend to his colleague and knows his wife and family. He recalls that the colleague has complained about losing big money in bad stocks. If the situation is as grim as Tian has heard, the colleague is on the verge of bankruptcy. He has been served notice to vacate his house. The family will undoubtedly have to move into an apartment and cut back on their lifestyle, causing stress that could topple an already troubled marriage. When the colleague mentions the black market, he looks at Tian in a way to mean he was not joking. Later he comes right out and speaks of big money. He states that he would be willing to bring Tian into a deal with him and take full responsibility if trouble with the law develops.

Part A: Circle each decision point in the narrative above.

Part B: Construct a decision tree, a diagram having a branch at each yes/no point. Label each branch as to what choice is available there.

In the ethical dilemma below, *Roberta's Choice*, three factors are intertwined: goods, rights, and duties. The facilitator's role is to help students unravel the issues by separating them into the three areas, looking at the factors in isolation, then placing them into a priority list. Note that adults will not usually find Roberta's choice a difficult decision, given the nature of medical law, but high school students will need time to discuss, clarify, and weigh outcomes before deciding what Roberta should do.

Classroom Activity 8-3: Considering Ethical Dilemma—Roberta's Choice

Roberta is a nurse in a large hospital. One of the patients in her care is a 34-year-old carpenter with a wife and three young children. Driving drunk, he caused a car accident which resulted in a young couple being seriously injured. His own injuries are severe: He is now partially blind and paralyzed at the waist and has potentially fatal injuries to internal organs. He wakes up briefly from sedation and tells Roberta he wants to have the machines keeping him alive removed so he can die.

Roberta knows of a patient in the hospital who is waiting for a heart transplant, as well as other patients who need other organs. In the state where Roberta lives, it is considered murder to disconnect a life support system without a court order. Obtaining the order could take weeks or months, and by that time the organs would not be usable. Roberta, however, knows a way to disconnect the machine with almost no chance of being caught.

Roberta has heard from a visitor that the man has a $250,000 life insurance policy. She knows that the company will not pay off if the insured person is murdered or disconnected from life support systems without a court order. After visiting hours have ended, the husband of the patient waiting for a heart transplant approaches Roberta in desperation. He says in so many words that he'll do anything to get a heart for his wife. He refers to Roberta's son, a senior in high school, and says he's in a position to offer a full scholarship to him at the college of his choice if Roberta will help get the transplant. What should Roberta do?

Part A: Identify all the people affected and the decisions to be made.

Part B: Write a one-page analysis of all the issues involved, and make and justify a recommendation for Roberta.

Classroom Activity 8-4: Analyzing Choices and Outcomes—Earthquake Prediction

Barry is a young civil engineer involved in the planning of a large dam project. By accident, some seismic data were taken in a peculiar manner. When Barry analyzed them, he appeared to stumble on the impossible: a means of predicting earthquakes several weeks before they occur. Barry now needs to somehow confirm his findings before releasing information about a means of prediction that geologists have been seeking for a century. Barry's colleague Allen, another scientist, could confirm Barry's conclusions. But if Barry's suspicion are right, Allen would likely use the findings to buy or sell stocks in companies that would be affected positively or adversely by a quake and make a huge profit in the process. Barry is considering telling his boss but worries that the dam construction project, which is already behind schedule, would be delayed even more. Having the least seniority on the staff, Barry would be the first to lose his job in a layoff (although it is uncertain whether a delay in construction would result in layoffs). Barry could call the governor, a man skeptical of all scientists who might not believe the truth even if he heard it. Barry could go to the press, possibly starting a panic that could kill more people than the quake, which Barry himself cannot be sure will happen. Barry could call some contacts at the university although they probably would want to hold off drawing conclusions about Barry's data until after the quake hit. What should Barry do?

How to Get Started Writing Ethical Dilemmas for Your Own Classroom

Barry Beyer (1978), an associate of Kohlberg's, provides four guidelines for writing ethical dilemmas.

1. Keep them as simple as possible. Dilemmas should involve only a few characters in a relatively straightforward situation. Otherwise, considerable time may be spent clarifying who people are and what the situation is.
2. Leave the questions open-ended and problematic, that is, having no obvious right answer.
3. Place two or more of these core ethical issues into opposition: punishment, property, loved ones, contracts, law, life, liberty, equal justice for all, truth, sex, and matters of conscience.
4. Having offered courses of actions, ask what the main character should do. Moral reasoning focuses on sorting out what a character should do and why.

Source Material for Choice Mapping Activities

Lickona (1991) presents a dozen fully discussed examples of ethical dilemmas for various age levels. Raw material for choice mapping activities can come from real-life situations, newspaper and other media accounts, role-playing activities, literature, or history. Here are two examples of ethical dilemmas related to the topic of personal conduct:

- Luis's friend has been acting strangely lately, very unlike himself. Luis finds out that his friend is using drugs and is involved over his head. What should Luis do?
- On the playground Sarah sees a big, mean boy stealing lunches and harassing kids. Should she tell anyone?

History and social studies courses are full of source material for ethical dilemmas. In fact, the development of ethical reasoning may be one of the most compelling reasons for including social studies in the curriculum. To identify material that might make the basis of a good ethical dilemma, first pose a question that grows out of the course material. For example, the following questions can be rewritten as ethical dilemmas.

- Should welfare recipients be required to work?
- Who should decide growth limits for your city?
- What's wrong with "insider trading" of stocks?
- Should people without children have to pay school taxes?
- The Stamp Act was a legal tax imposed by the British on the American colonists. Were the colonists right in refusing to pay the tax?
- During both World Wars, the Korea War, and the Vietnam War, every man who turned 18 was subject to the draft. Draft boards, composed of citizens appointed by the governor, decided who was drafted and who wasn't. The draft was legal, but was it right?
- Should President Truman have ordered the second atomic bomb dropped on Japan only three days after the first one?
- If a promising candidate for the U.S. Senate does a really bad thing, should a reporter who finds out about it expose it, knowing that it could destroy the candidate's political career, or keep quiet and let the people decide?
- The 18th Amendment to the U.S. Constitution banned the manufacture and sale of alcoholic drinks. Champagne, however, was not hard to buy, and enforcement was lax. Should a wedding party be subject to fines or worse for serving champagne at a wedding?

Once the question has been posed, turn it into a moral dilemma by choosing a main character, stating without elaboration the options available, and asking what the character should do.

Moral Dilemmas in Fiction

Virtually any quality story presents scenarios in which characters make important decisions. These situations are easily turned into discussions of ethical choice. Perhaps this is why storytelling is one of the oldest arts. In his thought-provoking book *On Moral Fiction*, best-selling novelist and scholar John Gardner concisely summarizes the function of art and literature:

> True art is *by its nature* moral. We recognize true art by its careful, thoroughly honest search for and analysis of values. It is not didactic because, instead of teaching by authority and force, it explores open-mindedly, to learn what it should teach. . . . Moral art tests values and rouses trustworthy feelings about the better and the worse in human action. (Gardner 1977, 19)

Some poems are beautiful statements of ethical dilemmas. "Stopping by Woods on a Snowy Evening" asks if a man has a higher obligation to himself or to his loved ones. Another Robert Frost poem, "Love and a Question," asks whether a newlywed couple should allow a wandering tramp to share their honeymoon cabin on a bitter winter's night. As we have seen in Module 5, Aesop's fables contain a simple situation, a decision, and an outcome. The result can be explored as a solution to the ethical problem presented.

Noted child psychiatrist and teacher Robert Coles uses literature to help patients and medical students deal with important issues of life. In *The Call of Stories: Teaching and the Moral Imagination* (1989), he tells from personal experience of the inestimable value of stories in helping people overcome obstacles in human relationships and in helping people face death. Here are the short story selections that Coles found rich in moral situations:

John Cheever	"The Bus to St. James" "The Housebreaker of Shady Hill" "The Sorrows of Gin"
Anton Chekhov	"Gooseberries" "Ward Six"
Richard Eberhart	"The Cancer Cells"
Jorie Graham	"At the Long Island Jewish Geriatric Home"
Philip Levine	"The Doctor of Starlight"
Flanery O'Connor	"The Artificial Nigger" "The Enduring Chill" "Everything That Rises Must Converge" "Good Country People" "The Lame Shall Enter First"
Tillie Olsen	"Hey, Sailor, What Ship?" "I Stand Here Ironing" "O Yes" "Tell Me a Riddle"
L. E. Sissman	"A Death Place" "Dying: An Introduction"

Leo Tolstoy	"The Death of Ivan Illych" "The Kreutzer Sonata" "Master and Man"
Lionel Trilling	"Of This Time, of That Place"
William Carlos Williams	*The Doctor Stories*

Novels, of course, contain dozens of situations that can be discussed as ethical dilemmas. In *Billy Budd* by Herman Melville, did Captain Vere have any other choice but to hang Billy as specified under naval law? In *The Adventures of Huckleberry Finn* (Huck's use of tobacco and habit of lying aside), is the free-spirited youngster a moral person, a rebel against any kind of authority, or just an impulsive teenager when he puts himself at risk by helping Joe escape? Robert Coles discusses more than 30 novels suitable for extensive study of ethical issues, books ranging from well-known classics such as *Pride and Prejudice* to *Catcher in the Rye* and Toni Morrison's *The Bluest Eye.*

Drama is an especially fertile source for discussions of ethical dilemmas because plays are the dance of human wills in conflict. The very nature of dramatic structure demands that a main character be brought to the brink of an important ethical decision and then be left alone to take action. In *All My Sons* by Arthur Miller, the question is raised "Should a son who discovers that his father has committed a terrible crime turn his own father over to the police, or should he conform to his mother's wishes and leave his father alone?" Lorraine Hansberry's drama *A Raisin the Sun* asks, "Can a son and brother commit an act so reckless and damaging to the family that they are justified in disowning him?"

Newspaper accounts can often be used in discussions of ethical choice. Generally, a case described in the newspaper will have to be reworked to get the right mix of issues and manageable degree of difficulty for the age and ability of the students. This means the teacher may want to write scenarios inspired by real cases, leaving out the distracting details of personality, fame, and side issues. What makes a good discussion is a situation in which two or more desirable alternatives carry equal weight (i.e., a scenario that pits two crucial values areas against each other). What values are crucial depends on the age of the students.

Potential Problems in Using Choice Mapping Activities

More than any other teaching tool, choice mapping activities have the potential to rouse emotions, both positive and negative. Any discussion of values and what constitutes goodness can be a valuable part of education. Jessica, a student I ran into five years after graduation, stopped me to say thanks, that a discussion and essay that we had done in a biology class was the single most memorable and valuable assignment she completed in all her high school years. The assignment sprang from a discussion on the brain. Briefly, the question was, "If Susan won the lottery and could have a black market surgeon implant a needle in the pleasure center of her brain, and she still had plenty of money for a staff of nurses to feed her intravenously and keep her under mild sedation, should she do it?"

To an adult this is an outrageous question. It would not take any thought to say "of course not." But for high school sophomores, the idea of being rid of worries and the uncertainties of the future made the pleasure coma sound appealing at first. *But it would mean giving up playing basketball, missing the prom, and never again seeing a rainbow. Come to think about it, it's just plain unnatural.* Students like Jessica came to an important realization about life itself: *You have to take the bad with the good, because there are plenty of good things, and you can't let the bad things dominate.*

This same activity would be inappropriate for sixth grade, out of context if it had not come from a discussion of the brain, and useless if I had expressed shock when some students endorsed the idea of the pleasure coma. In the case of choice mapping activities, the context, manner of presentation, and timing of the activity are probably as important to its success as the activity itself. Also, I avoid using words that might create mental and emotional blocks in students. Suppose I had introduced the topic by saying, "Today we're going to have a discussion on morality and the meaning of life." What if I had replied to supporters of the pleasure coma by saying, "How could you possibly believe that? That's very unnatural and disgusting." Suppose we were having a slow day and I decided to whip out the discussion of ethics to fill in some time. Any of these choices on my part could have been disastrous.

The Extremes

Teachers who have problems in the classroom often cause them. A local teacher sent home a survey with his fifth-grade class during a unit on health asking parents to identify any family history of alcohol or drug abuse, violent behavior, or mental illness. Parents burned up the central office switchboard with complaints. A sixth-grade teacher did the now infamous lifeboat activity. (With limited food and water and seven people in the lifeboat, who should be tossed overboard? A brief description of each person is provided, and students are asked to evaluate the importance of each individual.) You wonder sometimes what happens to common sense.

At the other extreme, some teachers, in talking about the Pilgrims, say they left England because they were unhappy there. This approach avoids having to deal with complaints about either advocating or knocking religion. (A more skilled teacher wouldn't fall into either trap.) *A truly democratic society that ensures liberty and justice for all cannot be built by avoiding controversy.* Teachers at all levels must realize that controversy is the single most critical factor in stimulating moral growth. Besides, a curriculum devoid of controversial issues is boring and ultimately dishonest. Teaching requires integrity and courage, always tempered by concern for the students' long-term best interests. It never hurts, before giving out an ethical dilemma or controversial assignment, to have a colleague give feedback on the suitability of the activity for the stated learning purpose and age group involved. If someone does question why you held a certain discussion—and it is their right to do so—be prepared to give your goals, rationale, and the ethical issues you're asking students to address.

A Closing Comment on Using Choice Mapping Activities

These last few paragraphs might have made you wary of using choice mapping activities. In my 26 year career, I have steered a careful course, and in dozens of choice mapping activities, I've had no serious problems, no administrative pressure, and no parent complaints. Quite the contrary, I have received many words of thanks and praise for "teaching students to think." Here is an analogy to take with you: Well-prepared mountain climbers and sailboat captains who respect nature rarely get into trouble. And so it is with teachers who incorporate fair, balanced, and appropriate discussions of ethical issues in the classroom.

REFERENCES

Berkowitz, L. 1964. *Development of Motives and Values in Children.* New York: Basic Books.

Beyer, Barry. 1978. Conducting Moral Discussions in the Classroom. In *Readings in Moral Education.* Edited by Peter Scharf. Minneapolis, MN: Winston Press.

Coles, Robert. 1989. *The Call of Stories: Teaching and the Moral Imagination.* Boston: Houghton Mifflin.

Einstein, Albert. 1954. On Education. In *Ideas and Opinions.* [Written in 1936.] Edited by Carl Seelig and others. New York: Dell.

Fraenkel, Jack R. 1978. The Kohlberg Bandwagon: Some Reservations. In *Readings in Moral Education.* Edited by Peter Scharf. Minneapolis, MN: Winston Press.

Gardner, John. 1977. *On Moral Fiction.* New York: Basic Books.

Gilligan, Carol. 1982. *In a Different Voice: Psychological Theory and Women's Development.* Cambridge, MA: Harvard University Press.

Kohlberg, Lawrence. 1971. From Is to Ought: How to Commit the Naturalistic Fallacy and Get Away with It in the Study of Moral Development. In *Cognitive Development and Epistemology.* Edited by T. Mischel. New York: Academic Press.

———. 1978a. The Cognitive-Developmental Approach to Education. In *Readings in Moral Education.* Edited by Peter Scharf. Minneapolis, MN: Winston Press.

Lickona, Thomas. 1991. *Educating for Character: How Our Schools Can Teach Respect and Responsibility.* New York: Bantam Books.

Peck, M. Scott. 1978. *The Road Less Traveled: A New Psychology of Love, Traditional Values, and Spiritual Growth.* New York: Simon & Schuster.

Piaget, Jean, and Barbel Inhelder. 1958. *The Growth of Logical Thinking from Childhood to Adolescence.* New York: Basic Books.

Public Agenda. 1994. *First Things First: What Americans Expect from Public Schools.* New York: Public Agenda.

Scharf, Peter. 1978. Creating Moral Dilemmas for the Classroom. In *Readings in Moral Education.* Minneapolis, MN: Winston Press.

FURTHER READING

Cutter, Mary Ann G. et al. 1992. *Mapping and Sequencing the Human Genome: Science, Ethics and Public Policy*. Colorado Springs, CO: BSCS and the American Medical Association.

Dworkin, Gerald. Analyzing Ethical Problems. In *Hard Choices*. Boston: Office of Radio and Television Learning.

Erickson, Lois V. 1978. The Development of Women: An Issue of Justice. In *Readings in Moral Education*. Minneapolis, MN: Winston Press.

Jackson, Philip W. 1993. *The Moral Life of Schools*. San Francisco: Jossey-Bass.

Kierkegaard, Soren. 1940. *Stages on Life's Way*. Trans. by Walter Lowrie. Princeton, NJ: Princeton University Press.

Kohlberg, Lawrence. 1978b. The Moral Atmosphere of the School. In *Readings in Moral Education*. Edited by Peter Scharf. Minneapolis, MN: Winston Press.

———. 1987. The Cognitive-Developmental Approach to Moral Education." In *Value Theory and Education*. Edited by Peter F. Carbove Jr. Malabar, FL: Robert Kreiger.

Mussen, Paul, and Nancy Eisenberg. 1977. *Roots of Caring, Sharing, and Helping: The Development of Pro-Social Behavior in Children*. San Francisco: W. H. Freeman.

Reimer, Joseph, Diana Paolitto, and Richard Hersh. 1983. *Promoting Moral Growth: From Piaget to Kohlberg*. New York: Longman.

Sommers, Christina, and Fred Sommers. 1993. *Vice and Virtue in Everyday Life: Introductory Readings in Ethics*. Fort Worth, TX: Harcourt Brace.

Wagner, Tony. October 9, 1996. Creating Community Consensus on Core Values: An Alternative to Character Education. *Education Week* xvi (6):36-38.

Module 9

Role-Playing and Enactments

If you really want to find out who you are, try playing someone else.

—James P. Downing

ENGAGING STUDENTS WITH PERFORMANCE ROLES

The key to effective teaching at all levels is to engage students in learning. The more engagement, the better. On the more elaborate end of the spectrum, a teacher can prepare an enactment such as the story of John Muir found at the end of this module and present it as a "guest lecture." Properly done, this can be a very effective and memorable lesson. An even higher level of engagement is possible when students participate in the enactment or even write and rehearse the script themselves. Student enactments involve emotions, movement, and visual and auditory stimuli as well as content. With forethought and sufficient preparation, enactments have a huge potential to help students remember what they've studied.

Student Skits

When done effectively, skits can meet many teaching goals: increasing involvement, encouraging student initiative, and practicing collaboration on a project. However, skits can easily degenerate into giggle sessions or mindless showing off. Too little planning, no script, a vague purpose, and insufficient rehearsal will invariably spell failure for a student skit. To eliminate these problems, provide a clear purpose, require a definite script, allow rehearsal time, and coach students to reduce self-consciousness in front of the group.

A workable format for student skits is to adapt the format of a game show or TV program to the unit of study. "Jeopardy" is known to just about everyone but is rather tame. "Let's Make a Deal" or "The Dating Game" are entertaining formats. For example, if a skit is to contrast elements in three different models of computers, instead of bachelors, the customer would try to win a date with computer #1, #2, or #3, played by members of the opposite sex of the customer.[1]

Staged Readings of Plays

Although the resource pool of plays about people of the sort studied in school is limited, there are a few good sources. *Plays of Great Achievers* (Kamerman 1992) contains short (10- to 20-page) plays about the following persons:

Clara Barton	(first president of the Red Cross)
Simon Bolivar	(South African leader)
Marie Curie	(discoverer of radium)
Thomas Edison	(inventor)
Albert Einstein	(physicist)
Leif Erickson	(Norwegian explorer)
Benito Juarez	(Mexican reformer)
Antoni van Leeuwenhoek	(maker of microscopes)
Horace Mann	(father of American public education)
Thomas Morton	(father of anesthesia)
Wolfgang Mozart	(composer)
Thomas Paine	(American political philosopher)
Louis Pasteur	(chemist and microbiologist)
Marco Polo	(Venetian traveler)
Paul Revere	(American patriot)
Wilhelm Roentgen	(discoverer of X-rays)
William Shakespeare	(playwright)
Katherine Stinson	(pioneer aviator)
Lucy Stone	(advocate of women's rights)
Mark Twain	(American writer)
Peter Zenger	(advocate of freedom of the press)

Mind of the Scientist by Michael Hoskin (1971) is a book based on a BBC television series. It contains 30-page dialogues with Charles Darwin, William Herschel, Louis Pasteur, Isaac Newton, and Galileo.

Analogical Enactments and Some Examples for Various Subjects

In *analogical enactments* students get out of their seats and play the role of armies, atoms, numbers, helping verbs, planets in orbits, or just about anything else where connections can be better understood on the concrete level. Political cartoons halfway resemble analogical enactments. For example, a cartoon might show a patient in a hospital bed with a pained look and a soaring fever. The banner across the patient reads: U.S. economy. On one side, dressed as a doctor, is the easily recognized caricature of the president, who says, "He'll be up and around in a matter of months if we give him the transfusion now." On the opposite side of the bed are other doctors, labeled "Congress," who say, "But if he's not better by November, *we're* dead."

The reader can quickly understand the complex interplay between politics and the economy by the use of analogy and labels that establish the analogical linkages. Analogical enactments carry the process of political cartooning one step further. Instead of making drawings, the students hang signs around their necks and move around, making concrete realities out of pure abstractions.

Here are a few examples of analogical enactments for various subjects.

High School Literature

The voyage of Odysseus: Locations around the room are tagged with signs showing Troy, Calypso's Island, Ithaca, etc., and people wear signs saying *Penelope, Calypso, Eurydice*, etc. To illustrate the basic facts of the story (which get fairly confusing in terms of location), a person wearing the sign *Odysseus* moves around the room telling the events of the story.

Elementary Math

Borrowing in subtraction is illustrated by cutouts of hamburgers or ice cream cones. Children walk up, remove the topmost cutouts, and change the remaining tally.

Ninth Grade Physical Science

To demonstrate quark theory, students make colored construction paper signs showing the names of various particles, for example, atoms, molecules, protons, neutrons, UP quarks, DOWN quarks, gluons, and gravitons. Each person in class has one or more signs. The universe is built up, step by step, by calling to the front various combinations of particles. For example, the proton is made of two UP quarks and one DOWN quark bound together by gluons. Atoms are built, then molecules, the planets, the galaxies and then the universe.

Foreign Language or Elementary School English

The various verb tenses are put on colored paper signs. "Helping" verbs such as *had, has,* and *will have* are required to perform certain tasks. This activity can also work with other parts of speech such as prepositions: *under, over, beside,* etc.

High School American Government

Consider the question "Why does deficit spending cause inflation?" Signs are made labeled *banks, consumer, big corporations, businessperson, government worker, war widow,* etc. Cutouts of money are stacked on the *government* table. The *government* gives away all its money, then starts borrowing from the *bank*. The other bank customers start an auction, bidding up the price of borrowing money. *Corporations* and *businessperson* raise prices to pay for their expensive loans, and the *consumer* gets fleeced.

ROLE-PLAYING

Playing roles is usually enjoyable. Rather than reading from an actual script, the characters play out scenarios focusing on personality types and everyday situations. Role-playing is an ideal activity for illustrating correct and incorrect problem-solving techniques, applying a step-by-step procedure, building good relationships, learning to get along with others, and resolving ethical dilemmas. Problems should be kept simple and situations exaggerated so the audience understands clearly the issue and the characters' responses to it.

Techniques for Role-Playing Activities

It is logistically easiest in most cases to write scenarios on index cards and hand them out to the players. The teacher should always allow time for rehearsal before asking students to get up in front of the class, unless they are seasoned performers. Group role-playing is "safer" than solo work.

Potential Problems in Using Role-Playing Activities

Role-playing requires that group members trust each other. Although students should be encouraged to participate in role-playing activities, it is counterproductive to demand that they do so if they have a real aversion to performing. Instead, arrange an alternative activity. The main problem that can undercut the value of the activity occurs when students never get into the role or drop the role and just react as themselves. For example, the activity might call for a student to act in an intolerant way. Some people have trouble playing such a role and lapse into playing themselves. This confuses the issue, and once students realize they are playing themselves, they become embarrassed. A bit of private rehearsal beforehand with teacher coaching provides a more effective outcome.

Classroom Activity 9-1: Role-Playing—Teenagers and the Law

Part A: Have a small group play out these scenarios in front of the class, showing a bad result. Then allow for whole-group discussion.

Part B: After the discussion, have the students play out the scenario again, this time illustrating a better result.

Situation #1: A teenager gets stopped by a police officer, not knowing why. The teenager feels persecuted. After inspecting the teenager's driver's license and registration, the officer says the car has a burned-out taillight.

Situation #2: Leaving a store after purchasing a pair of expensive running shoes, a teenager is confronted by a store detective and asked to produce a receipt. The teenager can't find it, and the store detective is not a good listener.

Situation #3: While getting an expired driver's license renewed, a teenager must wait in a long line to get the results of the test. Finally, it is corrected. The student failed. The clerk won't issue the driver's license. The teenager becomes upset.

ENACTMENTS

Any form of dramatic presentation in front of a group could be called an *enactment*. The degree of preparation and staging can range from a simple impromptu skit to a full one-act play.

No other lesson plan format generates more student involvement than group enactments. Imagine having the entire class in costume, reenacting a moment from history. Projects of this size generally necessitate the involvement of more than one teacher, but they can be accomplished by a single teacher with enough commitment. Projects of a lesser scale can be spun out of biographies and even paintings and documents. Some samples:

- Each student researches one of the signers of the Declaration of Independence and provides a simple costume, a scarf, a hat, or a cape. After all of the players have revealed who they are, the group positions itself as if sitting for a commemorative portrait.
- Given recordings of American folk music and the words to songs such as "Erie Canal," "I've Been Working on the Railroad," and "Drill Ye Terriers, Drill," students write fictional narratives about life in the nineteenth century, then string them together into an historical version of the Broadway musical *A Chorus Line*.
- *Spoon River Anthology* by Edgar Lee Masters (1963) is a series of character vignettes about life in small town America at the turn of the twentieth century. As a group enactment, students could provide simple costumes and read the set of poems aloud.
- Given a biography of a real person, such as Queen Elizabeth II or Thomas Jefferson, students the take parts of characters in that person's life, then tell her or his story in the format of a serial interview, something like the old TV show "This is Your Life."

Developing Scripts for Enactments

The possibilities for scripts are nearly inexhaustible, but before enacting scripts, you must set the tone for make-believe by leading off with some imagination activities and teacher or small group enactments. As with any complex skill, it is necessary to work up to enactments with simpler activities that have a high degree of success. For example, an ordinary biographical report can work as a scripted interview or even a fictional press conference. Once the students are comfortable in attempting enactments, they'll find a variety of scripts from which to choose.

Scripts from Interviews

Historical Interviews

In many cases an historical interview works best when the person interviewed is not the famous person, but a relative or friend of the famous person. This way, it is easier to work in revelations of intimate or unpleasant facts. Also, it avoids the problem of the deceased person telling us when he or she died. Here are a few historical interview suggestions.

- Two of Daniel Boone's best friends with somewhat different memories tell the story of his life.

- Amelia Earhart's nephew describes the events of her life and the search for her.
- Two of George Washington's slaves discuss their lives on his plantation, Mount Vernon.
- Jackie Kennedy's hairdresser describes the real life of the President's wife.

Fictional Interviews

Fictional interviews can be a lot of fun, and there are an infinite number from which to choose. Here are just a few.

- One of Jack London's characters
- Bugs Bunny, a Disney character, or Feifel from the film *An American Tale*
- Hamlet
- Dorothy from *The Wizard of Oz*

Contemporary Interviews

Students will need help in locating the appropriate resource materials to script contemporary interviews. Popular magazines such as *People* or *National Geographic*, or anecdotal biographies such as *Current Biography*, are better sources for this project than scholarly works, which contain few if any personal details on which to build a fully human character.

Scripts from Correspondence

Writing scripts creates a greater depth of understanding than writing reports. Early in the year, teachers can have students just write scripts; then after they become more comfortable with classmates, they can both write and enact their scripts.

Correspondence Between Characters from History

- During his first term as president, Abraham Lincoln corresponds with Thomas Jefferson to ask for advice.
- Newton attempts to explain gravity to Aristotle.
- Copernicus and Ptolemy discuss the path of a newly sighted comet around the sun.
- Euclid corresponds with Riemann about the new geometry.
- Henry VIII sends numerous memos to Cromwell concerning the "Thomas More Problem."

Correspondence Between Two Characters from a Play, Short Story, or Film

- Elliot writes a letter to ET on the subject of how Earth is getting along.
- Biff Loman and his brother, characters in *Death of a Salesman*, write letters concerning their father, Willy Loman.
- Winnie the Pooh writes to his grandma, describing his friends and his home in the woods.

Scripted Group Discussions

Probably the most famous example of a *scripted group discussion* was written by TV's Steve Allen, a skit master and comedian who presented an intriguing series of scripted round-table discussions involving famous people of the past. The seven PBS programs in the "Meeting of Minds" series are still available on both videocassette and audiocassette.

The first program includes Theodore Roosevelt, Thomas Paine, Thomas Aquinas, and Cleopatra. The remaining tapes each feature four speakers from history, ranging from the beloved (Socrates) to the hated (Marquis de Sade).

Part II: Ulysses S. Grant, Marie Antoinette, Thomas More, Karl Marx

Part III: Charles Darwin, Emily Dickinson, Attilla the Hun, Galileo

Part IV: Frederick Douglass, Empress Tz'u-hsi, Marchese di Bonesana Cesare Beccaria, Marquis de Sade

Part V: Martin Luther, Voltaire, Plato, Florence Nightingale

Part VI: Susan B. Anthony, Francis Bacon, Socrates, Emiliano Zapata

Part VII: St. Augustine, Thomas Jefferson, Empress Theodora of the Byzantine Empire, Bertrand Russell

The scripted discussion format works particularly well after studying a group of "isms." For example, in science suppose the topic was the six "isms" that have contributed to the growth of science: materialism, idealism, empiricism, rationalism, mysticism, and skepticism. Now suppose that a mysterious impenetrable sphere, unlike anything ever seen on Earth, was found and brought before a panel of distinguished guests. The students could write a scripted discussion in which each of six speakers supports a different one of the "isms."

Skill Development Activity 9-1: Setting up a Scripted Dialogue

Suppose the economy has turned sour. Unemployment and the deficit are up, wages are down, and there is civil unrest. Write a script for a dialogue among these five panelists: a capitalist, a socialist, a Marxist, an anarchist, and a monarchist.

Scripted Press Conference

A scripted press conference combines the interview and scripted discussion formats. Questions for the person interviewed are written on numbered index cards and handed out to the audience. Using index cards increases the participation level and makes the interview more realistic. One of my favorite examples of this lesson format was the Campfire Interview. A teacher turned the lights down, put on a recording of crickets, had the students sit in a circle on the floor in a campfire arrangement, and handed out index cards with questions for Geronomo on them. Wearing a hat and Indian blanket, the teacher appeared as Geronomo, now an old man. The students, playing the part of the next generation faced with the challenge of carrying on the tribe's identity and traditions after Geronomo was gone, asked him questions about his life and the traditions of his people.[2]

Scripts as Debates and Dialogues

The *scripted debate* is an especially good tool for bringing out similarities and differences between two or more opposing views. This project works especially well to tie together a unit of study as any debate contains a wide spectrum of content. The essential ingredient of any story or drama is conflict; no conflict, no drama. Debates always contain some level of conflict. The question is how to bring in dramatic conflict without turning it into actual conflict. In choosing or approving topics for the debate chosen by students, it is probably best to avoid those issues with already well-defined sides, for example, abortion, gun control, and gay rights. The purpose of this activity is to teach students to think on their feet, not defend previously established viewpoints, especially if the viewpoints are not really their own. Ideas for debates include these:

Aristotle (author Jim Downing) and Galileo (student Bill Kalinowski) debate motion

- Three members of a colonial family—a Tory, a patriot, and a moderate—have a spirited discussion in reaction to the Boston Tea Party.
- Caesar meets Antony to discuss military matters, governing, and Cleopatra.
- Charles Darwin and Lamarck debate changes in species over many generations.
- John Von Neumann and Thomas Edison debate the importance of mathematics that cannot apply to any practical problems.

How to Get Started Using Scripted Enactments in Your Classroom

Writing and performing a script are complex tasks that require a different approach from preparing for a test or writing a standard report. Fortunately, the process of writing and presenting a script, although requiring several skills, can be taught in layers.

An Overview of the Process

The first stage of writing a script is the same as preparing a report; it's a matter of research. Once the right source material has been located, notes are taken in the usual way, but before beginning the writing stage, the author must spend some time planning the structure of the script, in a manner parallel to organizing a piece of prose. The story spine consists of a major event or crucial decision and the events leading up to that decision. Once the string of major events has been identified, questions are created that will address these events. If the enactment is a conversation or an interview, the questions become part of the script. If the script will be a monologue, some of the questions can be absorbed into the character's speech: *Was I angry? Well, not exactly*. Props, such as a diary, or stage cues, such as the sound of birds, can be used to transition to other points. Stage cues can either be heard by the audience or silently incorporated into the actor's responses. Once the script is ready, staging is added and it is rehearsed.

Locating the Right Source Material for the Script

The first hurdle to leap in giving an assignment that combines factual content with fictional premise is locating the right kind of source material. In some instances the textbook or supplementary reader will contain all the source material you need. Biographies vary immeasurably, from the very dry *The Dictionary of Scientific Biography* (Gillispie 1970), an incredibly thorough, scholarly and anecdote-free work to Plutarch's *Lives* (of the Greeks and Romans) (1917), a highly entertaining work, beautifully written though interwoven with a few tall tales. The teacher may wish to create a file of articles for students to choose from, or at least a menu of sources. In my experience, librarians have been pleased to participate in the project by compiling a list of suitable sources.

Pulling the Initial Concept Together

After locating source materials, students may need a bit of direction. Collecting rough drafts of the script and skimming them for suitability spares the teacher the dilemma of dealing with a paper whose author completely misinterpreted the assignment. (The dilemma is whether to accept anything at all that has the faintest aroma of creativity or to tell the student his or her work has been for naught and must be redone to receive credit.)

Using Assignment Sheets for Scripts and Other Creative Projects

Story writing projects and scripts progress more smoothly if the teacher distributes an assignment sheet (or at least posts one the bulletin board) because it will prevent students from straying from the assignment. You may wish to grade and score some of the short writing projects, using a *grid grading chart*. In a nutshell, the grid grading chart resembles a toothbrushing chart where the youngster receives a check mark for each week's assignment. A predetermined number of check marks is required for each letter grade. There are only four levels: excellent, good, acceptable, and redo for credit.

Handling the Logistics of Staging Enactments

Overseeing scripted performances in costume may seem an impossible task for the average teacher to manage, but it can be done. A scripted enactment can be built up one layer at a time in the following order:

1. Complete research on the character and write an interview with that person.
2. Develop the character's costume, props, speech patterns and movement.
3. Create a dramatic story line in the G-O-D-O format.
4. Rewrite the interview, incorporating the story line and dropping the questioner from the interview.
5. Plan a bit of staging to enhance the performance and stimulate the imagination.

Potential Problems Using Scripted Dialogues

At the risk of stirring up needless worry by pointing out potential problems, I offer a few hints to avoid problems with writing scripts for interviews and enactments in the classroom.

Upstaging Content with Creative Panache

The hardest thing to convey to students is that the assignment has a dual purpose: to present both factual content and evidence of creativity. Uppermost in students' minds is the creative angle, however, so they may upstage their content with creative panache. Students may also entertain the false notion that creativity equals total freedom. It is important to stress to students that creative projects in the real world are subject to deadlines, formats, and budgets and that learning to work within constraints is part of the process of developing creative productivity. Whatever the constraints, make sure students know about them from the outset of the project. On the assignment sheet, it might be necessary to list the vocabulary words and topics to be included. Although this setup restricts the students' range of freedom, it may be necessary until the students can function more independently. Also keep in mind that when the format of the assignment is new, the Murphy's Law gremlins will be working overtime. But after a few months of practice with the format, students will come to understand it. Then you can give them more freedom to choose the best way to blend content and creativity into one unified piece.

Submitting Papers Out of Left Field

Even with an assignment sheet, it will take time for some students to get used to creative formats for writing. Expect to get an occasional paper so far removed from the stated assignment's goals that you won't even recognize what it is about. Remarkably, the student will be able to explain how assignment sheet A led to project Z, and then you'll marvel at the human mind's capacity for ingenious misinterpretation of the obvious. If this happens early in the school year, you may want to grade the assignment on effort rather than content, but later on, it might be good to offer the student a full explanation of what is expected and then provide a chance to redo the assignment.

Developing Constructive Assessment Tools

The creative merit of students' work should not be graded, although the routine elements and the assignment parameters of the project should be. In other words taking off points for spelling and punctuation errors (if specified at the outset of the assignment) will not destroy student creativity, although assessing the quality and appeal of their fictional characters could. Assessing the presence or absence of descriptors using the five senses and a G-O-D-O story plan is not destructive, as long as it was announced beforehand. As we have already seen, the assignment sheet and assessment tool must be designed together.

Managing Complexity

To avoid the problem of running out of gas halfway through the script, students should prepare notes covering the following aspects of writing a script:

- Identification of each speaker's point of view
- Identification of specific points of contrast or conflict
- Formulation of a character profile for each speaker
- Creation of a distinct story structure in G-O-D-O form

Final Touches: Adding Theatrical Staging

For any play reading, imaginary excursion, or enactment, a few simple changes in the room make a world of difference to the impact of the performance and provide heightened sensation that adds to students' capacity to remember information presented.

- *Backdrops.* A large sheet of black flannel hung behind center stage sets off the play from the room and allows the imagination to block out the regular classroom setting.
- *Lighting.* Any change in lighting—using candles, a table lamp, or even light from an overhead projector pointed toward the back wall to create indirect light—has an unexpectedly large impact on mood and readiness to participate. Perhaps the mere novelty of it perks up student attention.
- *Costumes.* Any change to a performer's attire can work wonders. A hat or bonnet, a vest, a shawl, boots or shoes appropriate to the character, and a small hand prop such as a book or pipe are sufficient to engage the imagination.
- *Sound effects and music.* To change a mood, nothing works as quickly as sounds and music. Even a simple sound effect such as ocean waves crashing over rocks, or crickets thrumming through the night creates an atmosphere of reality and readiness. If music is used, it must never upstage the activity, so keep it soft; solo instrumentals work best.
- *Props.* Objects used by actors on stage can help tell a story. A history teacher taught a lesson on the 1960s era by enacting an imaginary scene: A father cleaning the attic discovers a box of old newspaper clippings and uses them, along with questions from his son, to tell the story of Robert Kennedy. He concluded with a dramatic reading of the eulogy of Robert Kennedy by his brother Ted.[3] A treasure chest of old things served as the means for "Abe Lincoln's granddaughter," now herself an old woman, to retell the story of his life. Included were a Bible, a piece of slate, an ax, a toy soldier, a cannon, and a train painted black, representing the funeral train.[4]

Special Problems and Rewards of Enactments

Enactments don't tolerate half measures, especially when the teacher is the performer. They should be done fully or left as interviews. Kitsch performances or half-done parodies don't go over well. A world history teacher I know tried to play Louis XIV with a paper crown from Burger King and a ruler for a scepter. The students thought the lesson was a joke and didn't get caught up in it.

Scripted enactments require more preparation than any other format, but they also reap greater rewards. Not only are enactments engaging to put together and perform, they can become a means of boosting rapport with students. Young people know when you've made a special effort on their behalf. If the idea for a group enactment is well thought out, it is generally not too difficult to find parents or community volunteers to help with the costumes and logistics. Cross-disciplinary projects involving music, history, and language teachers, although a lot of work, produce some lifelong, positive memories for students and have a creative ripple effect far beyond what can be imagined.

A Sample Enactment

Note: This script was written by a fourth-grade teacher, Stan Converse, and enacted in his class. It is an exemplar of the enactment format rather than what is typical. Shorter, simpler scripts are possible using the techniques presented here.

Awaiting the Dawn: A Visit with John Muir

by Stan Converse[5]

The acting space is as large as a campsite. There is no stage scenery, except for a large black cloth that serves as a backdrop to the stage. The stage is set with a ring of stones containing a pile of twigs, under which has been placed a flashlight wrapped in red cloth. A tin can blackened with soot sits in the campfire. John enters carrying a well-worn notebook and squats beside the campfire. His costume is a pair of coveralls and a bandanna. He wears a light jacket and carries a cloth rucksack. He takes off his bandanna to use as a pot holder and pours an imaginary cup of tea into a tin cup, then sips it. From his rucksack, he takes up a pencil and writes as he speaks.

JOHN

"September 20th: I made my bed in a nook of a pine thicket. These are the best bedchambers the high mountains afford—snug as squirrel nests. I little expected company, but creeping in through a low side-door, I found five or six birds nestling among the tassels."

He looks up from his journal, listens to the birds, then speaks to them.

You're right; it's still dark out. Rising early is a thing I came by as a boy. Aye, that was a thing my father never sought to create. But that's the way it worked out. You've come a long way from Hickory Hill farm in the Wisconsin wilderness, Johnny Muir.

He silently writes again in his journal, then pauses to think.

When Father brought us from Scotland, my brother David and I were overjoyed with the farm in the Wisconsin forest. This sudden splash into pure wildness—baptism in Nature's warm heart—how utterly happy it made us! Nature streaming into us, teaching her wonderful, glowing lessons. Oh, that glorious Wisconsin wilderness.

John stands up, stretches, and looks around at the pre-dawn sky.

God's property—that's what my father called the farm we lived on—and Father was the overseer. One summer he set me to digging a well 90 feet deep, with only a hammer and mason's chisels. He would lower me into that dank, musty pit at dawn, haul me up for a noon meal, then lower me again to chip away until darkness fell and put an end to my labors.

One morning, as I reached the bottom of the well and stepped out of the bucket, I smelt a peculiar odor and felt faint. I choked, nearly overcome by the gas they call choke damp. I shouted for them to haul me up. The walls echoed so resoundingly with my shouts, I can almost still hear my words. Barely did I manage to stagger back into the bucket and call one last desperate time for my father and brother to pull me out. They hoisted me up and must have thought I was dead, for I had barely a breath left in my body. But the fresh air restored me, and being a person of generally strong constitution, I got over it. As soon as I was recovered, Father put me back to work finishing the well.

John surveys the imaginary eastern horizon, looking for the first streaks of the dawn.

Perhaps it was as a release from the long hours of work that I so loved to read, but Father had little use for books other than the Bible.

John changes his voice as he speaks his father's words and again when he replies as the child John.

"I'll have no irregularity within the family. You must go to bed."

"But my book is a church history, and I thought . . ."

"If you want to read, get up earlier in the morning. Late hours will not be kept in this house. But you may get up as early as you like."

I went to bed wishing that something might call me out of my sleep. In the morning I awoke as if to a trumpet blast, hurried downstairs, ignoring the cold in the freezing cellar, to see how much time I had won. Five glorious hours! I felt that I was simply rich beyond anything I could have dreamed or hoped for. Father had given his permission for me to rise early and read, and that is just what I did. I can hardly think of any other event in my life, any discovery I ever made that gave birth to joy so transportingly glorious as the possession of these five frosty hours.

John stirs the fire and sips tea.

I soon knew that if I were to be able to continue my reading on those cold mornings, I would need to build a fire. This was something Father would look upon as an extravagant expense of wood, so I set out to make my first invention: a self-setting sawmill to produce a greater amount of firewood. We had brought a few tools from Scotland, but many were of poor quality, and the only saw was coarse and bent.

John takes out a pocketknife, unfolds it, and begins to whittle.

First I had to make a set of tools and a workshop in the cellar. I soon completed the self-setting sawmill and right away commenced to work on many other inventions. I made many waterwheels, door locks and latches, thermometers, hygrometers, pyrometers, clocks, barometer, an automatic contrivance for feeding the horses at any required hour, a lamp-lighter and fire-lighter, an early or late rising machine.

John exudes pride of accomplishment. His recitation of the details of his devices with two addendums sounds a bit comical, but not to him.

I wanted a timekeeper that would tell the day of the week and the day of the month, as well as strike like a common clock and point out the hours; also to have an attachment whereby it could be connected with a bedstead to set me on my feet at any hour in the morning and also to start fires and light lamps. I carried small parts in my pocket to whittle at when I was out at work on the farm. When my timekeeper was nearly completed, Father found it behind the bedstead in the unused upstairs bedroom where I had hidden it.

John changes his voice as he speaks his father's words and his reply as a child.

"John, what is that thing you are making upstairs?" I didn't know what to call it, so that is how I replied. "You don't know what you are trying to do?" my father thundered.

"An early rising machine," I replied. When Father heard me, his hard stare at me softened a bit. "After getting up so extravagantly early all these last winter months, you're making a machine for getting up still earlier?" It seemed so ridiculous to my father that he very nearly laughed.

John takes off his jacket and packs it into his rucksack.

At the encouragement of a neighbor, I carried a few of my inventions in a bundle on my shoulder and boarded the train to Madison for the State Fair. My inventions raised quite a stir at the Fair, with crowds of spectators and many wonderful comments. I won a small award and soon after determined to stay in Madison and see if I couldn't get an education. I was desperately hungry and thirsty for knowledge and willing to endure anything to get it.

I worked in inventing and taking care of machinery for a while in the thickness of the Canadian forests. I came back eventually to a machine shop in Indianapolis, but that is where there was a terrible accident.

John acts out working on a lathe.

I was working on a milling machine, turning down the diameter of a shaft, when my file slipped.

John fumbles with the file and then grabs his right eye.

Suddenly, there was sharp stabbing pain. In an instant my right eye was gone. It was less the pain that hurt than the thought that my eye was closed forever on all God's beauty. After the accident, my left eye quickly went blind too, in a sympathetic reaction to the right eye's blindness. I was left in total darkness. The physician informed me I would never see again.

Darkness makes you think, and I had many weeks to think. Then my good friend, Miss Catherine Merrill, informed me of a specialist who might be able to help. It was a miracle, that's all. After several weeks of treatment, not knowing if I would ever see again, they took me for a walk in the woods. Oh what a glorious and memorable day. The sunlight filtered into those wonderful woods of Indianapolis in golden shafts descending through broken clouds. I came out of my darkness, and my course was set. I was determined to abandon the world of *man's* inventions to devote the rest of my life to studying the inventions of God.

With the income from my inventions, I might have become a millionaire, but I chose instead to become a tramp. My first step in that direction came on September 1, 1867. I set forth on foot, joyful, free, and seeing again, on a thousand mile walk to the Gulf of Mexico. I haven't words to speak of the magnificence of the hardwood forests in autumn. Crossing the Ohio at Louisville, I steered through the big city by compass without speaking a word to anyone.

My plan was simply to push on in a general southward direction by the wildest, leafiest, and least trodden way I could find, promising the greatest extent of virgin forest. That was a truly memorable journey through the South so recently ravaged by Civil War. Severe fever and lingering illness in Florida kept me from my original intention of proceeding to South America and the Amazon.

He rises and indicates the view he has been admiring.

Instead I opted for the drier climate of California's Sierra Nevada in what proved to be a most fortunate circumstance, for here truly is the crowning culmination of God's glorious creation.

John looks around at the coming dawn, then tends the fire.

It will be sunrise soon. The morning light will silhouette Half Dome and El Capitan.

John stands in awe, looking out on the majestic Sierras, the "Range of Light."

Probably more free sunshine falls on this majestic range than on any other in the world. It has the brightest weather, brightest glacier-polished rocks, more starshine, moonshine, and perhaps more crystal-shine than any other mountain chain, and its countless mirror lakes, having more light poured into them, glow, and spangle most. How ineffably superb, how spiritually fine is the morning-glow on the mountaintops and the alpenglow of evening. Well may the Sierra be named, not "The Snowy Range," as it is in Spanish, but "The Range of Light."

John perks up and turns to the wind, cupping his ear.

Ah, listen to the songs the wind sings in the boughs of these great redwoods. It will be a gloriously clear day. A good day to walk on a glacier. I find it curious that Mr. Whitney, after whom the tallest peak in the 48 states is named, would not see that this landscape was carved by glaciers. Gentle snow flowers falling silently for unnumbered centuries. If he had but walked the paths of the glaciers, he surely would have seen their unmistakable footprints polished into the rocks of the Tuolumne, or there, on Half Dome herself, matriarch of all the great rocks of Yosemite. One has but to walk here.

I hope those two young artists have found many sublime views for their sketches. Why those two fellows would wander into these mountains to find me I don't know, with me just preparing to descend to the valleys from a summer of studying the glaciers on the headwaters of the San Joaquin. I trust they didn't wander far from the camp I made for them. It wouldn't be good if they got themselves out into places where they don't belong. I know how easily it can happen, for that is just what happened to me one unlucky autumn day on Mt. Ritter.

John takes up his journal, finds an entry, and reads it.

"October 8. After leaving my companions two days ago, I set off to inspect the flanks of the mountain, with the intention of returning next summer to climb it.

"This season being fairly spent, I would not attempt to make the summit of Mt. Ritter now for fear a sudden October storm might leave me snowbound on the mountain, ill equipped to survive in cloud-darkness the cliffs and snow-covered crevasses. The sky being as clear this morning as a snow-fed brook, I have decided to set out to survey the flanks of Mt. Ritter and become acquainted with her so that in the future when I return, I might enjoy a gainful ascent."

John sets the journal aside and enacts the following story.

As far as I knew, Mt. Ritter was unclimbed and offered unknown challenges, and not planning a full ascent to the summit, I hadn't even taken along an ice ax for cutting steps on the glacier.

I succeeded in gaining the foot of the cliff on the eastern extremity of the glacier, and there discovered the mouth of a narrow avalanche gully, through which I began to climb, intending to follow it as far as possible, and at least obtain some fine wild views for my pains.

As I climbed the wilderness of crumbling spires and battlements, I often had to hammer a coating of ice off the rock, and I ignored the good sense which scolded me for continuing. I began to have a vague foreboding of what actually might befall me. I was not really afraid, but my instincts, usually so positive and true, seemed vitiated in some way, and were leading me astray. Unwittingly, I had quickly reached a point where I no longer dared to think of descending along the same route I had come up on, for the danger beneath seemed so great that I would rather trust to the unknown dangers above than the known perils below. What I had climbed was so steep that a single misstep would send me tumbling all the way to the glacier below. After attaining an elevation of about 12,800 feet, I found myself at the foot of a sheer drop, which seemed absolutely to bar further progress.

It was only about 45 or 50 feet high and somewhat roughened by fissures and projections; but these seemed so slight and insecure, I must either go straight up the cliff or turn back. Again the known dangers below seemed too great to consider returning down from this point, so I began to scale upwards again. I picked my holds with intense caution; they were so very small. About halfway to the top, I was suddenly brought to a dead stop, arms outspread, clinging to the face of the rock, unable to move hand or foot either up or down. My doom appeared fixed. I would surely fall. I clung to the rock face as if frozen to it. There would be a moment of bewilderment, I thought, and then a lifeless rumble down the one unforgiving precipice to the glacier below.

When this final danger flashed upon me, I became nerve-shaken for the first time since setting foot in the mountains. My mind seemed to fill with a stifling smoke. But this terrible eclipse lasted only a moment, then life blazed forth again with preternatural clearness. I seemed suddenly to become possessed of a new sense. The other self, bygone experiences, instinct, or Guardian Angel—call it what you will—came forward and assumed control. Then my trembling muscles became firm again, every rift and flaw in the rock was seen as through a microscope, and my limbs moved with a positiveness and precision with which I seemed to have nothing to do at all. Had I been borne aloft on wings, my deliverance could not have been more complete. Above me, walls of the cliff rose to still greater heights. The mountain's face seemed savagely hacked and torn. But the influx of strength I had received seemed inexhaustible.

I found a way to scale the peak's jagged slopes seemingly without effort, and soon stood upon the topmost crag in the blessed light. From the top of Mt. Ritter, my eyes were the first human eyes ever to behold the majesty of that sight!

I could not linger long at the top of the mountain, though I wished to spend a lifetime there. I found my way down from the summit through the forests of the far slope, but night drew near before I reached the base of the mountain. My camp lay many a rugged mile to the north; but despite the darkness, my ultimate safe return to camp was assured. It was now only a matter of endurance and ordinary mountain-craft.

After John's harrowing tale, he returns to the campfire, becalmed.

How glorious a greeting the sun gives the mountains! To behold this alone is worth the pains of any such errant excursion a thousand times over. This grand show is eternal. It is always sunrise somewhere in this valley; the dew is never all dried at once; a shower is forever falling; vapor, ever rising. Eternal sunrise, eternal sunset, eternal dawn and gloaming, on sea and continents and islands, each in its turn as the round earth rolls.

John pours the contents of the teapot on the fire, then spreads out the ashes with his foot. He stows his journal and takes up his rucksack.

I must be gone now, or I'll miss the first glorious rays as they flood the valley. In the moment of dawn the Range of Light shines in its most majestic hour. ♦

References for *Awaiting the Dawn:*

Muir, John. 1916. *Mountains of California.* Boston and New York: Houghton Mifflin.

———. 1916. *A Thousand Mile Walk to the Gulf.* Boston and New York: Houghton Mifflin.

———. 1917. *The Story of My Boyhood and Youth.* Boston and New York: Houghton Mifflin.

———. 1984. *Mountaineering Essays.* Salt Lake City: G. M. Smith.

April 1973. The Wilderness World of John Muir. *National Geographic.*

Wolfe, Lennie Marsh. 1945. *Son of the Wilderness: The Life of John Muir.* New York: Alfred A. Knopf.

NOTES

1. I am indebted to Sandy Gasseling for this clever idea.
2. The teacher was Jessica Rowland.
3. Mark van Cleave was the teacher.
4. This lesson was the work of Heather Wagner.
5. The author of this script, Stan Converse, is a teacher at Louisville Middle School in Boulder county, Colorado.

REFERENCES

Allen, Steve. *Meeting of Minds* series. Public Broadcasting Service. Dove Audio Audiotapes.

Gillispie, Charles Coulston, ed. 1970. *Dictionary of Scientific Biography*. New York: Charles Scriber's Sons.

Hoskin, Michael. 1971. *The Mind of the Scientist*. New York: Taplinger.

Johnstone, Keith. 1979. *Impro: Improvisation and the Theater*. New York: Theater Arts Books.

Kamerman, Sylvia E., ed. 1992. *Plays of Great Achievers*. Boston: Plays.

Masters, Edgar Lee. 1963. [Written in 1944.] *Spoon River Anthology*. New York: Macmillan.

Plutarch. 1917. *Plutarch's Lives*. Cambridge, MA: Harvard University Press.

FURTHER READING

Hery, Nancy Duffy. 1996. *Drama That Delivers: Real-Life Problems, Student Solutions*. Englewood, CO: Teacher Ideas Press.

Kase-Polisinsi, Judith, and Barbara Spector. Improvised Teaching: A Tool for Teaching Science. In *Youth Theater Journal* 7 (1):15–22.

Lallier, Katherine Grimes, and Nancy Robinson Marino. 1997. *The Persona Book: Curriculum-Based Enrichment for Educators*. Englewood, CO: Teacher Ideas Press.

Randak, Steve. October 1990. Historical Role-Playing. *The American Biology Teacher* 52 (7):439-42.

Module 10

Creative Teaching in the Real World

The dominant role of education at its beginning and at its end is freedom, but . . . there is an intermediate stage of discipline with freedom in subordination.
—Alfred North Whitehead, The Aims of Education and Other Essays

Author's note: This module will be presented in a different format, a fictional round-table discussion among a master teacher, Larry Sanders, and several undergraduates preparing to teach.

Sanders: Well, we're nearing the end of our journey. So what questions do you have?

Charlene: How about discipline? That's always a dangerous subject.

Prescott: We haven't gotten too much guidance on how to *grade* creatively.

Sanders: Creative grading. Never thought of it that way.

E. J.: I'm thinking that if I'm the only guy out there teaching creatively, it could be rough. I mean being new and calling too much attention to myself could backfire. The faculty could resent the new guy.

Franco: Curriculum. Do you think teachers should have control or what? Who determines what to teach?

Sanders: Wow. You guys get right to the real issues, don't you? Curriculum, that's as good a place to start as any. Later we'll talk about grading and discipline.

CURRICULUM

Sanders: In practice, you have two polar opposite approaches to curriculum. On one end, you have the French system, which is totally standardized. I've heard that in France, every child is studying the same thing at the same time. The Ministry of Education publishes lesson plan books and timetables, and every teacher covers the same arithmetic problems on the same day. That's probably an exaggeration, but there's no question that it's centralized and standardized. The standardized curriculum approach holds for the British system, too, both in the home islands and abroad in the former British colonies. Curriculum in high school follows a two-step plan: the O, or ordinary levels and the A, the advanced levels. A booklet for each subject specifies the topics and level of depth in the subject that the teacher is to cover. There's no doubt that passing the Biology Level A Exam means that you know high school-level biology. This system is similar to the Advanced Placement system used across the United States.

E. J.: What's the O level test like?

Sanders: Very long. Depending on the subject, it can take days.

Charlene: One long exam?

Sanders: No, it's really a battery of exams. In the sciences, there are actually what we call lab practicals; you actually have to manipulate equipment and make measurements.

Franco: Is the test all memorization?

Sanders: No. There are some open-ended questions, including coming up with a hypothesis and suggesting experiments.

E. J.: It doesn't sound so bad to me. Why don't we adopt something like that?

Sanders: Good question. I suppose it's too confining for the average independent-minded American. Also, it's used in the British system as a sorting tool, to track people into university or nonuniversity careers. That's called "elitist" over here. The United States is one of the few countries of the world committed to universal education. Sorting students for future education is not a major part of our system, because nearly everyone can exercise the option to go on to higher education—everything from community colleges to the Ivy League—if they so choose.

Franco: What sense does that make, giving everyone diplomas? Sure, 85 percent of the population gets a diploma now, but what's a diploma worth?

Choosing the Curriculum

Prescott: Calm down, Franco. I think the main factor against the British system in the United States is philosophical. After all, John Dewey, that quintessential American educator, talked about allowing the students to participate in the formation of their own end purposes.

Charlene: I'm not sure I understand that, Prescott. Could you give an example?

Prescott: Sure, let's say you're studying physics. There are many current discoveries reported in the newspaper. Did you see the article over the weekend that they just recently discovered a huge black hole at the core of a nearby galaxy, a trillion times heavier than our sun? Or for that matter, what about relativity? It's not a practical subject at all, but most people want to know all about warped space and time travel. Call it the science fiction impulse. It's things like that that drew great scientists into their subjects, not the desire to learn about the mysteries of heat transfer.

Sanders: Yes, the British system would produce motivation problems here. Maybe in some countries, you can send the unmotivated students away, but in the United States, there is no *away*.

Franco: But isn't the opposite extreme even worse? I mean it's chaos in our schools, every man for himself. You have the self-indulgent chemistry teacher baking pies in class and the geography teacher studying Euro Disneyland instead of looking at globes.

Sanders: Yeah, I suppose that can happen. But I think what's going on is more like teachers—especially in small schools—getting assigned to teach subjects they haven't been prepared to teach. In some cases, they haven't a clue what's important to teach or how to go about it.

Franco: So what about those scope and sequence charts? Don't a lot of school districts have those? Are you supposed to follow the guidebook, maybe not to the extent of the British system, but that's how you're evaluated, right?

Sanders: Well, not exactly. Only the better-organized districts have such a curriculum guide, and even if you're supposed to follow it, I don't think there's much enforcement. Actually, supervision of teachers is nearly nonexistent. Help for teachers with problems is inadequate, and the mentoring process for new teachers is terrible. There you are, fresh out of college, and you sink or swim. It's OK in the respect that you're trying out your own ideas, but it's not always the best for students. The one reform I'd like to see put in place is that every new teacher have a specially trained veteran teacher as a mentor. The mentor teacher would have either fewer classes or receive additional pay. This would be, in my opinion, the single most effective way to spend dollars to improve education.

Curriculum Reform

Charlene: What are the reforms you spoke of?

Sanders: I'm sure you've all heard of *A Nation at Risk* (1983), which was published back in the early 1980s. That report spawned numerous new plans. Now, nearly two decades later, there are some very attractive curriculum reforms that have managed to navigate between the shoals of over-regimentation and curriculum haphazardness. I'm speaking of the *Curriculum and Evaluation Standard for School Mathematics* (1989) and the *Benchmarks for Scientific Literacy* (1993). Others subject areas are still in progress. These reform projects have taken the position, continuing my analogy, of erecting a lighthouse to point the way without taking over the wheel. The breadth of the *Benchmarks for Science Literacy* is remarkable. Here are some chapter titles: The Nature of Technology, The Human Organism, Human Society, The Mathematical World, and The Designed World. As for the specific benchmarks of progress, let me read you a few examples:

By the end of second grade, students should know that

- when a science investigation is done the way it was done before, we expect to get a very similar result, and
- science investigations generally work the same way in different places.

By the end of fifth grade, students should know that

- results of similar scientific investigations seldom turn out exactly the same. Sometimes this is because of unexpected differences in the things being investigated, sometimes because of unrealized differences in the methods used or in the circumstances in which the investigation is carried out, and sometimes just because of uncertainties in observations. It is not always easy to tell which.

By the end of eighth grade, students should know that

- scientific knowledge is subject to modification as new information challenges prevailing theories and as a new theory leads to looking at old observations in a new way.

By the end of twelfth grade, students should know that

- from time to time, major shifts occur in the scientific view of how the world works. More often, however, the changes that take place in the body of scientific knowledge are small modifications of prior knowledge. Change and continuity are persistent features of science.

Sanders: Some states and school districts have adopted their own versions of the standards. Here are the K-12 geography standards from the *Colorado Model Content Standards for Geography* (1995):

Standard #1: Students know how to use and construct maps, globes, and other geographical tools to locate and derive information about people, places, and environments.

Standard #2: Students know the physical and human characteristics of places and can use this knowledge to define and study regions and their patterns of change.

Standard #3: Students understand how physical processes shape Earth's surface patterns and systems.

Standard #4: Students understand how economic, political, cultural, and social processes interact to shape patterns of human populations, interdependence, cooperation, and conflict.

Standard #5: Students understand the effects of interactions between human and physical systems, and the changes in meaning, use, distribution, and importance of resources.

Standard #6: Students apply knowledge of people, places, and environments to understand the past and present and to plan for the future.

Sanders: Following each standard is a list of two to five concepts that are embedded in the standard. The standards are broad, but not vague. Personally, I don't think many teachers of geography will feel constrained by these and the other standards. How could you call it geography if you're not doing those?

Prescott: Won't teaching these standards require a new kind of teaching?

Sanders: Yes. There will be more activities and more process skills. The topical approach will become more interdisciplinary and more integrated, less dichotomized within a discipline. Not Algebra II and Geometry with Trigonometry, but Integrated Math, not Western Civilization and Great Books, but World Studies. I'm happy to say that everything I've been saying in this course is right in keeping with the new teaching required by the content standards movement. So, Prescott don't worry. You may start out your career being the only one to use the new teaching, but in time you'll be surrounded by new teachers using more creative and constructionist modes of teaching.

DISCIPLINE

Sanders: Charlene wanted to talk about discipline.

Franco: I just dread all the hassles. Isn't there someplace I can get a job where I can just *teach?*

Sanders: You mean just convey content and not deal with human beings? In a real sense discipline *is* teaching, and more importantly, you're helping young people grow up. I guess I don't see discipline as something apart from teaching.

Charlene: But can't the bratty ones get on your nerves? Didn't you ever want to just clobber them?

Sanders: Yes, I have wanted to clobber them sometimes, but on the other hand, working with problem kids and seeing a huge turnaround in their behavior by the end of the year is very satisfying, too. It's those kids on whom you can have the greatest influence. They need your help growing up more than they need your knowledge.

E. J.: OK, so what's your secret to discipline?

Maintaining Good Order Without Coercion

Sanders: No secret, really. You have to have a curriculum that is appropriate for the students and capable of engaging them; that will forestall many problems. After ensuring the curriculum is suitable, you'll want to follow three steps:

1. Build a good rapport to prevent problems.
2. Establish the right relationship with the kid causing a problem.
3. Be skilled at applying techniques for changing behavior.

Prescott: You make it sound so easy.

Sanders: Well, it's not easy, but it can be learned. After enough practice, it becomes second nature. Good teachers have a lot fewer problems in the first place even though they give more work and have higher standards, which may make them less popular at the time than more fun colleagues. But a year later, when students realize that they have learned a lot, the good teacher's popularity rises retroactively.

Charlene: So what's the key to popularity?

Sanders: Well, I'd hate to shift the discussion to being popular—you'll figure that out if that's the teacher you want to be. But there are a few tricks of the trade that make a big difference in creating a special feeling between yourselves and your students. Be concerned, fair, and flexible. Don't snap at kids even when they deserve it, and be capable of giving them a good romp.

E. J.: What's a good romp?

Sanders: My favorite romp was in C. S. Lewis's book *The Lion, the Witch, and the Wardrobe.* Aslan the lion is a powerful, yet gentle fellow who likes to get on the kids' level and do the things they love. It may feel a little silly sometimes for an adult to be on a kid's level, but that's something children, or college students for that matter, really warm up to.

Franco: Sorry, but I just can't see myself like *Conrack* out there playing tackle football with the boys. I hope you're not suggesting I take my class out and roll around on the ground with them like a pile of puppies.

Sanders: No, that's not it. I guess more than roughhousing around like puppies, a romp is a *feeling.* That feeling can occur on any level, from preschool to graduate school because it is a feeling of belonging. The feeling is more than just fun; it's a sense that the separateness has receded, that the spiritual warmth of the moment transcends all barriers, that age groups and individual background have no significance. In Nietzsche's words, when he was speaking about the Dionysian energy of creativity, "Each one feels himself not only united, reconciled, fused with his neighbor, but as one with him" (Nietzsche 1966, 37). A romp is the unbridled exuberance of learning; it's the joy of life, a natural form of spiritual pleasure that has no specific subject matter or confinement to circumstance.

Relating to the Problem Student

Charlene: OK, maybe building a rapport, being fair, and giving a good romp can reduce discipline problems, but it won't stop them all.

Sanders: No, it won't. Many routine problems crop up, most of them due to immaturity. You'll be asking yourself. "Why can't these children clean up after themselves?" You'll have some sassy students, some irresponsible with equipment, some insensitive, some late, others who burst out with comments or actions, and some who can't seem to get their work in at all. "Don't these kids' parents teach them anything about responsibility at home?" you'll wonder. Well, sadly, there are quite a few parents who don't care for their children and avoid real interaction. Others have demanding jobs that prevent much supervision of their children. Happily, there are many parents who do a splendid job, and sometimes you'll be impressed by the remarkable maturity these students show. Then too, there are many students going through family trouble, which you won't know about, and it affects their behavior. All you can see is a disruptive youngster, who, you begin to believe, deliberately devises ways to make your life miserable. But in reality, the troubled students' behavior doesn't originate with you but grows from inside them and out of their circumstances. Your choice is whether to make an effort to be understanding and empathic or not.

I once had a student, a tough guy senior, who wore muscle shirts to display his 20-inch biceps. By the end of April, he was flunking, and without credit in Biology, he would not graduate. Aware of the stakes, he still came late to class without his materials; made rude, challenging remarks to me; and seldom turned in a paper except when it was done in class. He had a chip on his shoulder. (I found out later that his father had abandoned the family without a word the year before.) I talked gently to him, never raising my voice, always sitting side by side, never towering over him. I didn't feel threatened by him, because I believe that except for a few hardened cases, all students need adult approval and at worst want to play a game of bluff.

Students in high adolescence behave a lot like Holden Caulfield in *Catcher in the Rye*. Holden hates phonies, yet he, more than any other character, puts on a front in public. I assumed this muscle man Derek was bluffing; he meant me no harm. I had several quiet one-on-one talks with him, reminding him of his ability and calling attention to his many inappropriate acts. He listened without saying much. I told Derek the simple truth, that he had plenty of ability and if he would make up his work, I would grade it, but it would be too late after the end of the week. Even if he turned in all his makeup work, still, he had to make a "C" on the final, and that would be that, no charity. Derek didn't seem especially appreciative, but grumbled as usual. Nevertheless, he got his overdue work in, and it was done properly. He passed the final with a 73%. Frankly, I was glad to be done with him. A few days later, at the graduation ceremony, I saw a very different Derek. With a broad smile, he dashed across the field to me and gave me a bear hug, lifting me off the ground. "Mom, come here," he called to a stylish lady five strides behind him. "I want you to meet the teacher who got me through high school." I was quite surprised. I had no prior indication that Derek was capable of anything positive, much less affection and appreciation.

After two decades of teaching, I still believe that as far as children are concerned, there are none you can write off. You can't be sure that a difficult young person will completely turn his or her life around. But if you don't assume it can happen, you make the chances even smaller. If you do assume every young person is redeemable, then you must try to help them make a positive turnaround.

Franco: Excuse me, but that's a rescuer mentality, isn't it? Aren't you taking away their freedom to fail?

Sanders: I intervened, but I didn't lower my standards, except with regards to accepting late work. I gave Derek a choice, not charity. My choice in the situation was between sacrificing a little in the way of rules and allowing a student with a chip on his shoulder to put it down. I think it was a fair trade.

To summarize, the way you speak to students, regardless of what they dish out—and they will really try to hurt you sometimes—should be confident, calm, simple, and unambiguous. You should frame the outcome as a choice the student has to make, not something you'll do to him or her. You shouldn't make threats, but illuminate the short- and long-term consequences to the student for continuing that specific behavior. If you grant the young person unconditional dignity and identify his or her choices, you won't trigger a clash of wills. You have legal clout, but used to excess it can have a chilling effect on the whole class, and you suffer a small gain and a large loss. I've put a few pointers here in writing.

Guidelines for Disciplinary Conferencing with Students

- *Expect immature responses.* If students weren't immature, they wouldn't have caused problems in the first place.
- *Develop empathy for the child's situation.* With an immature ego structure, how can the student get what he or she wants? It must be very upsetting to be unable to sort things out. State that you feel some sympathy for something in the child's situation.
- *Never compromise the student's dignity* by using insults or demeaning remarks. There is no justification for such behavior and nothing to gain, other than the petty pleasure of putting someone down, a behavior inappropriate to a professional in a helping role.
- *Be aware of your telepathy through nonverbal channels.* What you're thinking will be transmitted to the student via your body language and other nonverbal channels. Do you mean to convey messages of devaluation of the young person, or do you want to send messages disapproving of the *behavior* without devaluing the *child*? Are your tactics relationship-preserving or relationship-terminating?
- *Maintain an "alert detachment."* Students sometimes engage in a bizarre game because they see the situation entirely differently. Their pride is at stake. For them victory is having control over you, and they define control as getting you upset. A real joy for some would be to make you so upset you broke into tears and left the room. As a professional, you can't afford to do that. Inform students of your intent calmly; never let them see you sweat. Don't threaten or bluff; know your authority and use it wisely. Remember that "this too shall pass" (unless you make it worse, then it will go on and on).
- *Gradually escalate consequences.* Don't come down suddenly on a student like a ton of bricks. Consequences should be necessary restraints or a natural result of the student's behavior. Penalties should involve restitution, not contrived make-work activities such as sweeping the floor as punishment for cheating.

Self-Observation by Students

If you sense a student doesn't mean to cause a problem but simply isn't aware enough to monitor his or her own behavior, you might want to have the student keep a record of his or her behavior in class. Figure 10.1 presents a form you could use.

Self-Evaluation of Cooperative Learning

Until further notice, you will be required to keep a self-evaluation of cooperative learning. Cooperative learning is based on these categories:

Organization: having study materials, keeping an organized notebook, keeping the Grade Record Sheet up to date

Participation: effective class participation, attention in class, note taking, willingness to recite, cooperation with class rules

Partnerships: working with lab partners (neither dominating nor withdrawing) and working with class partner (helping partner get caught up in case of absence)

Group Dynamic: positive group dynamic including self-monitoring (not interrupting, dominating, or remaining 100 percent silent), and facilitating discussion

Readiness to Learn: punctuality, attendance, having homework ready on time, prompt conferencing with teacher when confused or behind

Write a complete sentence on each line describing your behavior for that category.

Date ____________________ Name ______________________________________

ORGANIZATION ____

PARTICIPATION ____

PARTNERSHIPS ____

GROUP DYNAMIC ____

READINESS TO LEARN ____

Fig. 10.1. Self-Evaluation of Cooperative Learning

UNC

Changing Behavior

Sanders: I have to say something more practical about changing behavior other than drawing the student into a conversation about his or her behavior and asking for voluntary compliance. Whether a student displays anger, rudeness, irresponsibility, or impulsiveness, your first task is to call the problem behavior to the student's attention in a depersonalized, calm way and explain why, for the group's sake and for the sake of the student, that behavior X should be changed to behavior Y. Many times students are quite glad to know that the behavior wasn't "cool," and although they don't thank you for calling the matter to their attention, they may change (allowing for a bit of relapse before the change becomes stable). The first obstacle to overcome is getting through the Plexiglas cube that students live in. Remember that to them you're part of the background. Somehow, you must step forward into the foreground.

Written Notice of Disciplinary Action

If the student doesn't respond to your oral instruction, it may be necessary to express yourself in writing. (See figure 10.2 on p. 188.) This will certainly get most students' cooperation. Also, you're providing documentation for administrative purposes that you have taken a positive action to change the behavior. Of course, overuse of this form will deflate its value. Use it when there has been no progress after verbal reprimands.

It is surely evident that school policies vary widely by district and state. It is always necessary to verify that your actions will be supported by the administration and higher authorities. Be clear and firm. Don't bluff, don't act capriciously, and don't go out on a limb by taking drastic measures that may come back to slap you in the face. Don't convey spite or dislike for the child, and you're bound to see progress.

Sanders: If a student is impulsive, he or she needs not only the self-awareness to recognize that the problem behavior is about to occur but the self-control to modify or eliminate that behavior. Here is where behaviorist tools work; in many cases, behavior modification is the surest way to build a positive habit. For the slightest increment of progress, an acknowledgment is made. "Johnny, you were on time today; that's good." After a few occasions of self-restraint by the student, a reward is in order. Reinforcement of the desired behavior is necessary to stabilize it.

Franco: Excuse me, but why should you have to acknowledge that a student has done just what he is supposed to? And giving a reward for ordinary things seems like an awfully complicated and draining way to get kids to sit still and shut up.

Sanders: Hmm. Maybe I've developed my discipline strategy over many years by trying things like ordering kids to sit still and shut up and finding out that it doesn't work; in fact, it will often backfire and create tension and even more headaches. I'm interested in the most efficient way to get the job done. I think the many-small-steps approach works best. As far as thinking a teacher shouldn't have to reward students for doing their job, I offer for consideration the possibility that presuppositions about what should occur can create a lot of stress in you.

Name of student__________________________ Date ____________________

Course Title__________________________ Mr. Sanders' Telephone 432-1234

Notification of Disciplinary Action

This is to notify you that your conduct in class has not been satisfactory in recent days. Below, you will find a list of the infraction(s) that have occurred. Be advised that you have now reached the second step in the disciplinary code. The steps in this code are:

For lesser offenses

1st Offense: Verbal reprimand

2nd Offense: Written notification of offenses

3rd Offense: Removal from class for the rest of the period in which the infraction occurs, and the following class period, with no chance for makeup work. A conference with an administrator will be set up; a contract will be written, when it is appropriate, specifying conditions for continuation in the class; and parents will be notified that credit in the class is at risk.

4th Offense: Conference with administrator and parent to determine why student should be allowed to continue in the class.

5th Offense: Permanent removal from the class.

Lesser offenses include repeated talking after being asked to stop, not paying attention to the lesson, put-downs, dishonesty (including copying homework), making jokes that detract from the lesson, interrupting, pranks, horseplay, or any other behavior that tends to obstruct progress of the lesson or disregards the rights, feelings, or safety of others.

For greater offenses, a student will begin immediately with step 3 or 4, depending on the nature of the offense. Greater offenses include lying, willful disobedience, defiance, fits of temper or sustained outbursts, cheating, stealing, or rude or hostile behavior toward the teacher or a student.

Specific offense(s): ____

Remember, the purpose of the disciplinary code is to ensure the cooperation necessary for maximal learning. Please take the necessary steps to remedy your conduct so that no further steps will be needed.

Parent or guardian signature __________________________________

Fig. 10.2. Notification of Disciplinary Action

Franco: Aren't you just being politically correct? Where's the right of the teacher to teach and not coddle?

Sanders: Well, you'll have to decide what level of nurturing is appropriate for your students. I hasten to add that you need to convey to your students respect and empathy and that you're looking after these young people in a caring spirit. I hope you don't see this as coddling. I feel genuinely good about treating kids with gentleness. You might have a different personal presence and convey a tougher persona. But even if you're tough, the students must feel you care about them and their learning, or they'll resent you and then will take perverse pleasure in tormenting you. You'll play into their scheme. You won't shut off their misbehavior but, instead, drive it underground. Students can create little codes and conspire to make endless mischief. I heard a class brag that they drove a teacher to quit. Just remember, they outnumber you. It takes much less energy to understand the nature of the child and go with the grain as much as possible than to fight it.

Charlene: What about scoldings and punishment in general?

Sanders: Scoldings may be appropriate sometimes, for example, when a boy has tormented a girl to tears after being told to stop, then folds his arms with a smug smile. You need to get through to him. A scolding should not last long (under one minute) and must be clear, informative, and private—out of the sight and earshot of others—not an opportunity to unload your pent-up anger. As for punishment, I believe in applying punishment sparingly, again because it seldom changes behavior. By punishment, I mean deliberately inflicting discomfort, even pain, on someone as a means of registering disapproval of the existing behavior, as opposed to correcting bad behavior. Unless a teacher explains to the student why the *behavior* is unacceptable and does so *without degrading the student* at a personal level, the teacher's effort will almost surely fail to accomplish anything and has a good chance of making the behavior worse. When treated as a matter of *policy*, not *personality*, penalties for cheating or other bad behavior are appropriate, but these penalties should be made clear beforehand. If someone mishandles equipment after being told how to handle it properly, and breaks it, *restitution* (repairing or replacing the item) is called for.

A preferred way to change behavior is to let natural consequences take their course. If a student forgets his or her lunch for the third time, he or she will have to do without. Being hungry or having to mooch off someone else is the natural consequence for that act. If someone is late to school on the day of the field trip, the natural consequence is to be left behind. In using natural consequences, make sure there is no genuine hardship involved and that you don't convey spite. You can convey sympathy for the student who misses the bus, but you don't have to hold up the trip.

Skill Development Activity 10-1: Practicing the Principles of Effective Discipline

Select an appropriate discipline tool to deal with each problem and explain your choice.

1. Bobbie is interested in a mechanical model on display. Bobbie takes it down to play with it and handles it roughly. You caution him not to handle it, because it's a look-at model, not a handling toy. Minutes later, you hear a crash. Bobbie has dropped and broken the model.

2. An older boy teases a smaller boy about his new haircut, which didn't turn out well. You overhear the boys and ask the older boy politely how he would feel if someone made fun of him that way. Later, the boys are fighting again, and you caution them more strongly this time. By afternoon recess, a fight has broken out, and much to your surprise, the older boy has a bloody nose.

3. A bright student seems to spoil every class discussion by blurting out the answer as soon as you ask the question. You have asked the student to raise her hand and wait to be called on before speaking, but she continues to barely wait for the question to be out of your mouth before jumping in with an answer.

4. A student comes to class late repeatedly after lunch, despite your requests and insistence that he be on time. His attitude is basically that *it's not important to me and I won't do it.*

5. You ask a student to please take the microscope out of the cabinet and replace it properly. She explodes and says you should get off her case. "Why is every teacher in this school picking on me?"

6. After your junior English class is over, with the room empty, you speak to a girl for the second time about her talking to classmates at the wrong time and her loud outbursts of laughing and constant chatting instead of doing her work. She looks you directly in the eye and says, "If you don't like something I do, that's your problem, not mine," then coolly walks out even after you ask her to wait.

7. A student says she will come in after school on Monday to get the notes for Wednesday's exam. She doesn't make it on Monday but says she'll be there on Tuesday. She doesn't come in Tuesday. She comes to the exam on Wednesday and says she's not taking the exam because you wouldn't give her the notes.

(See Appendix 4: Comments on Skill Development Activities 10-1 and 10-2 (pp. 209-10) for the author's ideas for dealing with these situations.)

Skill Development Activity 10-2: More Practice with Effective Discipline

Use role-playing to illustrate these situations and discuss how each can be turned into a teaching opportunity. (See Appendix 4 (pp. 209-10) for author's responses.)

1. During a discussion in science of the age of the planet Earth, the teacher mentions that the time of creation was once put by an archbishop at 4004 B.C. Shawn makes a comment about "stupid Christians." After the teacher's reprimands him, Shawn adds, "You must be one of them."

2. During a group project, Sandi hauls off and slugs Baron, one of the football team's linemen. The teacher speaks to Sandi. Sandi claims Baron called her a dumb broad.

3. The teacher finds that Jon's homework paper is identical in every detail (including the placement of work on the page) to Arthur's homework paper. When asked about it, Jon makes up an implausible excuse. The evidence is presented, but Jon holds firm.

4. It is now four weeks before the end of the semester. Amber is failing math. She has turned in only four of nine homework papers, even though most of them were done partially or totally in class. When Amber is contacted about her situation, she says, "No offense, but you're a boring teacher. I got an 'A' last year in math because Mr. Awesome was a great teacher."

5. The science teacher finds a broken beaker in the wastebasket and asks Roberto—the student with a sheepish look on his face—if he knows anything about it. Roberto says, "Why did you pick out me?" The teacher gives a reasonable nonaccusative response and says that whoever broke the beaker should put it in the container for broken glass and let the teacher know. Roberto says he's going to tell his social worker that the teacher is racist and always harassing him.

6. The teacher has observed Fiona handing out Halloween candy to several students around her, and says, looking right at Fiona that all students are to put away all food, including candy. A moment later, Fiona hands a candy bar to a boy beside her. The teacher approaches Fiona and reports seeing her give the candy to the other student. Fiona flatly denies having had any candy at all.

GRADING AND ASSESSMENTS

Sanders: Grading has limitations as a learning and assessment tool. Although grading is one form of holding students accountable for what they learn, scored assessments can be overused. Excessive grading can create anxiety, which interferes with learning. Too little grading can make a course seem like a joke. The problem for the teacher is to develop an assessment system that provides feedback and indicates the level of achievement without de-motivating students.

You heard me say before that grading and assessments should not be tacked on at the end of a unit but should be organically connected. An instructional unit is a *tout ensemble*, meaning that all parts of your plan affect all other parts. The learning objectives, student tasks, teacher presentations, and assessments must be developed together. Designing anything from automobiles to software is a cyclic process. Designing educational activities produces better results when the components of the system have a chance to interplay and rebalance. The means of assessment should be built into the unit plan from the start. Once the entire unit plan has been developed, the teacher presents the tasks or assignments.

The tasks, once chosen, must be clearly defined and explained with due consideration for constraints. Guidelines for creative assignments must be stated explicitly and clearly, as creative assignments are a new type of assignment to most students, and this makes students more inclined to freelance. Emphasize that using creativity does not grant total freedom to produce any desired product. The idea is to use creativity to organize factual content, not replace it. Grading an integrative student project, one with both factual content and creativity, might focus on the content and evidence of using steps in the creative process. In other words, for the model of the Coliseum, the grade could be based on the factual accuracy; the accompanying paperwork showing the research; the project design, including intermediate steps; and the time spent on the model, with fewer points going toward the aesthetic quality of the product itself (which may require manual dexterity, practice with the artistic medium, etc., to look really good).

Assessments in General

Charlene: You know, I don't see how grades got started in the first place. Why is everything so point-oriented. Is it like money; you just have to have more?

Sanders: Throughout much of the twentieth century, grading has been used as a scheme to sort people out for future careers and to identify those individuals suited for intellectual pursuits and leadership, others for management, and the bottom of the curve for manual labor. But in the age when America has seen her smokestack industries and many manufacturing interests move offshore, the basis of the economy has changed from manufacturing to service. The old way of schooling won't fit the needs of the new global economy. Students must demonstrate a broad range of abilities and skills, not just bookish knowledge and the ability to score well on pencil-and-paper tests. All the workforce, starting with today's students, must be provided incentives to continue to enlarge their mental abilities and develop teamwork skills to respond to a changing economic climate. Furthermore, much of the existing grading process is not helpful to learning; it creates needless anxiety, which blocks true learning.

Prescott: Do you think we should go to ungraded instruction?

Sanders: No. But a teacher needs a variety of assessment tools to evaluate a broad range of what is learned. We have already seen Bloom's version of the types of knowledge the student may be asked to learn: facts, skills, concepts, applications, principles, and evaluating. Each of these types of learning requires a different mode of assessment. Traditionally, all kinds of learning have been assessed by means of pencil-and-paper tests. Of course, students can do well on an exam and not have the capacity to apply their knowledge, which raises the question if it is true learning.

Charlene: Other than motivation, what is the purpose of assessments, anyway?

Sanders: The purpose of an assessment is to determine if learning has taken place and, if so, how much. Assessments provide feedback to the teacher on the effectiveness of the instruction—whether the material presented got across to the students—and how well the class learned. Obviously, students need to be held accountable for the quality, thoroughness, and timeliness of their work. At the same time, pencil-and-paper tests as a means of assessing student work are often not providing information about the learning, and they may even be a false kind of assessment in that they appear to measure something that they are not. Here are a few examples of nonpencil-and-paper assessments.

Demonstration of a Skill

Students perform a given task, for example, using a piece of lab equipment. Students can do a *walk-about* assessment, in which they move around the room identifying numbered specimens or performing tasks with equipment. To demonstrate writing skill, students actually produce a logical, error-free letter to the editor or a government official. Students may be asked to go to the board and make a drawing, manipulate props, place concept words on index cards into a flowchart, give an oral explanation, tutor another student, or build a model. In biology this could mean taking all the internal organs out of the human torso model and having the student replace them correctly. An assessment for the skill may be simply observing that it was completed at a satisfactory level.

An Assessment Grid

The *assessment grid* is a useful tool for keeping track of skills demonstrated. Instead of averaging a set of somewhat arbitrary numbers to obtain a grade, the teacher can compile a skill list and a set-up grid with the skills listed on one edge and the students' names listed on the other. To complete the course requirements (and avoid a grade of "incomplete" at the end of the semester) the student must demonstrate all the skills on the assessment grid at a satisfactory level or above. The grid contains a list of each specific skill the student is to demonstrate. The teacher observes and notes whether the skills are present or absent. In the elaborated version of the assessment grid, adjectives replace numbers, for example, *satisfactory, more than satisfactory,* and *superior.* In some cases the list might be expanded to include these adjectives: *no evidence, minimal, partial, complete, irrelevant, issue mentioned, minimal evidence cited, supporting evidence evident,* and *evidence substantial and elaborated.*

Oral Quizzes

The teacher asks individual students about their work on a one-to-one basis. This format can work well in assessing makeup work.

Manipulatives

Manipulatives are a fun way for students to demonstrate understanding. For example, the student is asked to organize a set of 3" x 5" cards with vocabulary or other material into some logical arrangement. The student keeps practicing until he or she can do the task. Other manipulatives apply to students of all age groups: study prints, floor cards, or magnetic-strip backed cards. Cards hung with colored clothespins on a long piece of twine stretched across the room can also be used by students to actively demonstrate understanding.

Portfolios

Each student collects samples of his or her work into a packet, folder, or computer file documenting progress through stages of development and final product. Although this approach to assessment has become increasingly popular in recent years, it too has advantages and disadvantages. The advantages are that it clearly shows a diversity of work—not just pencil-and-paper products—and reflects growth over a long period of time. At the beginning of the year the student can set goals and state what products he or she will produce to prove that these goals were met. This *planning and proving* process engages the student as a full partner in his or her own education.

On an even more comprehensive scale, software is already available for producing portfolios that document a whole school career. A student in first grade sets up an electronic portfolio complete with scanned pictures and physical measurements. Compositions of various types of work, even artwork, can be scanned in and kept on one disk. In succeeding years, the portfolio is enlarged all the way through graduation. Of course, this convenient type of record not only demonstrates skills achieved but serves as a great self-esteem builder and helps the formation of one's identity.

The big question for portfolios is what gets put into the folder or file and what requirements, if any, apply to it. Without requirements, students can fill a portfolio with what they already do well and avoid what they need to work on. For a low-motivation student, the portfolio might represent the few quality items produced, not the true picture of what is typical.

A smaller, but still important question concerns how the portfolios are managed and stored over the long term, maintained, and—yes—graded. Most teachers find it difficult enough to make time during the school year to develop new curriculum and reflect on one's strengths and weakness the way each and every teacher should. Having to oversee and assess a class's portfolios presents a time problem that must be addressed before portfolios become standard assessment tools. Portfolios are a valuable supplement to the student's record but not an adequate record by themselves for either a course or a school career.

Journals

A written journal kept by students over the semester provides a cumulative, anecdotal record of activities done, student self-observation, and milestones accomplished. Students should understand who will read the journal and how it will be used as an assessment.

Exhibits, Models, and Other Tangible Products

When students work many hours making a sky map, or a kaleidoscope, or a model of the cross-section of a typical leaf, they incorporate many process steps along the way. If such a project is to be graded, the teacher should distribute an assignment sheet telling which of these process steps will be graded (e.g., the research, the care and effort made evident, or the general appearance). An oral quiz on the project or perhaps an oral report to the class may be appropriate.

Walk-Abouts

Students move from station to station to examine a specimen, name a piece of equipment, or interpret a photograph. Walk-abouts are an excellent way to assess skill with a physical object, but if the assessment is to be a solo work, a management plan is required beforehand to ensure a smooth flow of students from station to station and eliminate opportunities to cheat.

Ungraded Practice

Prescott: You know, I think ungraded practice is a good idea for certain uses. I mean, like for doing physics problems in a new unit. Should you really be graded for everything? How are you supposed to learn how to do it *before* you do it?

Charlene: Yes, and in English, too, it really has potential. Nothing causes creativity to dry up faster than grading a creative project or performance without providing opportunities to improve them beforehand. I went to a theater workshop where we had small groups, *rehearsal circles*, with four or fewer students, to practice in a low-risk setting. After we practiced and helped each other, we gave our presentations to the larger group. It really helped.

Sanders: Yes. If student creativity is to thrive, it must be nurtured in an environment where it is not too risky to try a wild idea and have it fail.

Franco: Now just a second. . . .

Prescott: As usual, Franco's the skeptic.

Sanders: Well, that's OK. Someone should be. Go on, Franco.

Franco: I don't think I could have learned to write by having the teacher check off my paragraphing skills.

Giving Helpful Feedback Without Grading

Sanders: OK, but is grading the answer?

Franco: Part of it.

Sanders: Why?

Franco: For feedback.

Sanders: How is grading related to feedback? Can't you have feedback without grading?

Franco: I don't see how.

Sanders: The goal for a teacher is to help the student produce a better product. If not a better version of the same product, then a better product the next time. So a teacher can give coached practice either verbally or on the work handed in.

E. J.: But that sounds like a lot of work.

Sanders: You handle the same project three times rather than handle three different projects. In terms of bookkeeping, it's a little *less* involved. Otherwise, it's the same time spent.

Giving Feedback for Creative Work

Charlene: But creative writing needs much more than help with construction. How can you teach things like creativity?

Sanders: The evaluator should concentrate on giving honest reactions to the project. As King Henry says in *A Man for All Seasons*, "For we artists, though we love praise, yet we love truth better." The goal for the educator is to give support and fair criticism to students, and help them improve their work. This can often be accomplished by asking questions: "Is this meant to be this way?" "I'm not sure what this means; could it be expanded with more specifics?" An evaluator should not come to the project just as it is being finished and then suggest how to redo the whole project according to a different premise or whole new energy. If the teacher is there at all stages giving constructive feedback, the student will not have the awful feeling of anxiety-induced creative block. Rather than direct the student toward a teacher-initiated idea, the teacher should inquire about less effective parts and ask what makes them so. Then let the student introduce improvements or suggest his or her new courses of action.

Peer Criticism

E. J.: Can't students help each other get better?

Sanders: Yes, but peer criticism is not appropriate for all age groups and settings. It requires a high degree of group solidarity and restraint. When it is appropriate, definite guidelines must be established; these guidelines must be rehearsed (perhaps through role-playing), and they must be modeled and enforced by the teacher. In teaching students to give constructive feedback to each other, stress the importance of helpful, not fault-finding language to state the critique. Near neutral wording is vital, not "you should" but "I felt," not "this didn't work" but "my reaction was." Courtesy requires granting the creator his or her premise; that is, evaluators should accept that the project was worth doing. Because it is easier for anyone to accept nondogmatic guidance, peer coaches should be trained to give honest, but gentle feedback on their reactions and refrain from making unsolicited suggestions. The writer or artist should be the one to come up with ways to improve the work.

Assessments for Creative Work

Rita: I hope to find a job teaching art. There's no content to judge as there is with history assignments, and if *I* assign the subject matter of the work, I'm infringing on the student's creativity. How can I grade art?

Sanders: Yes, you're right, Rita. Creative work for the history classroom is integrative, that is, it has a content and a process as well as a product.

Grading Guides or Rubrics

Franco: But if you can score gymnastics, diving, and figure skating, why can't you score art? They do it all the time in galleries. Even cooking is judged by panels of expert judges who tend to agree fairly closely.

Sanders: For gymnastics and diving, manuals assign degrees of difficulty for each stunt, as well as the compulsory elements. The panel of judges estimates the closeness of fit of a stunt or routine with the established guidelines. In the instance in which a creative project is to be scored, you can hand out guidelines as to format and elements to include. Adopting the objective approach allows creative works to be fairly judged at least on the stated criteria. For this to happen, you will need a grading guide or rubric, which can take different forms, and should be customized to fit the project. A rubric is simply a formalized structure with clearly delineated categories and criteria for evaluation. The best way to reduce the degree of subjectivity of grading is to use a scoring system with either prose descriptors or checklists of contents. It may be helpful to use many categories with a small point value attached to each. This allows the teacher to count up points rather than estimate quality, thus, removing the appearance of arbitrariness. For judging novice creators, it is better to assign more points for the creative elements being present and fewer points for the way they fit together to produce a desired effect. Even the great artists have difficulty producing a unified work, and novices will likely seem inept at matching, balancing, and proportioning their final product.

Levels of Creativity

For more original creative projects, such as those in your art class, it is important first to establish on what level the creative project is being done. The purpose of the project depends on the level of creativity that it involves: expressive, productive, innovative, ingenious, or emergent (Taylor 1975).

For *expressive creativity*, the rationale for doing the project is solely the joy of it. Assessing how enjoyable the project was might involve oral feedback or a survey.

Productive creativity focuses on completing the project, meaning that all its elements are intact. To assess this kind of project, a checklist of completed items can be employed. The assessor rates each element in the project on an *evident/not evident* basis, perhaps with brief comments. This approach is especially important if nonfiction content has been assigned. Assessment focuses in large part on the accuracy and completeness of the content.

Innovative creativity refers to the combining of existing elements in a new way. Any art or writing project involves selecting familiar elements and reorganizing them into a new combination. In art this means using techniques skillfully and blending elements into a pleasing whole. Because the combination is new, not the elements, assessment can focus on the proportions, balance, tempo, and rhythm of the mix. Projects such as inventions are judged on use of materials and how efficiently they accomplish their stated goal. For example, science fair projects or cultural fair projects illustrate innovative creativity because they take existing elements (e.g., the scientific cycle, household materials, natural samples) and combine them in unique ways. The project can be judged by how clearly formed the hypothesis or concept is and how clearly the results are presented.

Ingenious creativity involves coming up with a new element. This level of creativity includes original research or a wholly new device, process, intellectual scheme, or genre of art. In both science and art, panels of experts review work and determine the level of quality. In advanced classes, peer review could be part of the assessment process.

Emergent creativity refers to a new idea or device that so changes the situation that a whole new system is required to accommodate it. The automobile, computer chip, and birth control pill are inventions of this type. The automobile changed transportation but in the process reduced the population density in cities. Likewise, the computer chip and the Pill have changed the way we live. Concepts such as the expanding universe altered completely our picture of the world and even our identity as a species. Incorporating the notion of human rights in U.S. foreign policy has changed international relations forever.

Franco: I can go along with your levels of creativity up to a point, but, whoa, do you really think anyone in your classroom is going to come up with something so new it will really bring about a transformation?

Sanders: Actually, yes. But I'd like to postpone the answer to your question for a bit.

Conclusions About Assessments

Sanders: I leave you with a brief list of questions to ask yourself in designing a unit and selecting a means of assessment.

- Does the task fit the assessment and *vice versa?*
- Does the assessment reflect the content and skill objectives stated?
- Will this task or activity be scored or unscored?

- Could the assessment be interdisciplinary, for example, a letter to the editor about re-cycling?
- Does the assessment itself have some positive value as a worthwhile learning experience?
- Could the assessment be done as a formalized oral response rather than written one?

IMPLEMENTING CREATIVE TEACHING

Sanders: Now we've come to the end of our time together, and I can say it's been really stimulating. I've gotten many new ideas from you and have great faith in your ability to develop your own teaching styles. There are no ready-to-wear teaching models, only custom-tailored ones. You have to combine the best elements and skills from others with your special gifts; you have to adapt and blend, and in a word, create new teaching. The best teaching model to employ is *yours* when you have developed skill in the practice of creative teaching. Here is where you must find your own creativity and make it work for you and for your students.

To answer Franco's question, emergent creativity—the kind that brings about something so entirely new that it transforms the whole situation—can come from *you*, the teacher. If you work at creative teaching, at first you will make progress on Levels 1 and 2: expressive and productive creativity. In time you will begin to discover ways to be innovative and ingenious. And someday with luck, you'll suddenly feel different about teaching. You will have rediscovered wonder. It will totally transform your classroom and make a real difference in your life and in the lives of your students. And some night in that profound moment between turning off the lamp on your night table and falling asleep, you'll reflect on your life with a smile and realize that teaching is the most rewarding and noble profession in the world.

REFERENCES

Benchmarks for Scientific Literacy. 1993. American Association for the Advancement of Science Project 2061. New York: Oxford University Press.

Colorado Model Content Standards for Geography. 1995. Denver: Colorado State Board of Education.

Curriculum and Evaluation Standards for School Mathematics. 1989. Reston, VA: National Council of Teachers of Mathematics.

Nietzsche, Freidrich. 1966. The Birth of Tragedy out of the Spirit of Music. In *Basic Writings of Nietzsche*. Translated and edited by Walter Kaufmann. New York, Random House.

Taylor, I. A. 1975. A Retrospective View of Creativity Investigation. In *Perspectives in Creativity*. Edited by I. A. Taylor and J. W. Getzels. Chicago: Aldine.

FURTHER READING

Dreikurs, Rudolph. 1964. *Children, the Challenge*. New York: Duell, Sloan and Pearce.

Science for All Americans. 1990. American Association for the Advancement of Science Project 2061. New York: Oxford University Press.

APPENDIX 1: Suggested Readings for Socratic Seminars

GRADES K-3

Joy Adamson, *Born Free*

Aesop's *Fables*

May H. Arbuthnot, compiler, *The Arbuthnot Anthology of Children's Literature*

Pearl Buck, *The Big Wave*

Bennett Cerf, *Bennett Cerf's Book of Riddles*

Harold Courtlander, "Janot Cooks for the Emperor" from *Piece of Fire and Other Haitian Tales*

Edward Curtis, *The Girl Who Married the Ghost and Other Tales from the North American Indian*

Hardie Gramatky, *Little Toot*

Rudyard Kipling, *Just So Stories*

Dorothy Kunhardt, *Pat the Bunny*

A. A. Milne, *Winnie the Pooh*

Anno Mitsumasa, *Anno's Journey*

Iona Opie and Peter Opie, eds., *The Oxford Book of Children's Verse* and *The Oxford Nursery Rhyme Book*

Carl Sandburg, *The Sandburg Treasury: Prose and Poetry for Young People*

Jose Marie Sandez-Silva, *The Boy and the Whale*

Maurice Sendak, *In the Night Kitchen* and *Outside over There*

Dr. Seuss, *The Cat in the Hat*, *If I Ran the Zoo*, and *Green Eggs and Ham*

James Thurber, *Many Moons*

Dorothy Van Woerkem, *Hidden Messages*

Uchida Yoshiko, "The Wedding of the Mouse" from *The Sea of Gold and Other Tales of Japan*

GRADES 4-8

Louisa May Alcott, *Little Women*

Isaac Asimov, "The Feeling of Power" from *Nine Tomorrows*

James M. Barrie, *Peter Pan*

Alice Elizabeth Chase, *Looking at Art*

C. S. Forester, *Captain Horatio Hornblower*

Paul Gallico, *The Snow Goose*

E. E. Hale, *The Man Without a Country*

Edith Hamilton, *The Greek Way* and *The Roman Way*

Helen Keller, *The Story of My Life*

Rudyard Kipling, *The Jungle Book*

C. S. Lewis, *The Chronicles of Narnia*

Voltaire, "Micromegas" in *The Portable Voltaire*

GRADES 9-12

Edwin A. Abbott, *Flatland*

Mortimer Adler, *The American Testament*

Aristotle, *Nichomachian Ethics*

Marcus Aurelius, *Meditations*

Frances Bacon, "Of Beauty, " "Of Great Places, " and "Of Youth and Age"

James Baldwin, *The Fire Next Time*

The Declaration of Independence

William Golding, *Lord of the Flies*

J. B. S. Haldane, "On Being the Right Size" in *The World of Mathematics*, vol. 2, edited by James R. Neuman

Alexander Hamilton, *The Federalist Papers*

Martin Luther King Jr., "I Have a Dream" in *The World's Great Speeches*

Plutarch, *The Lives of the Noble Grecians and Romans*

James Thurber, *My World—And Welcome to It*

APPENDIX 2: Multicultural Readings and Authors

BOOKS AND STORIES

Level	Title	Author
pre K-2	*The Legend of the Bluebonnet: An Old Tale of Texas*	Tomie DePaola
pre K-2	*Crow Chief*	Paul Goble
pre K-3	*Iktomi and the Berries*	Paul Goble
K-3	*The Rooster Who Could Understand Japanese*	Yoshiko Uchida
K-3	*Momo's Kitchen*	Taro & Mitsu Yashima
K-3	*Umbrella*	Taro & Mitsu Yashima
K-12	*Lon Po Po: A Red Riding Hood Story from China*	Ed Young
2 & up	*Cyclops*	Leonard Everett Fisher
2 & up	*At the Crossroads*	Rachel Isadora
2 & up	*The King's Equal*	Katherine Paterson
3-6	*Traveling to Tondo: A Tale of the Nkundo of Zaire*	Verna Aardema
3-6	*The Magic Boat*	Demi
3-6	*Everybody Cooks Rice*	Nora Dooley
3-6	*Miko: Little Hunter of the North*	Bruce Donehower
3-6	*Tonight Is Carnival*	Arthur Dorros
3-6	*The Amish*	Doris Faber
3-6	*Irene and the Big, Fine Nickel*	Irene Smalls-Hector
3-6	*Coconut Kind of Day: Island Poems*	Lynn Joseph
3-6	*On the Go*	Ann Morris
3-6	*Further Tales of Uncle Remus*	Julius Lester
3-6	*The Grandchildren of the Incas*	Matti Pitkanen

3-6	*The Golden Cockerel and Other Fairy Tales*	Aleksandr Pushkin
3-6	*Escape from Slavery*	Doreen Rappaport
3-6	*Tar Beach*	Faith Ringgold
3-6	*Tailypo*	Jan Wahl
3-6	*The Fourth Question: A Chinese Tale*	Rosalind Wang
3-6	*All of You Was Singing*	Ed Young
3-8	*El Chino*	Allen Say
3 & up	*Love Flute*	Paul Goble
4-7	*In the Year of the Boar and Jackie Robinson*	Betty Bao Lord
4-12	*The Dark Way: Stories from the Spirit World*	Virginia Hamilton
4-12	*Haroun and the Sea of Stories*	Salmon Rushdie
5-8	*The Land I Lost: Adventures of a Boy in Vietnam*	Nhuong Quang Huynh
5-8	*The Best Bad Thing*	Yoshiko Uchida
5-8	*The Happiest Ending*	Yoshiko Uchida
5-8	*A Jar of Dreams*	Yoshiko Uchida
5-10	*Scorpions*	Walter Dean Myers
5-10	*The Rainbow People*	Laurence Yep
5-12	*The People Could Fly*	Virginia Hamilton
5-12	*Other People's Myths*	Wendy O'Flaherty
6-9	*The Invisible Thread*	Yoshiko Uchida
6-12	*Beauty*	Robin McKinley
6-12	*Now Is Your Time: The African-American Struggle for Freedom*	Walter Dean Myers
6-12	*This Same Sky: A Collection of Poems from Around the World*	Naomi Shihib Nye, ed.
6-12	*Journey Home*	Yoshiko Uchida
7-12	*I Know Why the Caged Bird Sings*	Maya Angelou
7-12	*Celine*	Brock Cole
7-12	*Granny Was a Buffer Girl*	Berlie Doherty
7-12	*The Owl Service*	Alan Garner
7-12	*Fallen Angels*	Walter Dean Myers
7-12	*White Wolf Woman*	Teresa Pijoan

7-12	*Somehow Tenderness Survives: Stories of Southern Africa*	Hazel Rochman
7-12	*The Fat Girl*	Marilyn Sachs
7-12	*Trail of Stones*	Gwen Strauss
8-12	*What Hearts*	Bruce Brooks
9-12	*Weetzie Bat*	Francesca Lia Block
9-12	*Under All Silences: Shades of Love*	Ruth Gordon, comp.
9-12	*The Woman Warrior*	Maxine Hong Kingston
10-12	*Beloved*	Toni Morrison
11 & up	"A Stranger in the Village"	James Baldwin
11 & up	"The Circular Ruins"	Jorge Luis Borges
11 & up	"Last of the Menu Girls"	Denise Chavez
11 & up	"A Religious Conversion, More or Less"	Eldridge Cleaver
11 & up	"Sanchez"	Richard Dokey
11 & up	"Letter from the Birmingham Jail"	Martin Luther King Jr.
11 & up	"The Ones Who Walk Away from Omelas"	Ursula LeGuin
11 & up	*The Labyrinth of Solitude*	Octavio Paz
11 & up	*The Joy Luck Club*	Amy Tan

AUTHORS WHO SPECIALIZE IN PRIMARY BOOKS ABOUT OTHER CULTURES

African American

Ashley Bryan
Jeannette Caines
Donald Crews
Pat Cummings
Valerie Flournoy
Jan Spivey Gilchrist
Nikki Giovanni
Julius Lester
Patricia McKissack
James Ransome

Chinese and Chinese American

Cheng Hou-Tien
Jade Snow Wong
Paul Yee

Latino and Latino American

Alma Flor Ada
George Anacona
Patricia De Garza
Carmen Lomas Garza
Jorge Maestro

Japanese and Japanese American

Satomi Ichikawa
Fumiko Takeshita
Taro Yashima

Vietnamese and Vietnamese American

Quyen Van Duong
Vo-Dinh Mai

Native American

Joseph Bruchac

SELECTED SOURCES FOR MULTICULTURAL READINGS

Andronik, Catherine. May/June 1994. A Sampling of Recent Books That Reflect Our Diversity. *Library Talk* 13–18.

Bodart, Joni Richards. May/June 1964. Talking Multicultural Books. *Library Talk* 12–13.

Harris, Violet, ed. 1993. *Teaching Multicultural Literature in Grades K–12.* Norwood, MA: Christopher Gordon.

Galda, Lee, and Janet Cotter. February 1992. Exploring Cultural Diversity. *Reading Teacher* 45 (6):452–56.

Galda, Lee et al. February 1993. One World, One Family. *Reading Teacher* 46 (5):410–19.

Johnson, Ingrid, and Margaret Macky. November–December 1995. Multicultural Books for Readers 10–18. *The Emergency Librarian* 23 (2):24–30.

Lewis, Valerie. February 1994. The Multicultural Connection. *Instructor* 37–49.

Rochman, Hazel. 1993. *Against Borders: Promoting Books for a Multicultural World.* Chicago: American Library Association.

APPENDIX 3: Preparing Slides and Transparencies from Books

There may be times when you want to use slides and transparencies in teaching creative lessons. You can make slides and transparencies from photographs, but keep in mind that copyright restrictions apply. Copies must not be made to avoid purchase, to sell, or with the intent to build a permanent collection. However, if you own a book and want to blow up a picture to a size large enough for a group of your students to see (and you don't charge them an admission fee to see the slides), making reproductions of those photos is not difficult and should be considered fair use for an educational purpose.

With today's photocopying machines, color transparencies for overheard projectors can be made in a jiffy. The disadvantages are (1) the cost ($2.50 each) and (2) the conditions under which they will be viewed (the relatively bright light of the classroom). If you plan on using just a few transparencies, the convenience factor offsets the cost, but if you plan on using a larger number of transparencies, you'd be better off purchasing Ektachrome slide. The cost per slide is about 50 cents for a roll of 24 exposures and as low as 40 cents (including both film and developing) for a roll of 36 exposures.

If you are new to photography, you may want to first ask your media specialist if someone is available to do the whole process for you. Many media centers are equipped with copy stands, cameras, and lenses; all you provide are the originals to be re-photographed and the film.

Materials Needed

1. A *single lens reflex (SLR) camera* such as a Minolta or Nikon. (Recently I purchased a used Minolta for under $100.) Make sure that it has an onboard light meter and variable shutter speed control.

2. *Close-up rings* or a *macro lens* for close-up work. A regular lens is usually 55 mm, which will not focus to close range.

3. *Ektachrome film.* This kind of film is preferred because it can be developed locally. Kodachrome is fine, except the developing process is patented and only a few labs throughout the country are licensed to use it. Therefore, you have to anticipate at least a week's turnaround time. Be sure to get a film with the word *chrome* in it; otherwise you are not taking slides (positives) but pictures developed from negatives.

4. *Natural light.* I prefer to wait for a sunny day, place the photos to be made into slides in bright sunlight, adjust the camera to the proper exposure and take the shot. Bright sunlight ensures the right color balance. Beware of glare, though, which sometimes will not show up in the viewfinder. Bright but cloudy days produce enough light to get a good picture but not a bright enough light to get a glare. You can achieve this indirect lighting effect in bright sunlight by taking a piece of white poster board or white paper and allowing the light to reflect off the white side onto the picture to be rephotographed. Overcast days, although workable, sometimes do not provide enough light to really saturate the colors, and as a result, the slides look dull. Beware of any kind of indoor lighting. Light from bulbs looks yellow on film, fluorescent light looks blue, and your slides will have an unnatural tint unless you use a correcting filter.

A note about light exposure: Because a light meter averages the light from the entire view, you may have a problem if the photos have a lot of contrast. To solve this problem, take a light meter reading very close to the part of the picture that you want to appear just right (e.g., a face), then back up to the right distance and ignore the light meter, which will say the light is not right. Alternatively, you can take several shots, varying the exposure above and below the average value, then use only the exposure that turns out right.

APPENDIX 4: Comments on Skill Development Activities 10-1 and 10-2

Discipline is not a craft; it is an art that requires reading body language and nonverbal cues and knowing the student's general pattern of behavior. Though your disciplinary style must fit your persona, as a rule, it is better to ask the student questions that will help him or her come to the appropriate realization than to do all the talking.

ACTIVITY 10-1

1. Bobbie is apparently an impulsive boy. First, Bobbie needs to acknowledge verbally all the relevant facts here: he was told not to handle the model, he handled it anyway, and he broke it, though not intentionally. A teacher might ask: Where was his decison point? How might he have behaved differently in this situation? Who should fix or replace the model? Bobbie needs to realize that his impulsive behavior harms himself and others, and he needs to accept responsibility for fixing the damage he did.

2. The children have worked out a solution to the situation themselves, but not within official limits. A teacher cannot ignore this fight for several reasons, one of which is the necessity of maintaining evenhandedness. However, I would be inclined toward administering the smallest reasonable consequence.

3. After a short conversation stating exactly what is expected and why, the teacher could assign this obviously bright student the task of keeping a daily "Self-Observation of Cooperative Learning" log for at least a week. At that point the teacher could again confer with the student concerning her observations and progress.

4. The student knows the expectation of punctuality but as yet is not motivated to act on this knowledge. A behavior contract could be set up specifying the consequence of repeated offenses. Confronting the undertone of defiance at this stage might provoke even more of it. If an outburst of defiance occurs, address it by having a conference with the student, then setting up a behavior contract if necessary.

5. If the teacher has a good relationship with the student, the teacher should talk privately with her after she has calmed down and ask what is bothering her. Alternatively, the teacher could talk with the school counselor.

6. This girl's behavior is so inappropriate and defiant that the Dean of Students should be contacted right away and the student not permitted back into class until a disciplinary conference has been held to remedy the problem. Her presence in class will create pervasive tension that will undermine the classroom atmosphere.

7. Something deep is probably bothering this student. In talking to her privately, the teacher should review the relevant facts and make sure she agreed about what was said, being careful not to become argumentative. In the conversation with her, if the teacher senses an opportunity to ask what the real problem is, he or she should follow through. Otherwise, consult with the student's counselor and postpone any decision about the test until more information is available.

ACTIVITY 10-2

1. A ground rule concerning no put-downs has presumably already been stated. The teacher should restate the rule, the reason for it, and the consequence for another offense, perhaps working one-on-one with the student in the hall.

2. Clear rules concerning no put-downs or slugging should be stated, and a consequence for other such offenses made clear.

3. Set up times later to talk with each student. This allows the students time to worry about what you're going to do. Before going into the meeting with the students, make photocopies of everything and discuss the situation with the Dean of Students to ensure support. Meet with the least guilty student first but don't play the students against each other. In the conference avoid accusations or a hostile, judgmental tone. State that you expect honesty. Ask for an explanation. Make confessing as easy as possible, and if you get a confession, praise the honest behavior, making it clear that a confession does not absolve cheating. If the students don't confess—many never do—implement an approriate penalty matter-of-factly, without a scolding. Make clear the consequences of future similar behavior.

4. Presumably, Amber has not taken advantage of your offers to help, and her parents have been notified of her failure in writing and preferably by phone as well. Amber is goading you; ignore the bait. Don't condescend. Perhaps you can share a sympathetic anecdote from your own schooling and emphasize the eventual, if not immediate, value of learning the material. Ask if passing means anything to her and point out the consequences of failing that she may not recognize. Specify what is needed to pass and ask if she is willing to do these things. If not, hold your ground; this is her problem.

5. Contact the social worker and find out what is behind this behavior that is clearly out of proportion to the situation. Avoid any debate, especially in front of other students.

6. Talk to Fiona's mother. Fiona's lying is probably not limited to school. You and the mother together can probably come up with a plan to help Fiona admit to her behavior and begin to monitor it.

REFERENCES

Abra, Jock. 1988. *Assaulting Parnassus: Theoretical Views of Creativity*. Lanham, MD: University Press of America.

Adams, James L. 1974. *Conceptual Blockbusting: A Guide to Better Ideas*. San Francisco: W. H. Freeman.

Adler, Mortimer. 1981. *Six Great Ideas*. New York: Collier.

———. 1982. *The Paideia Proposal: An Educational Manifesto*. New York: Collier.

———. 1983. *Paideia: Problems and Possibilities*. New York: Collier.

———. 1984. *Paideia Program: An Educational Syllabus*. New York: Collier.

Allen, Steve. 1992. *Meeting of Minds* series. Public Broadcasting Service. Dove Audio audiotapes.

Amabile, Teresa. 1983. *The Social Psychology of Creativity*. New York: Springer-Verlag.

Amabile, Teresa, and Beth Hennessey. 1988. The Conditions of Creativity. In *The Nature of Creativity: Contemporary Psychological Perspectives*. Edited by Robert J. Sternberg. New York: Press Syndicate of the University of Cambridge.

Andronik, Catherine. May/June 1994. A Sampling of Recent Books That Reflect Our Diversity. *Library Talk* 13–18.

Arieti, Silvano. 1976. *Creativity: The Magic Synthesis*. New York: Basic Books.

Ausubel, David. 1960. The Use of Advance Organizers in the Learning and Retention of Meaningful Verbal Material. *Journal of Educational Psychology* 51:267-72.

Barron, Frank. 1952. The Psychology of the Creative Writer. In *The Creative Process*. Edited by B. Ghiselin. New York: New American Library.

———. 1967. The Psychology of the Creative Writer. In *Explorations in Creativity*. Edited by R. L. Mooney and T. A. Razik. New York: Harper & Row.

———. 1976. The Psychology of Creativity. In *The Creativity Question*. Edited by Albert Rothenburg and Carl R. Hausman. Durham, NC: Duke University Press.

Benchmarks for Scientific Literacy. 1993. American Association for the Advancement of Science Project 2061. New York: Oxford University Press.

Berkowitz, L. 1964. *Development of Motivation and Values in Children*. New York: Basic Books.

Beyer, Barry. 1978. Conducting Moral Discussions in the Classroom. In *Readings in Moral Education*. Edited by Peter Scharf. Minneapolis, MN: Winston Press.

Bloom, Benjamin. 1956. *Taxonomy of Educational Objectives: Handbook I: Cognitive Domain*. New York: David McKay.

———. 1976. *Human Characteristics and School Learning*. New York: McGraw-Hill.

Bodart, Joni Richards. May/June 1964. Talking Multicultural Books. *Library Talk* 12–13.

Bolt, Robert. 1960. *A Man for All Seasons*. New York: Random House.

Brooks, Jacqueline Grennon, and Martin G. Brooks. 1993. *In Search of Understanding: The Case for Constructivist Classrooms*. Alexandria, VA: Association for Supervision and Curriculum Development.

Bower, G. H. 1981. Mood and Memory. *American Psychologist* 36:129-48.

Coles, Robert. 1989. *The Call of Stories: Teaching and the Moral Imagination.* Boston: Houghton Mifflin.

Colorado Model Content Standards for Geography. 1995. Denver: Colorado State Board of Education.

Conroy, Pat. 1972. *The Water Is Wide.* New York: Dell.

Crutchfield, Richard. 1967. Instructing the Individual in Creative Thinking. In *Explorations in Creativity.* Edited by R. L. Mooney and T. A. Razik. New York: Harper & Row.

———. 1973. The Creative Process. In *Creativity: Theory and Research.* Edited by Morton Bloomberg. New Haven, CT: College and University Press.

Csikszentmihalyi, M. 1990. *Flow: The Psychology of Optimum Experience.* Grand Rapids, MI: Harper & Row.

cummings, e e. 1991. *Complete Poems: 1904-1962.* Edited by George J. Firmage. New York: Liveright.

Curriculum and Evaluation Standards for School Mathematics. 1989. Reston, VA: National Council of Teachers of Mathematics.

Cutter, Mary Ann G., and others. 1992. *Mapping and Sequencing the Human Genome: Science, Ethics, and Public Policy.* Colorado Springs, CO: BSCS and the American Medical Association.

Davis, Gary A., and Margaret A. Thomas. 1989. *Effective Schools and Effective Teachers.* Boston: Allyn & Bacon.

deBono, Edward. 1985. *Six Thinking Hats.* Boston: Little, Brown.

———. 1992. *Serious Creativity.* New York: Harper Business Books.

Dewey, John. 1938, 1963. *Experience and Education.* New York: Collier.

Dreikurs, Rudolph. 1964. *Children, the Challenge.* New York: Duell, Sloan and Pearce.

Dubrovin, Vivian. 1994. *Storytelling for the Fun of It: A Handbook for Children.* Masonville, CO: Storycraft.

Dworkin, Gerald. Analyzing Ethical Problems. In *Hard Choices.* Boston: Office of Radio and Television Learning.

Eastman, Arthur E., ed. 1984. *The Norton Reader: An Anthology of Expository Prose.* 6th ed. New York: W. W. Norton.

Einstein, Albert. 1954. On Education. In *Ideas and Opinions.* [Written in 1936.] Edited by Carl Seelig and others. New York: Dell.

Elkind, David. 1970. *Children and Adolescents: Interpretive Essays on Jean Piaget.* New York: Oxford University Press.

Erickson, Lois V. 1978. The Development of Women: An Issue of Justice. In *Readings in Moral Education.* Minneapolis, MN: Winston Press.

Field, Syd. 1982. *Screenplay: The Foundations of Screenwriting.* New York: Dell.

Filley, Alan C. 1975. *Interpersonal Conflict Resolution.* Glenview, IL: Scott, Foresman.

Fraenkel, Jack R. 1978. The Kohlberg Bandwagon: Some Reservations. In *Readings in Moral Education.* Edited by Peter Scharf. Minneapolis, MN: Winston Press.

Franck, Frederick. 1973. *The Zen of Seeing.* New York: Random House.

Freud, Sigmund. 1958. *On Creativity and the Unconscious: Papers on the Psychology of Art, Literature, Love, Religion.* New York: Harper & Row.

———. 1960. Wit and Its Relation to the Unconscious. In *The Comic in Theory and Practice.* Edited by Jack Enck and others. Englewood Cliffs, NJ: Prentice-Hall.

Gagne, Robert. 1965. *Conditions of Learning.* New York: Holt, Rinehart & Winston.

Galda, Lee, and Janet Cotter. February 1992. Exploring Cultural Diversity. *Reading Teacher* 45 (6):452–56.

Galda, Lee, and others. February 1993. One World, One Family. *Reading Teacher* 46 (5):410–19.

Gardner, Howard. 1982. *Art, Mind, and Brain: A Cognitive Approach to Creativity*. New York: Basic Books.

———. 1993. *Multiple Intelligences: The Theory in Practice*. New York: Basic Books.

Gardner, John. 1977. *On Moral Fiction*. New York: Basic Books.

Getzels, J. V., and M. Csikszentmihalyi. 1975. From Problem-Solving to Problem-Finding. In *Perspectives in Creativity*. Edited by I. A. Taylor and J. V. Getzels. Chicago: Aldine.

Gilligan, Carol. 1982. *In a Different Voice: Psychological Theory and Women's Development*. Cambridge, MA: Harvard University Press.

Gillispie, Charles Coulston, ed. 1970. *Dictionary of Scientific Biography*. New York: Charles Scriber's Sons.

Goleman, Daniel, P. Kaufman, and M. Ray. 1992. *The Creative Spirit*. New York: E. P. Dutton.

Hamachek, Don E. 1968. *Motivation in Teaching and Learning*. Washington, DC: National Education Association.

Hardy, Barbara N. 1975. *Teller and Listeners: The Narrative Imagination*. London: Althone Press.

Harris, Violet J., ed. 1993. *Teaching Multicultural Literature in Grades K-8*. Norwood, MA: Christopher Gordon.

Hery, Nancy Duffy. 1996. *Drama That Delivers: Real-Life Problems, Student Solutions*. Englewood, CO: Teacher Ideas Press.

Highet, Gilbert. 1950. *The Art of Teaching*. New York: Vintage Books.

Hoskin, Michael. 1971. *The Mind of the Scientist*. New York: Taplinger.

Jackson, Philip W. 1993. *The Moral Life of Schools*. San Francisco: Jossey-Bass.

Johnson, Ingrid, and Margaret Macky. November–December 1995. Multicultural Books for Readers 10-18. *The Emergency Librarian* 23 (2):24–30.

Johnstone, Keith. 1979. *Impro: Improvisation and the Theater*. New York: Theater Arts Books.

Joyce, Bruce, and Marsha Weil. 1986. *Models of Teaching*. 3d ed. Englewood Cliffs, NJ: Prentice-Hall.

Jung, Carl G. 1957. *The Undiscovered Self*. New York: Mentor.

Kamerman, Sylvia E., ed. 1992. *Plays of Great Achievers*. Boston: Plays.

Karplus, Robert. 1964. The Science Curriculum Improvement Study—Report to the Piaget Conference. *Journal of Research in Science Teaching* 2 (3):236-400.

Kase-Polisinsi, Judith, and Barbara Spector. Improvised Teaching: A Tool for Teaching Science. In *Youth Theater Journal* 7 (1):15–22.

Kierkegaard, Soren. 1940. *Stages on Life's Way*. Trans. by Walter Lowrie. Princeton, NJ: Princeton University Press.

Kleinke, Chris L. 1978. *Self-Perception: The Psychology of Personal Awareness*. San Francisco: W. H. Freeman.

Kohlberg, Lawrence. 1971. From Is to Ought: How to Commit the Naturalistic Fallacy and Get Away with It in the Study of Moral Development. In *Cognitive Development and Epistemology*. Edited by T. Mischel. New York: Academic Press.

———. 1978a. The Cognitive-Developmental Approach to Education. In *Readings in Moral Education*. Edited by Peter Scharf. Minneapolis, MN: Winston Press.

———. 1978b. The Moral Atmosphere of the School. In *Readings in Moral Education*. Minneapolis, MN: Winston Press.

———. 1987. The Cognitive-Developmental Approach to Moral Education. In *Value Theory and Education*. Malabar, FL: Robert Kreiger.

Kubie, Lawrence. 1967. Blocks to Creativity. In *Explorations in Creativity*, Edited by R. L. Mooney and T. A. Razik. New York: Harper & Row.

La Fay, Howard. January 1962. Easter Island and Its Mysterious Monuments. *National Geographic* 121 (1).

Labinowicz, Ed. 1980. *The Piaget Primer*. Menlo Park, CA: Addison-Wesley.

Lajos, Egri. 1960. *The Art of Dramatic Writing*. New York: Simon & Schuster.

Lallier, Katherine Grimes, and Nancy Robinson Marino. 1997. *The Persona Book: Curriculum-Based Enrichment for Educators*. Englewood, CO: Teacher Ideas Press.

Lazarus, R. 1991. *Emotion and Adaptation*. Oxford: Oxford University Press.

Lewis, Valerie. February 1994. The Multi-Cultural Connection. *Instructor* 103 (6):37–49.

Lickona, Thomas. 1991. *Educating for Character: How Our Schools Can Teach Respect and Responsibility*. New York: Bantam Books.

Lincoln, Wanda, and Murray Suid. 1986. *The Teacher's Quotation Book: Little Lessons in Learning*. Palo Alto, CA: Dale Seymour Publications.

Lomboroso, Cesare. [1864]/1976. Genius and Insanity. In *The Creativity Question*. Edited by Albert Rothenburg and Carl R. Hausman. Durham, NC: Duke University Press.

Lozanov, Gregorii. 1978. *Suggestology and Outlines of Suggestopedeia*. New York: Gordon and Breach.

Luria, Alexandr. 1976. *Cognitive Development: Its Cultural and Social Foundations*. Cambridge, MA: Harvard University Press.

Maslow, Abraham. 1964. *Religions, Values, and Peak Experiences*. New York: Penguin Books.

———. 1967. The Creative Attitude. In *Explorations in Creativity*. Edited by R. L. Mooney and T. A Razik. New York: Harper & Row.

May, Rollo. 1975. *The Courage to Create*. New York: Bantam Books.

Masters, Edgar Lee. 1963. *Spoon River Anthology*. [Written in 1944.] New York: Macmillan.

Masters, J., R. Barden, and M. Ford. 1979. Affective States, Expressive Behavior, and Learning in Children. *Journal of Personality and Social Psychology* 37:380-90.

McPherson, John. 1993. *High School Isn't Pretty*. Kansas City, MO: Andrews and McMeel.

Montessori, Maria. 1964. *The Montessori Method*. [Written in 1912.] New York: Schocken Books.

———. 1965. *Dr. Montessori's Own Handbook*. [Written in 1915.] New York: Schocken Books.

Mussen, Paul, and Nancy Eisenberg. 1977. *The Roots of Caring, Sharing, and Helping: The Development of Pro-Social Behavior in Children*. San Francisco: W. H. Freeman.

Nation at Risk, A: The Imperative of Educational Reform: A Report to the Nation and Secretary of Education, United States Department of Education. 1983. Washington, DC: The Commission.

Nietzsche, Friedrich. 1966. The Birth of Tragedy out of the Spirit of Music. In *Basic Writings of Nietzsche*. Translated and edited by Walter Kaufman. New York: Random House.

Noll, James William, ed. 1995. *Taking Sides: Clashing Views on Controversial Educational Views*. Guilford, CT: Duskin.

Olson, Robert W. 1980. *The Art of Creative Thinking: A Practical Guide*. New York: Barnes & Noble.

Osborne, A. F. 1953. *Applied Imagination*. New York: Charles Scribner's Sons.

Ostrander, Sheila, and Lynn Schroeder. 1979. *Superlearning*. New York: Delta Books.

Papert, Seymour, and Idit Harel. 1991. *Constructionism: Research Reports and Essays, 1985-1990 by the Epistemology and Learning Research Group*. Norwood, NJ: Ablex.

Peck, M. Scott. 1978. *The Road Less Traveled: A New Psychology of Love, Traditional Values, and Spiritual Growth*. New York: Simon & Schuster.

Piaget, Jean, and Barbel Inhelder. 1958. *The Growth of Logical Thinking from Childhood to Adolescence.* New York: Basic Books.

Plutarch. 1917. *Plutarch's Lives.* Cambridge, MA: Harvard University Press.

Public Agenda. 1994. *First Things First: What Americans Expect from Public Schools.* New York: Public Agenda.

Randak, Steve. October 1990. Historical Role-Playing. *The American Biology Teacher* 52 (7): 439–42.

Ravetch, Irving, and Harriet Frank Jr. 1974. *Conrack.* Produced by Martin Ritt and Harriet Frank Jr. 20th Century Fox. 111 minutes. Videotape.

Reimer, Joseph, Diana Paolitto, and Richard Hersh. 1993. *Promoting Moral Growth: From Piaget to Kohlberg.* New York: Longman.

Rochman, Hazel. 1993. *Against Borders: Promoting Books for a Multicultural World.* Chicago: American Library Association.

Rousseau, Jean Jacques. 1962. *Emile.* Translated by William Boyd. New York: Bureau of Publications, Teacher's College, Columbia University.

Rubin, Louis, J. 1985. *Artistry in Teaching.* New York: Random House.

Russ, Sandra. 1993. *Affect and Creativity: The Role of Affect and Play in the Creative Process.* Hindsdale, NJ: Lawrence Erlbaum.

Sandburg, Carl. 1970. Good Morning, America. In *The Collected Poems of Carl Sandburg.* New York: Harcourt Brace Jovanovich.

Scharf, Peter. 1978. Creating Moral Dilemmas for the Classroom. In *Readings in Moral Education.* Minneapolis, MN: Winston Press.

Schuster, D. H. 1978. Review of *Suggestology and Outlines of Suggestopedeia, Journal of Accelerative Learning and Teaching* 3 (1):57–61.

Science for All Americans. 1990. American Association for the Advancement of Science Project 2061. New York: Oxford University Press.

Seger, Linda. 1987. *Making a Good Script Great.* New York: Henry Holt.

———. 1990. *Creating Unforgettable Characters.* New York: Henry Holt.

Smiley, Sam. 1971. *Playwriting: The Structure of Action.* Englewood Cliffs, NJ: Prentice-Hall.

Sommers, Christina, and Fred Sommers. 1993. *Vice and Virtue in Everyday Life: Introductory Readings in Ethics.* Fort Worth, TX: Harcourt Brace.

Spiegel, Victor. 1992. *AZTEC: The World of Moctezuma.* Antenna and Denver Museum of Natural History. Audiotape.

Springer, Sally, and Georg Deutsch. 1981. *Left Brain, Right Brain.* San Francisco: W. H. Freeman.

Starko, Alane Jordan. 1995. *Creativity in the Classroom: Schools of Curious Delight.* White Plains, NY: Longman.

Starratt, Robert J. 1994. *Building an Ethical School: A Practical Response to the Moral Crisis in Schools.* London and Washington, DC: Falmer Press.

Stechen, Edward. 1955. *The Family of Man.* New York: The Museum of Modern Art.

Steichen, Edward, photograph collector. 1955. *The Family of Man.* New York: The Museum of Modern Art.

Steinbeck, John. 1965. *Of Mice and Men.* [Originally published 1937.] New York: Viking Penguin.

———. 1995. *The Pearl.* New York: Viking Penguin.

Sternburg, Robert, ed. 1988. *The Nature of Creativity: Contemporary Psychological Perspectives.* New York: Press Syndicate of the University of Cambridge.

Tardif, Twila, and Robert Sternberg. 1988. What Do We Know About Creativity? In *The Nature of Creativity: Contemporary Psychological Perspectives*. Edited by Robert J. Sternberg. New York: Press Syndicate of the University of Cambridge.

Taylor, I. A. 1975. A Retrospective View of Creativity Investigation. In *Perspectives in Creativity*. Edited by I. A. Taylor and J. W. Getzels. Chicago: Aldine.

Torrance, E. Paul. 1962. *Guiding Creative Talent*. Englewood Cliffs, NJ: Prentice-Hall.

———. 1963. Creativity. In *What Research Says to the Classroom Teacher*. Washington, DC: National Education Association.

———. 1967. The Nurture of Creative Talents. In *Explorations in Creativity*. Edited by R. L. Mooney and T. A. Razik. New York: Harper & Row.

———. 1976. Education and Creativity. In *The Creativity Question*. Edited by Albert Rothenburg and Carl R. Hausman. Durham, NC: Duke University Press.

Vygotsky, Lev. 1978. *Mind in Society: The Development of Higher Psychological Processes*. Translated from the 1930 original. Cambridge, MA: Harvard University Press.

———. 1994. Imagination and Creativity in the Adolescent. *The Vygotsky Reader*. Edited by Rene van der Veer and Jaan Valsiner. Cambridge, MA: Blackwell.

Wadsworth, Barry. 1971. *Piaget's Theory of Cognitive Development*. New York: David McKay.

Wagner, Tony. October 9, 1996. Creating Community Consensus on Core Values: An Alternative to Character Education. *Education Week* xvi (6):36–38.

Index

About the Author

James P. Downing has taught many subjects (and coached several sports) in grades 7 through 12 in public and private schools over the last 26 years and has given dozens of workshops on creative teaching. In addition to teaching physics, astronomy, and geology at Boulder High School, Jim teaches a course in Creative Teaching at the University of Colorado in Boulder. In 1996 Jim was listed in *Who's Who Among America's Teachers*. A one-time English major, Jim has an active interest in the humanities: His stage play *The Sand-Reckoner*, based on the life of Archimedes, was produced on stage in Denver. In addition to playwriting, Jim is an enthusiastic photographer, author of two juvenile fantasy adventure novels, an avid guitar player (having once played in various cabaret groups), and a passionate solar eclipse chaser, making treks to many remote locations to view nature's most mysterious sky show. Jim is also a volunteer with Habitat for Humanity. (Photo by Mia Mindell.)